Life in Society

New to This Edition

The following readings are new to this edition:

Fourth Edition

Life in Society

Readings to Accompany
SOCIOLOGY
A Down-to-Earth Approach
Tenth Edition

Edited by
James M. Henslin
Southern Illinois University, Edwardsville

Allyn and Bacon

Boston ■ Columbus ■ Indianapolis ■ New York ■ San Francisco ■ Upper Saddle River
Amsterdam ■ Cape Town ■ Dubai ■ London ■ Madrid ■ Milan ■ Munich ■ Paris ■ Montreal ■ Toronto
Delhi ■ Mexico City ■ Sao Paulo ■ Sydney ■ Hong Kong ■ Seoul ■ Singapore ■ Tapei ■ Tokyo

Senior Editor: Brita Mess
Editorial Assistant: Elaine Almquist
Marketing Manager: Kelly May
Marketi++ng Assistant: Gina Lavagna
Production Editor: Judy Fiske
Manufacturing Buyer: Debbie Rossi
Cover Administrator: Joel Gendron
Editorial Production and Composition Service: Omegatype Typography, Inc.

Library of Congress Cataloging-in-Publication Data
Life in society : readings to accompany Sociology, a down-to-earth approach, tenth edition / edited by James M. Henslin.—4th ed.
        p.   cm.
  Includes bibliographical references and index.
  ISBN-13: 978-0-205-78041-9 (pbk.)
  ISBN-10: 0-205-78041-5 (pbk.)
  1. Sociology.   I. Henslin, James M.   II. Henslin, James M. Sociology.
  HM586.L54   2011
  301—dc22

                                                    2010000110

Printed in the United States of America

22 2021

Allyn & Bacon
is an imprint of

PEARSON

www.pearsonhighered.com

ISBN 10: 0-205-78041-5
ISBN 13: 978-0-205-78041-9

For my sons—may they have success as they pursue their distinctive visions for the present and the future.

Contents

Preface

It is gratifying to see that students and instructors alike have responded so favorably to *Sociology: A Down-to-Earth Approach*. Since many instructors want to give their students the opportunity to read original sociological research, I have designed this brief anthology as a companion for *Sociology*. Because the readings follow the text's outline chapter for chapter and I have chosen a single reading for each chapter, it is easy to incorporate these selections into the course. Adopters of the *Core Concepts* version of *Sociology: A Down-to-Earth Approach* can use this reader by simply adapting these readings to the *Core's* table of contents.

As always, a selection may have several subthemes. This allows a reading to be incorporated into a different chapter than the one I have assigned it, or to be included in the course even though a particular chapter is not assigned. I have also written a short introduction to each selection and an introduction for each of the five parts.

I think that you'll find these selections both interesting and valuable in teaching the sociological perspective. If you have any suggestions for the next edition of this reader, please let me know.

As always, I look forward to hearing from you.

Jim Henslin
henslin@aol.com

1 The Sociological Perspective

All of us, at least to some degree, want to understand social life. If nothing else, we want to understand why people react to us as they do. We may want to know why some people boast and tell lies, while others undergo personal hardship in order to tell the truth. These are important questions, and they affect our everyday lives. So do issues on a much broader scale, such as why the stock market crashes, why credit is hard or easy to get, why certain types of jobs are drying up around us, why we need more and more education to get a good job, why so many marriages break up, why people are prejudiced, why people are marrying later, or why cohabitation, which most people used to consider shameful, is now common and largely acceptable. Then, too, there is the perplexing question of why nations go to war despite the common sentiment that war is evil and should be avoided.

The tool that sociology offers in our quest for understanding is called *the sociological perspective* (also called *the sociological imagination*). Basically, the sociological perspective means that no behavior or event stands in isolation. Rather, it is connected to other events that surround it. To understand any particular behavior or event, we need to view it within the context in which it occurs. The sociological perspective sensitizes us to the need to uncover these connections.

Back in the 1950s and 1960s, sociologist C. Wright Mills noted that world events were coming to play an increasingly significant role in our personal lives. More than ever, this is true today. What transpires in other countries—even on the other side of the globe—has profound effects on our own lives. An economic downturn in Europe, for example, can pinch our economy—and may force us to put our lives on hold. When a country such as China or India undergoes rapid industrialization and exports goods ferociously, it changes the cost of the goods we buy and threatens domestic industries. When jobs are hard to get—or we can get only low-paying jobs, despite our education and other qualifications—we may decide that it is better to postpone getting married, no matter how much we are in love. Reluctantly, we may even determine that it is prudent to move back in with our parents. Similarly, if our country goes to war in some far-off region, perhaps in a country we hadn't even heard of before, many people's lives are disrupted, some even shattered.

Economies surge, then tumble. Empires grow to a peak of power, then overreach and decline. Wars come and go, a strange and unwelcome intruder that casts its dead and mutilated into our midst, fearful warnings that inevitably go unheeded. The Internet becomes a part of our lives, changing the way we do business, even the ways we communicate, do our homework, and, for some, how we make dates and meet our husbands, wives, and lovers. Even morals change, and what was once considered wrong comes to be accepted as an ordinary part of everyday life.

Such events form a shaping context that affects us profoundly. This context influences both the ways we look at the world and how we see ourselves. Our aspirations and our other "innermost" desires do not originate within us. Instead, if we view them from the sociological perspective, we see that they are transplanted inside us. The social origin of these transplantings, though, ordinarily remains beyond our field of vision. We tend to perceive only what we experience directly—our feelings, our interactions, our friendships, our problems. The shaping context of these vital forces in our lives we perceive but dimly.

In short, we cannot understand our lives merely by looking inside ourselves—at our own abilities, emotions, desires, or aspirations. Nor is it sufficient to consider only our family, friends, associates, or even our neighborhood or the social institutions such as school and church that influence us. Though they are important, we have to also consider a world far beyond our immediate confines.

All these—our personal feelings, our everyday interactions, and events around the globe—come together in *the sociological perspective*. Learning to see ourselves and others from this perspective is a fascinating journey, perhaps the most promising aspect of our introduction to sociology.

To begin our journey, we open this anthology with a selection that has become a classic in sociology. Peter Berger invites you to consider the excitement of exploring social life and beginning to view it from the sociological perspective. We follow this with a reading by Napoleon Chagnon, who recounts his fascinating adventure with a tribe in South America. In the third selection, Gwynne Dyer examines techniques that the U.S. Marine Corps uses to turn ordinary boys into soldiers who will not hesitate to kill when the order is given. In the fourth article, Helene Lawson and Kira Leck analyze how people use the Internet for dating. In the concluding selection, we follow Kathleen Blee as she does participant observation and interviewing of dangerous people. Her frank analysis of her research into racist organizations is a far cry from what can be a "dry" analysis of sociological methods.

Invitation to Sociology

Peter L. Berger

introduction ■ ■ ■ ■ ■

To grasp *the sociological perspective* is to see the world in a new light. It can even change the way you see the world that you now take for granted. If you peer beneath the surface of human relationships, for example, your angle of vision changes and other realities begin to emerge. Consider something as common and familiar as friendship. If you place the sociological lens on friendship, you find that it is far from a simple matter. The implicit understandings on which friendship is based begin to emerge, and you uncover a complex system of rights and obligations. As you probe beneath the surface, you expose friendship's reciprocal obligations—how, for example, you acquire a social debt when your friend does something for you, in what way you are expected to repay this debt, and what the consequences are if you fail to do so. Although seldom stated, such implicit understandings inhabit the taken-for-granted assumptions that rule relationships. Violate them, and you risk damaging or even severing the friendship.

Uncovering realities that lie beneath the surface and attaining a different understanding of social life are part of the fascination of sociology. Regardless of a sociologist's topic—whether as comfortable as friendship or as jarring as the role of women in the organized hate movement (Reading 5)—as Berger points out in this selection, the sociologist's overriding motivation is curiosity, a desire to know more about some aspect of social life, to discover what is really going on in some setting.

Thinking Critically

As you read this selection, ask yourself:

1. What is the difference between a sociologist and a pollster?

2. What does Berger mean by this statement? "Statistical data by themselves do not make sociology."

3. What does Berger mean when he says that sociology is a game? If sociology is a game, can it be taken seriously?

It is gratifying from certain value positions (including some of this writer's) that sociological insights have served in a number of instances to improve the lot of groups of human beings by uncovering morally shocking conditions or by clearing away collective illusions or by showing that socially desired results could be obtained in more humane fashion. One might point, for example, to some applications of sociological knowledge in the penological practice of Western countries. Or one might cite the use made of sociological studies in the Supreme Court decision of 1954 on racial segregation in the public schools. Or one could look at the applications of other sociological studies to the humane planning of urban redevelopment. Certainly the sociologist who is morally and politically sensitive will derive gratification from such instances. But, once more, it will be well to keep in mind that what is at issue here is not sociological understanding as such but certain applications of this understanding. It is not difficult to see how the same understanding could be applied with opposite intentions. Thus the sociological understanding of the dynamics of racial prejudice can be applied effectively by those promoting intragroup hatred as well as by those wanting to spread tolerance. And the sociological understanding of the nature of human solidarity can be employed in the service of both totalitarian and democratic regimes. . . .

One image [of the sociologist is that of] a gatherer of statistics about human behavior. . . . He* goes out with a questionnaire, interviews people selected at random, then goes home [and] enters his tabulations [into computers]. . . . In all of this, of course, he is supported by a large staff and a very large budget. Included in this image is the implication that the results of all this effort are picayune, a pedantic restatement of what everybody knows anyway. As one observer remarked pithily, a sociologist is a fellow who spends $100,000 to find his way to a house of ill repute.

This image of the sociologist has been strengthened in the public mind by the activities of many agencies that might well be called parasociological, mainly agencies concerned with public opinion and market trends. The pollster has become a well-known figure in American life, inopportuning people about their views from foreign policy to toilet paper. Since the methods used in the pollster business bear close resemblance to sociological research, the growth of this image of the sociologist is understandable. . . . The fundamental sociological question, whether concerned with premarital petting† or with Republican votes or with the incidence of gang knifings, is always presumed to be "how often?" or "how many?". . . .

Now it must be admitted, albeit regretfully, that this image of the sociologist and his trade is not altogether a product of fantasy. . . . [A good] part of the so-

From *Invitation to Sociology* by Peter L. Berger, copyright © 1963 by Peter L. Berger. Used by permission of Doubleday, a division of Random House, Inc.

*Some classic articles in sociology that are reprinted in this anthology were written when "he" and "man" were generic, when they referred to both men and women. So it is with "his," "him," and so on. Although the writing style has changed, the sociological ideas have not. At each instance you might want to mentally substitute he/she, his/her, man/woman, and so forth.

†A term that used to be common to refer to making out, especially to the male touching the female's sexual organs.

ciological enterprise in this country continues to consist of little studies of obscure fragments of social life, irrelevant to any broader theoretical concern. One glance at the table of contents of the major sociological journals or at the list of papers read at sociological conventions will confirm this statement. . . .

Statistical data by themselves do not make sociology. They become sociology only when they are sociologically interpreted, put within a theoretical frame of reference that is sociological. Simple counting, or even correlating different items that one counts, is not sociology. There is almost no sociology in the Kinsey reports. This does not mean that the data in these studies are not true or that they cannot be relevant to sociological understanding. They are, taken by themselves, raw materials that can be used in sociological interpretation. The interpretation, however, must be broader than the data themselves. So the sociologist cannot arrest himself at the frequency tables of premarital petting or extramarital pederasty. These enumerations are meaningful to him only in terms of their much broader implications for an understanding of institutions and values in our society. To arrive at such understanding the sociologist will often have to apply statistical techniques, especially when he is dealing with the mass phenomena of modern social life. But sociology consists of statistics as little as philology consists of conjugating irregular verbs or chemistry of making nasty smells in test tubes.

Sociology has, from its beginnings, understood itself as a science. . . . [T]he allegiance of sociologists to the scientific ethos has meant everywhere a willingness to be bound by certain scientific canons of procedure. If the sociologist remains faithful to his calling, his statements must be arrived at through the observation of certain rules of evidence that allow others to check on or to repeat or to develop his findings further. It is this scientific discipline that often supplies the motive for reading a sociological work as against, say, a novel on the same topic that might describe matters in much more impressive and convincing language. . . .

The charge that many sociologists write in a barbaric dialect must . . . be admitted. . . . Any scientific discipline must develop a terminology. This is self-evident for a discipline such as, say, nuclear physics that deals with matters unknown to most people and for which no words exist in common speech. However, terminology is possibly even more important for the social sciences, just because their subject matter *is* familiar and just because words *do* exist to denote it. Because we are well acquainted with the social institutions that surround us, our perception of them is imprecise and often erroneous. In very much the same way most of us will have considerable difficulty giving an accurate description of our parents, husbands or wives, children or close friends. Also, our language is often (and perhaps blessedly) vague and confusing in its references to social reality. Take for an example the concept of *class,* a very important one in sociology: There must be dozens of meanings that this term may have in common speech—income brackets, races, ethnic groups, power cliques, intelligence ratings, and many others. It is obvious that the sociologist must have a precise, unambiguous definition of the concept if his work is to proceed with any degree of scientific rigor. In view of these facts, one can understand that some sociologists have been tempted to invent altogether new words to avoid the semantic traps of the vernacular usage.

Finally, we would look at an image of the sociologist not so much in his professional role as in his being, supposedly, a certain kind of person. This is the image of the sociologist as a detached, sardonic observer, and a cold manipulator of men. Where this image prevails, it may represent an ironic triumph of the sociologist's own efforts to be accepted as a genuine scientist. The sociologist here becomes the self-appointed superior man, standing off from the warm vitality of common existence, finding his satisfactions not in living but in coolly appraising the lives of others, filing them away in little categories, and thus presumably missing the real significance of what he is observing. Further, there is the notion that, when he involves himself in social processes at all, the sociologist does so as an uncommitted technician, putting his manipulative skills at the disposal of the powers that be.

This last image is probably not very widely held. . . . The problem of the political role of the social scientist is, nevertheless, a very genuine one. For instance, the employment of sociologists by certain branches of industry and government raises moral questions that ought to be faced more widely than they have been so far. These are, however, moral questions that concern all men in positions of responsibility. . . .

How then are we to conceive of the sociologist? The sociologist is someone concerned with understanding society in a disciplined way. The nature of this discipline is scientific. This means that what the sociologist finds and says about the social phenomena he studies occurs within a certain rather strictly defined frame of reference. One of the main characteristics of this scientific frame of reference is that operations are bound by certain rules of evidence. As a scientist, the sociologist tries to be objective, to control his personal preferences and prejudices, to perceive clearly rather than to judge normatively. This restraint, of course, does not embrace the totality of the sociologist's existence as a human being, but is limited to his operations *qua* sociologist. Nor does the sociologist claim that his frame of reference is the only one within which society can be looked at. For that matter, very few scientists in any field would claim today that one should look at the world only scientifically. The botanist looking at a daffodil has no reason to dispute the right of the poet to look at the same object in a very different manner. There are many ways of playing. The point is not that one denies other people's games but that one is clear about the rules of one's own. The game of the sociologist, then, uses scientific rules. As a result, the sociologist must be clear in his own mind as to the meaning of these rules. That is, he must concern himself with methodological questions. Methodology does not constitute his goal. The latter, let us recall once more, is the attempt to understand society. Methodology helps in reaching this goal. In order to understand society, or that segment of it that he is studying at the moment, the sociologist will use a variety of means. Among these are statistical techniques. Statistics can be very useful in answering certain sociological questions. But statistics does not constitute sociology. As a scientist, the sociologist will have to be concerned with the exact significance of the terms he is using. That is, he will have to be careful about terminology. This does not have to mean that he must invent a new language of his own, but it does mean that he cannot naively use the language of everyday discourse. Finally, the interest of the sociologist is primarily theoretical. That is, he is interested in understanding for its own sake. He may be aware of or even concerned with the practical applicability and consequences of his findings, but at that point he leaves the sociological frame of reference as such and moves into realms of values, beliefs and ideas that he shares with other men who are not sociologists. . . .

[W]e would like to go a little bit further here and ask a somewhat more personal (and therefore, no doubt, more controversial) question. We would like to ask not only what it is that the sociologist is doing but also what it is that drives him to it. Or, to use the phrase Max Weber used in a similar connection, we want to inquire a little into the nature of the sociologist's demon. In doing so, we shall evoke an image that is not so much ideal-typical in the above sense but more confessional in the sense of personal commitment. Again, we are not interested in excommunicating anyone. The game of sociology goes on in a spacious playground. We are just describing a little more closely those we would like to tempt to join our game.

We would say then that the sociologist (that is, the one we would really like to invite to our game) is a person intensively, endlessly, shamelessly interested in the doings of men. His natural habitat is all the human gathering places of the world, wherever men come together. The sociologist may be interested in many other things. But his consuming interest remains in the world of men, their institutions, their history, their passions. And since he is interested in men, nothing that men do can be altogether tedious for him. He will naturally be interested in the events that engage men's ultimate beliefs, their moments of tragedy and grandeur and ecstasy. But he will also be fascinated by the commonplace, the everyday. He will know reverence, but this reverence will not prevent him from wanting to see and to understand. He may sometimes feel revulsion or contempt. But this also will not deter him from wanting to have his questions answered. The sociologist, in his quest for understanding, moves through the world of men without respect for the usual lines of demarcation. Nobility and degradation, power and obscurity, intelligence and folly—these are equally *interesting* to him, however unequal they may be in his personal values or tastes. Thus his questions may lead him to all possible levels of society, the best and the least known places, the most respected and the most despised. And, if he is a good sociologist, he will find himself in all these places because his own questions have so taken possession of him that he has little choice but to seek for answers.

It would be possible to say the same things in a lower key. We could say that the sociologist, but for the grace of his academic title, is the man who must listen to gossip despite himself, who is tempted to look through keyholes, to read other people's mail, to open closed cabinets. Before some otherwise unoccupied psychologist sets out now to construct an aptitude test for sociologists on the basis of sublimated voyeurism, let us quickly say that we are speaking merely by way of analogy. Perhaps some little boys consumed with curiosity to watch their maiden aunts in the bathroom later become inveterate sociologists. This is quite uninteresting. What interests us is the curiosity that grips any sociologist in front of a closed door behind which there are human voices. If he is a good sociologist, he will want to open that door, to understand these voices. Behind each closed door he will anticipate some new facet of human life not yet perceived and understood.

The sociologist will occupy himself with matters that others regard as too sacred or as too distasteful for dispassionate investigation. He will find rewarding the company of priests or of prostitutes, depending not on his personal preferences but on the questions he happens to be asking at the moment. He will also concern himself with matters that others may find much too boring. He will be interested in the human interaction that goes with warfare or with great intellectual discoveries, but also in the relations between people employed in a restaurant or between a group of little girls playing with their dolls. His main focus of attention is not the ultimate significance of what men do, but the action in itself, as another example of the infinite richness of human conduct. So much for the image of our playmate.

In these journeys through the world of men the sociologist will inevitably encounter other professional Peeping Toms. Sometimes these will resent his presence, feeling that he is poaching on their preserves. In some places the sociologist will meet up with the economist, in others with the political scientist, in yet others with the psychologist or the ethnologist. Yet chances are that the questions that have brought him to these same places are different from the ones that propelled his fellow-trespassers. The sociologist's questions always remain essentially the same: "What are people doing with each other here?" "What are their relationships to each other?" "How are these relationships organized in institutions?" "What are the collective ideas that move men and institutions?" In trying to answer these questions in specific instances, the sociologist will, of course, have to deal with economic or political matters, but he will do so in a way rather different from that of the economist or the political scientist. The scene that he contemplates is the same human scene that these other scientists concern themselves with. But the sociologist's angle of vision is different. When this is understood, it becomes clear that it makes little sense to try to stake out a special enclave within which the sociologist will carry on business in his own right. There is, however, one traveler whose path the sociologist will cross more often than anyone else's on his journeys. This is the historian. Indeed, as soon as the sociologist turns from the present to the past, his preoccupations are very hard indeed to distinguish from those of the historian. However, we shall leave this relationship to a later part of our considerations. Suffice it to say here that the sociological journey will be much impoverished unless it is punctuated frequently by conversation with that other particular traveler.

Any intellectual activity derives excitement from the moment it becomes a trail of discovery. In some fields of learning this is the discovery of worlds previously unthought and unthinkable. This is the excitement of the astronomer or of the nuclear physicist on the antipodal boundaries of the realities that man is capable of conceiving. But it can also be the excitement of bacteriology or geology. In a different way it can be the excitement of the linguist discovering new realms of human expression or of the anthropologist exploring human customs in faraway countries. In such discovery, when undertaken with passion, a widening of awareness, sometimes a veritable transformation of consciousness, occurs. The universe turns out to be much more wonder-full than one had ever dreamed. The excitement of sociology is usually of a different sort. Sometimes, it is true, the sociologist penetrates into worlds that had previously been quite unknown to him—for instance, the world of crime, or the world of some bizarre religious sect, or the world fashioned by the exclusive concerns of some group such as medical specialists or military leaders or advertising executives. However, much of the time the sociologist moves in sectors of experience that are familiar to him and to most people in his society. He investigates communities, institutions and activities that one can read about every day in the newspapers. Yet there is another excitement of discovery beckoning in his investigations. It is not the excitement of coming upon the totally unfamiliar, but rather the excitement of finding the familiar becoming transformed in its meaning. The fascination of sociology lies in the fact that its perspective makes us see in a new light the very world in which we have lived all our lives. This also constitutes a transformation of consciousness. Moreover, this transformation is more relevant existentially than that of many other intellectual disciplines, because it is more difficult to segregate in some special compartment of the mind. The astronomer does not live in the remote galaxies, and the nuclear physicist can, outside his laboratory, eat and laugh and marry and vote without thinking about the insides of the atom. The geologist looks at rocks only at appropriate times, and the linguist speaks English with his wife. The sociologist lives in society, on the job and off it. His own life, inevitably, is part of his subject matter. Men being what they are, sociologists too manage to segregate their professional insights from their everyday affairs. But it is a rather difficult feat to perform in good faith.

The sociologist moves in the common world of men, close to what most of them would call real. The categories he employs in his analyses are only refinements of the categories by which other men live—power, class, status, race, ethnicity. As a result, there is a deceptive simplicity and obviousness about some sociological investigations. One reads them, nods at the familiar scene, remarks that one has heard all this before and don't people have better things to do than to waste their time on truisms—until one is suddenly brought up against an insight that radically questions everything one had previously assumed about this familiar scene. This is the point at which one begins to sense the excitement of sociology.

Let us take a specific example. Imagine a sociology class in a Southern college where almost all the students are white Southerners. Imagine a lecture on the subject of the racial system of the South. The lecturer is talking here of matters that have been familiar to his students from the time of their infancy. Indeed, it may be that they are much more familiar with the minutiae of this system than he is. They are quite bored as a result. It seems to them that he is only using more pretentious words to describe what they already know. Thus he may use the term "caste," one commonly used now by American sociologists to describe the Southern racial system. But in explaining the term he shifts to traditional Hindu society, to make it clearer. He then goes on to analyze the magical beliefs inherent in caste taboos, the social dynamics of commensalism and connubium, the economic interests concealed within the system, the way in which religious beliefs relate to the taboos, the effects of the caste system upon the industrial development of the society and vice versa—all in India. But suddenly India is not very far away at all. The lecture then goes back to its

Southern theme. The familiar now seems not quite so familiar any more. Questions are raised that are new, perhaps raised angrily, but raised all the same. And at least some of the students have begun to understand that there are functions involved in this business of race that they have not read about in the newspapers (at least not those in their hometowns) and that their parents have not told them—partly, at least, because neither the newspapers nor the parents knew about them.

It can be said that the first wisdom of sociology is this—things are not what they seem. This too is a deceptively simple statement. It ceases to be simple after a while. Social reality turns out to have many layers of meaning. The discovery of each new layer changes the perception of the whole.

Anthropologists use the term "culture shock" to describe the impact of a totally new culture upon a newcomer. In an extreme instance such shock will be experienced by the Western explorer who is told, halfway through dinner, that he is eating the nice old lady he had been chatting with the previous day—a shock with predictable physiological if not moral consequences. Most explorers no longer encounter cannibalism in their travels today. However, the first encounters with polygamy or with puberty rites or even with the way some nations drive their automobiles can be quite a shock to an American visitor. With the shock may go not only disapproval or disgust but a sense of excitement that things can *really* be that different from what they are at home. To some extent, at least, this is the excitement of any first travel abroad. The experience of sociological discovery could be described as "culture shock" minus geographical displacement. In other words, the sociologist travels at home—with shocking results. He is unlikely to find that he is eating a nice old lady for dinner. But the discovery, for instance, that his own church has considerable money invested in the missile industry or that a few blocks from his home there are people who engage in cultic orgies may not be drastically different in emotional impact. Yet we would not want to imply that sociological discoveries are always or even usually outrageous to moral sentiment. Not at all. What they have in common with exploration in distant lands, however, is the sudden illumination of new and unsuspected facets of human existence in society. This is the excitement and, as we shall try to show later, the humanistic justification of sociology.

People who like to avoid shocking discoveries, who prefer to believe that society is just what they were taught in Sunday School, who like the safety of the rules and the maxims of what Alfred Schuetz has called the "world-taken-for-granted," should stay away from sociology. People who feel no temptation before closed doors, who have no curiosity about human beings, who are content to admire scenery without wondering about the people who live in those houses on the other side of that river, should probably also stay away from sociology. They will find it unpleasant or, at any rate, unrewarding. People who are interested in human beings only if they can change, convert or reform them should also be warned, for they will find sociology much less useful than they hoped. And people whose interest is mainly in their own conceptual constructions will do just as well to turn to the study of little white mice. Sociology will be satisfying, in the long run, only to those who can think of nothing more entrancing than to watch men and to understand things human. . . .

To be sure, sociology is an individual pastime in the sense that it interests some men and bores others. Some like to observe human beings, others to experiment with mice. The world is big enough to hold all kinds and there is no logical priority for one interest as against another. But the word "pastime" is weak in describing what we mean. Sociology is more like a passion. The sociological perspective is more like a demon that possesses one, that drives one compellingly, again and again, to the questions that are its own. An introduction to sociology is, therefore, an invitation to a very special kind of passion.

The Fierce People

Napoleon Chagnon

introduction

The many cultures of humans are fascinating. Every human group has a culture, whether that group is an urban gang in the United States or a tribe in the jungles of South America. Culture encompasses us like an envelope encloses a letter. It exposes us to what is within the envelope and limits us from seeing what lies beyond it. It is difficult to exaggerate the significance of culture. Our culture gives us language, the conceptual apparatus by which we divide and view the world. It provides statuses for people to occupy and guidelines for how we should act within those statuses and how we are expected to interact with others based upon their statuses. It gives us a system of beliefs and a framework for interpreting life, ways even for viewing the self. In short, culture provides the basic rules for human interaction and the framework from which we view life. Understand a people's culture, then, and you come a long way to understanding why they think and act in the ways they do.

Understanding and appreciation are quite different matters. To understand a group does not necessarily mean that you appreciate them. This distinction will become apparent as you read this selection by Chagnon, who recounts his harrowing stay with the Yanomamö, a tribe in South America. His account makes it apparent how uncomfortable he felt during his lengthy fieldwork. See if you can understand why.

Thinking Critically

As you read this selection, ask yourself:

1. Why didn't Chagnon develop an appreciation for the way of life of the Yanomamö?

2. Why was Chagnon so stingy with his food and so reluctant to accept food from others?

3. How does the culture of the Yanomamö compare with your own culture? The differences are probably readily apparent, but look also for similarities.

The Yanomamö Indians live in southern Venezuela and the adjacent portions of northern Brazil. Some 125 widely scattered villages have populations ranging from 40 to 250 inhabitants, with 75 to 80 people the most usual number. In total numbers their population probably approaches 10,000 people, but this is merely a guess. Many of the villages have not yet been contacted by outsiders, and nobody knows for sure exactly how many uncontacted villages there are, or how many people live in them. By comparison to African or Melanesian tribes, the Yanomamö population is small. Still, they are one of the largest unacculturated tribes left in all of South America.

But they have a significance apart from tribal size and cultural purity: The Yanomamö are still actively conducting warfare. It is in the nature of man to fight, according to one of their myths, because the blood of "Moon" spilled on this layer of the cosmos, causing men to become fierce. I describe the Yanomamö as "the fierce people" because that is the most accurate single phrase that describes them. That is how they conceive themselves to be, and that is how they would like others to think of them.

I spent nineteen months with the Yanomamö during which time I acquired some proficiency in their language and, up to a point, submerged myself in their culture and way of life. The thing that impressed me most was the importance of aggression in their culture. I had the opportunity to witness a good many incidents that expressed individual vindictiveness on the one hand and collective bellicosity on the other. These ranged in seriousness from the ordinary incidents of wife beating and chest pounding to dueling and organized raiding by parties that set out with the intention of ambushing and killing men from enemy villages. One of the villages was raided approximately twenty-five times while I conducted the fieldwork, six times by the group I lived among. . . .

This is not to state that primitive man everywhere is unpleasant. By way of contrast, I have also done limited fieldwork among the Yanomamö's northern neighbors, the Carib-speaking Makiritare Indians. This group was very pleasant and charming, all of them anxious to help me and honor bound to show any visitor the numerous courtesies of their system of etiquette. In short, they approached the image of primitive man that I had conjured up, and it was sheer pleasure to work with them. . . .

My first day in the field illustrated to me what my teachers meant when they spoke of "culture shock." I had traveled in a small, aluminum rowboat propelled by a large outboard motor for two and a half days. This took me from the Territorial capital, a small town on the Orinoco River, deep into Yanomamö country. On the morning of the third day we reached a small mission settlement, the field "headquarters" of a group of Americans who were working in two Yanomamö villages. The missionaries had come out of these villages to hold their annual conference on the progress of their mission work, and were conducting their meetings when I arrived. We picked up a passenger at the mission station, James P. Barker, the first non-Yanomamö to make a sustained, permanent contact with the tribe (in 1950). He had just returned from a year's furlough in the United States, where I had earlier visited him before leaving for Venezuela. He agreed to accompany me to the village I had selected for my base of operations to introduce me to the Indians. This village was also his own home base, but he had not been there for over a year and did not plan to join me for another three months. Mr. Barker had been living with this particular group about five years.

We arrived at the village, Bisaasi-teri, about 2:00 P.M. and docked the boat along the muddy bank at the terminus of the path used by the Indians to fetch their drinking water. It was hot and muggy, and my clothing was soaked with perspiration. It clung uncomfortably to my body, as it did thereafter for the remainder of the work. The small, biting gnats were out in astronomical numbers, for it was the beginning of the dry season. My face and hands were swollen from the venom of their numerous stings. In just a few moments I was to meet my first Yanomamö, my first primitive man. What would it be like? I had visions of entering the village and seeing 125 social facts running about calling each other kinship terms and sharing food, each waiting and anxious to have me collect his genealogy. I would wear them out in turn. Would they like me? This was important to me; I wanted them to be so fond of me that they would adopt me into their kinship system and way of life, because I had heard that successful anthropologists always get adopted by their people. I had learned during my seven years of anthropological training at the University of Michigan that kinship was equivalent to society in primitive tribes and that it was a moral way of life, "moral" being something "good" and "desirable." I was determined to work my way into their moral system of kinship and become a member of their society.

My heart began to pound as we approached the village and heard the buzz of activity within the circular compound. Mr. Barker commented that he was anxious to see if any changes had taken place while he was away and wondered how many of them had died during his absence. I felt into my back pocket to make sure that my notebook was there and felt personally more secure when I touched it. Otherwise, I would not have known what to do with my hands.

I looked up and gasped when I saw a dozen burly, naked, filthy, hideous men staring at us down the shafts of their drawn arrows! Immense wads of green tobacco were stuck between their lower teeth and lips making them look even more hideous, and strands of dark-green slime dripped or hung from their noses. We arrived at the village while the men were blowing a hallucinogenic drug up their noses. One of the side effects of the drug is a runny nose. The mucus is always saturated with the green powder and the Indians usually let it run freely from their nostrils. My next discovery was that there were a dozen or so vicious, underfed dogs snapping at my legs, circling me as if I were going to be their next meal. I just stood there holding my notebook, helpless and pathetic. Then the stench of the decaying vegetation and filth struck me and I almost got sick. I was horrified. What sort of a welcome was this for the person who came here to live with you and learn your way of life, to become friends with you? They put their weapons down when they recognized Barker and returned to their chanting, keeping a nervous eye on the village entrances.

We had arrived just after a serious fight. Seven women had been abducted the day before by a neighboring group, and the local men and their guests had just that morning recovered five of them in a brutal club fight that nearly ended in a shooting war. The abductors, angry because they lost five of the seven captives, vowed to raid the Bisaasi-teri. When we arrived and entered the village unexpectedly, the Indians feared that we were the raiders. On several occasions during the next two hours the men in the village jumped to their feet, armed themselves, and waited nervously for the noise outside the village to be identified. My enthusiasm for collecting ethnographic curiosities diminished in proportion to the number of times such an alarm was raised. In fact, I was relieved when Mr. Barker suggested that we sleep across the river for the evening. It would be safer over there.

As we walked down the path to the boat, I pondered the wisdom of having decided to spend a year and a half with this tribe before I had even seen what they were like. I am not ashamed to admit, either, that had there been a diplomatic way out, I would have ended my fieldwork then and there. I did not look forward to the next day when I would be left alone with the Indians; I did not speak a word of their language, and they were decidedly different from what I had imagined them to be. The whole situation was depressing, and I wondered why I ever decided to switch from civil engineering to anthropology in the first place. I had not eaten all day, I was soaking wet from perspiration, the gnats were biting me, and I was covered with red pigment, the result of a dozen or so complete examinations I had been given by as many burly Indians. These examinations capped an otherwise grim day. The Indians would blow their noses into their hands, flick as much of the mucus off that would separate in a snap of the wrist, wipe the residue into their hair, and then carefully examine my face, arms, legs, hair, and the contents of my pockets. I asked Mr. Barker how to say "Your hands are dirty"; my comments were met by the Indians in the following way: They would "clean" their hands by spitting a quantity of slimy tobacco juice into them, rub them together, and then proceed with the examination.

Mr. Barker and I crossed the river and slung our hammocks. When he pulled his hammock out of a rubber bag, a heavy, disagreeable odor of mildewed cotton came with it. "Even the missionaries are filthy," I thought to myself. Within two weeks everything I owned smelled the same way, and I lived with the odor for the remainder of the fieldwork. My own habits of personal cleanliness reached such levels that I didn't even mind being examined by the Indians, as I was not much cleaner than they were after I had adjusted to the circumstances.

So much for my discovery that primitive man is not the picture of nobility and sanitation I had conceived him to be. I soon discovered that it was an enormously time-consuming task to maintain my own body in the manner to which it had grown accustomed in the relatively antiseptic environment of the northern United States. Either I could be relatively well fed and relatively comfortable in a fresh change of clothes and do very little fieldwork, or, I could do considerably more fieldwork and be less well fed and less comfortable.

It is appalling how complicated it can be to make oatmeal in the jungle. First, I had to make two trips to the river to haul the water. Next, I had to prime my kerosene stove with alcohol and get it burning, a tricky procedure when you are trying to mix powdered milk and fill a coffee pot at the same time: the alcohol prime always burned out before I could turn the kerosene on, and I would have to start all over. Or, I would turn the kerosene on, hoping that the element was still hot enough to vaporize the fuel, and not start a small fire in my palm-thatched hut as the liquid kerosene squirted all over the table and walls and ignited. It was safer to start over with the alcohol. Then I had to boil the oatmeal and pick the bugs out of it. All my supplies, of course, were carefully stored in Indian-proof, ratproof, moisture-proof, and insect-proof containers, not one of which ever served its purpose adequately. Just taking things out of the multiplicity of containers and repacking them afterward was a minor project in itself. By the time I had hauled the water to cook with, unpacked my food, prepared the oatmeal, milk, and coffee, heated water for dishes, washed and dried the dishes, repacked the food in the containers, stored the containers in locked trunks and cleaned up my mess, the ceremony of preparing breakfast had brought me almost up to lunch time.

Eating three meals a day was out of the question. I solved the problem by eating a single meal that could be prepared in a single container, or, at most, in two containers, washed my dishes only when there were no clean ones left, using cold river water, and wore each change of clothing at least a week to cut down on my laundry problem, a courageous undertaking in the tropics. I was also less concerned about sharing my provisions with the rats, insects, Indians, and the elements, thereby eliminating the need for my complicated storage process. I was able to last most of the day on *café con leche,* heavily sugared espresso coffee diluted about five to one with hot milk. I would prepare this in the evening and store it in a thermos. Frequently, my single meal was no more complicated than a can of sardines and a package of crackers. But at least two or three times a week I would do something sophisticated, like make oatmeal or boil rice and add a can of tuna fish or tomato paste to it. I even saved time by devising a water system that obviated the trips to the river. I had a few sheets of zinc roofing brought in and made a rain-water trap. I caught the water on the zinc surface, funneled it into an empty gasoline drum, and then ran a plastic hose from the drum to my hut. When the drum was exhausted in the dry season, I hired the Indians to fill it with water from the river.

I ate much less when I traveled with the Indians to visit other villages. Most of the time my travel diet consisted of roasted or boiled green plantains that I obtained from the Indians, but I always carried a few cans of sardines with me in case I got lost or stayed away longer than I had planned. I found peanut butter and crackers a very nourishing food, and a simple one to prepare on trips. It was nutritious and portable, and only one tool was required to prepare the meal, a hunting knife that could be cleaned by wiping the blade on a leaf. More importantly, it was one of the few foods the Indians would let me eat in relative peace. It looked too much like animal feces to them to excite their appetites.

I once referred to the peanut butter as the dung of cattle. They found this quite repugnant. They did not know what "cattle" were, but were generally aware that I ate several canned products of such an animal. I perpetrated this myth, if for no other reason than to have some peace of mind while I ate. Fieldworkers develop strange defense mechanisms, and this was one of my own forms of adaptation. On another occasion I was eating a can of frankfurters and growing very weary of the demands of one of my guests for a share in my meal. When he asked me what I was eating, I replied: "Beef." He then asked, "What part of the animal are you eating?" to which I replied, "Guess!" He stopped asking for a share.

Meals were a problem in another way. Food sharing is important to the Yanomamö in the context of displaying friendship. "I am hungry," is almost a form of greeting with them. I could not possibly have brought enough food with me to feed the entire village, yet they seemed not to understand this. All they could see was that I did not share my food with them at each and every meal. Nor could I enter into their system of reciprocities with respect to food; every time one of them gave me something "freely," he would dog me for months to pay him back, not with food, but with steel tools. Thus, if I accepted a plantain from someone in a different village while I was on a visit, he would most likely visit me in the future and demand a machete as payment for the time that he "fed" me. I usually reacted to these kinds of demands by giving a banana, the customary reciprocity in their culture—food for food—but this would be a disappointment for the individual who had visions of that single plantain growing into a machete over time.

Despite the fact that most of them knew I would not share my food with them at their request, some of them always showed up at my hut during mealtime. I gradually became accustomed to this and learned to ignore their persistent demands while I ate. Some of them would get angry because I failed to give in, but most of them accepted it as just a peculiarity of the subhuman foreigner. When I did give in, my hut quickly filled with Indians, each demanding a sample of the food that I had given one of them. If I did not give all a share, I was that much more despicable in their eyes.

A few of them went out of their way to make my meals unpleasant, to spite me for not sharing; for example, one man arrived and watched me eat a cracker with honey on it. He immediately recognized the honey, a particularly esteemed Yanomamö food. He knew that I would not share my tiny bottle and that it would be futile to ask. Instead, he glared at me and queried icily, "Shaki![1] What kind of animal semen are you eating on that cracker?" His question had the desired effect, and my meal ended.

Finally, there was the problem of being lonely and separated from your own kind, especially your family. I tried to overcome this by seeking personal friendships among the Indians. This only complicated the matter because all my friends simply used my confidence to gain privileged access to my cache of steel tools and trade goods, and looted me. I would be bitterly disappointed that my "friend" thought no more of me than to finesse our relationship exclusively with the intention of getting at any locked up possessions, and my depression would hit new lows every time I discovered this. The loss of the possession bothered me much less than the shock that I was, as far as most of them were concerned, nothing more than a source of desirable items; no holds were barred in relieving me of these, since I was considered something sub-human, a non-Yanomamö.

The thing that bothered me most was the incessant, passioned, and aggressive demands the Indians made. It would become so unbearable that I would have to lock myself in my mud hut every once in a while just to escape from it: Privacy is one of Western culture's greatest achievements. But I did not want privacy for its own sake; rather, I simply had to get away from the begging. Day and night for the entire time I lived with the Yanomamö I was plagued by such demands as: "Give me a knife, I am poor!"; "If you don't take me with you on your next trip to Widokaiya-teri, I'll chop a hole in your canoe!"; "Don't point your camera at me or I'll hit you!"; "Share your food with me!"; "Take me across the river in your canoe and be quick about it!"; "Give me a cooking pot!"; "Loan me your flashlight so I can go hunting tonight!"; "Give me medicine . . . I itch all over!"; "Take us on a week-long hunting trip with your shotgun!"; and "Give me an axe, or I'll break into your hut when you are away visiting and steal one!" And so I was bombarded by such demands day after day, months on end, until I could not bear to see an Indian.

It was not as difficult to become calloused to the incessant begging as it was to ignore the sense of urgency, the impassioned tone of voice, or the intimidation and aggression with which the demands were made. It was likewise difficult to adjust to the fact that the Yanomamö refused to accept "no" for an answer until or unless it seethed with passion and intimidation—which it did after six months. Giving in to a demand always established a new threshold; the next demand would be for a bigger item or favor, and the anger of the Indians even greater if the demand was not met. I soon learned that I had to become very much like the Yanomamö to be able to get along with them on their terms: sly, aggressive, and intimidating.

Had I failed to adjust in this fashion I would have lost six months of supplies to them in a single day or would have spent most of my time ferrying them around in my canoe or hunting for them. As it was, I did spend a considerable amount of time doing these things and did succumb to their outrageous demands for axes and machetes, at least at first. More importantly, had I failed to demonstrate that I could not be pushed around beyond a certain point, I would have been the subject of far more ridicule, theft, and practical jokes than was the actual case. In short, I had to acquire a certain proficiency in their kind of interpersonal politics and to learn how to imply subtly that certain potentially undesirable consequences might follow if they did such and such to me. They do this to each other in order to establish precisely the point at which they cannot goad an individual any further without precipitating retaliation. As soon as I caught on to this and realized that much of their aggression was stimulated by their desire to discover my flash point, I got along much better with them and regained some lost ground. It was sort of like a political game that everyone played, but one in which each individual sooner or later had to display some sign that his bluffs and implied threats could be backed up. I suspect that the frequency of wife beating is a component of this syndrome, since men can display their ferocity and show others that they are capable of violence. Beating a wife with a club is considered to be an acceptable way of displaying ferocity and one that does not expose the male to much danger. The important thing is that the man has displayed his potential for violence and the implication is that other men better treat him with respect and caution.

After six months, the level of demand was tolerable in the village I used for my headquarters. The Indians and I adjusted to each other and knew what to expect with regard to demands on their part for goods, favors, and services. Had I confined my fieldwork to just that village alone, the field experience would have been far more enjoyable. But, as I was interested in the demographic pattern and social organization of a much larger area, I made regular trips to some dozen different villages in order to collect genealogies or to recheck those I already had. Hence, the intensity of begging and intimidation was fairly constant for the duration of the fieldwork. I had to establish my position in some sort of pecking order of ferocity at each and every village.

For the most part, my own "fierceness" took the form of shouting back at the Yanomamö as loudly and as passionately as they shouted at me, especially at first, when I did not know much of their language. As I became more proficient in their language and learned more about their political tactics, I became more sophisticated in the art of bluffing. For example, I paid one young man a machete to cut palm trees and make boards from the wood. I used these to fashion a platform in the bottom of my dugout canoe to keep my possessions dry when I traveled by river. That afternoon I was doing informant work in the village; the long-awaited mission supply boat arrived, and most of the Indians ran out of the village to beg goods from the crew. I continued to work in the village for another hour or so and went down to the river to say "hello" to the men on the supply boat. I was angry when I discovered that the Indians had chopped up all my palm boards and used them to paddle their own canoes across the river. I knew that if I overlooked this incident I would have invited them to take even greater liberties with my goods in the future. I crossed the river, docked amidst their dugouts, and shouted for the Indians to come out and see me. A few of the culprits appeared, mischievous grins on their faces. I gave a spirited lecture about how hard I had worked to put those boards in my canoe, how I had paid a machete for the wood, and how angry I was that they destroyed my work in their haste to cross the river. I then pulled out my hunting knife and, while their grins disappeared, cut each of their canoes loose, set them into the current, and let them float away. I left without further ado and without looking back.

They managed to borrow another canoe and, after some effort, recovered their dugouts. The headman of the village later told me with an approving chuckle that I had done the correct thing. Everyone in the village, except, of course, the culprits, supported and defended my action. This raised my status.

Whenever I took such action and defended my rights, I got along much better with the Yanomamö. A good deal of their behavior toward me was directed with the forethought of establishing the point at which I would react defensively. Many of them later reminisced about the early days of my work when I was "timid" and a little afraid of them, and they could bully me into giving goods away.

Theft was the most persistent situation that required me to take some sort of defensive action. I simply could not keep everything I owned locked in trunks, and the Indians came into my hut and left at will. I developed a very effective means for recovering almost all the stolen items. I would simply ask a child who took the item and then take that person's hammock when he was not around, giving a spirited lecture to the others as I marched away in a faked rage with the thief's hammock.

Nobody ever attempted to stop me from doing this, and almost all of them told me that my technique for recovering my possessions was admirable. By nightfall the thief would either appear with the stolen object or send it along with someone else to make an exchange. The others would heckle him for getting caught and being forced to return the item.

With respect to collecting the data I sought, there was a very frustrating problem. Primitive social organization is kinship organization, and to understand the Yanomamö way of life I had to collect extensive genealogies. I could not have deliberately picked a more difficult group to work with in this regard: They have very stringent name taboos. They attempt to name people in such a way that when the person dies and they can no longer use his name, the loss of the word in the language is not inconvenient. Hence, they name people for specific and minute parts of things, such as "toenail of some rodent," thereby being able to retain the words "toenail" and "(specific) rodent," but not being able to refer directly to the toenail of that rodent. The taboo is maintained even for the living: One mark of prestige is the courtesy others show you by not using your name. The sanctions behind the taboo seem to be an unusual combination of fear and respect.

I tried to use kinship terms to collect genealogies at first, but the kinship terms were so ambiguous that I ultimately had to resort to names. They were quick to grasp that I was bound to learn everybody's name and reacted, without my knowing it, by inventing false names for everybody in the village. After having spent several months collecting names and learning them, this came as a disappointment to me: I could not cross-check the genealogies with other informants from distant villages.

They enjoyed watching me learn these names. I assumed, wrongly, that I would get the truth to each question and that I would get the best information by working in public. This set the stage for converting a serious project into a farce. Each informant tried to outdo his peers by inventing a name even more ridiculous than what I had been given earlier, or by asserting that the individual about whom I inquired was married to his mother or daughter, and the like. I would have the informant whisper the name of the individual in my ear, noting that he was the father of such and such a child. Everybody would then insist that I repeat the name aloud, roaring in hysterics as I clumsily pronounced the name. I assumed that the laughter was in response to the violation of the name taboo or to my pronunciation. This was a reasonable interpretation, since the individual whose name I said aloud invariably became angry. After I learned what some of the names meant, I began to understand what the laughter was all about. A few of the more colorful examples are: "hairy vagina," "long penis," "feces of the harpy eagle," and "dirty rectum." No wonder the victims were angry.

I was forced to do my genealogy work in private because of the horseplay and nonsense. Once I did so, my informants began to agree with each other and I managed to learn a few new names, real names. I could then test any new informant by collecting a genealogy from him that I knew to be accurate. I was able to weed out the more mischievous informants this way. Little by little I extended the genealogies and learned the real names. Still, I was unable to get the names of the dead and extend the genealogies back in time, and even my best informants continued to deceive me about their own close relatives. Most of them gave me the name of a living man as the father of some individual in order to avoid mentioning that the actual father was dead.

The quality of a genealogy depends in part on the number of generations it embraces, and the name taboo prevented me from getting any substantial information about deceased ancestors. Without this information, I could not detect marriage patterns through time. I had to rely on older informants for this information, but these were the most reluctant of all. As I became more proficient in the language and more skilled at detecting lies, my informants became better at lying. One of them in particular was so cunning and persuasive that I was shocked to discover that he had been inventing his information. He specialized in making a ceremony out of telling me false names. He would look around to make sure nobody was listening outside my hut, enjoin me to never mention the name again, act very nervous and spooky, and then grab me by the head to whisper the name very softly into my ear. I was always elated after an informant session with him, because I had several generations of dead ancestors for the living people. The others refused to give me this information. To show my gratitude, I paid him quadruple the rate I had given the others. When word got around that I had increased the pay, volunteers began pouring in to give me genealogies.

I discovered that the old man was lying quite by accident. A club fight broke out in the village one day, the result of a dispute over the possession of a woman. She had been promised to Rerebawa, a particularly aggressive young man who had married into the village. Rerebawa had already been given her older sister and was enraged when the younger girl began having an affair with another man in the village, making no attempt to conceal it from him. He challenged the young man to a club fight, but was so abusive in his challenge that the opponent's father took offense and entered the village circle with his son, wielding a long club. Rerebawa swaggered out to the duel and hurled insults at both of them, trying to goad them into striking him on the head with their clubs. This would have given him the opportunity to strike them on the head. His opponents refused to hit him, and the fight ended. Rerebawa had won a moral victory because his opponents were afraid to hit him. Thereafter, he swaggered around and insulted the two men behind their backs. He was genuinely angry with them, to the point of calling the older man by the name of his dead father. I quickly seized on this as an opportunity to collect an accurate genealogy and pumped him about his adversary's ancestors. Rerebawa had been particularly nasty to me up to this point, but we became staunch allies: We were both outsiders in the local village. I then asked about other dead ancestors and got immediate replies. He was angry with the whole group and not afraid to tell me the names of the dead. When I compared his version of the genealogies to that of the old man, it was obvious that one of them was lying. I challenged his information, and he explained that everybody knew that the old man was deceiving me and bragging about it in the village. The names the old man had given me were the dead ancestors of the members of a village so far away that he thought I would never have occasion to inquire about them. As it turned out, Rerebawa knew most of the people in that village and recognized the names.

I then went over the complete genealogical records with Rerebawa, genealogies I had presumed to be in final form. I had to revise them all because of the numerous lies and falsifications they contained. Thus, after five months of almost constant work on the genealogies of just one group, I had to begin almost from scratch!

Discouraging as it was to start over, it was still the first real turning point in my fieldwork. Thereafter, I began taking advantage of local arguments and animosities in selecting my informants, and used more extensively individuals who had married into the group. I began traveling to other villages to check the genealogies, picking villages that were on strained terms with the people about whom I wanted information. I would then return to my base camp and check with local informants the accuracy of the new information. If the informants became angry when I mentioned the new names I acquired from the unfriendly group, I was almost certain that the information was accurate. For this kind of checking I had to use informants whose genealogies I knew rather well: They had to be distantly enough related to the dead person that they would not go into a rage when I mentioned the name, but not so remotely related that they would be uncertain of the accuracy of the information. Thus, I had to make a list of names that I dared not use in the presence of each and every informant. Despite the precautions, I occasionally hit a name that put the informant into a rage, such as that of a dead brother or sister that other informants had not reported. This always terminated the day's work with that informant, for he would be too touchy to continue any further, and I would be reluctant to take a chance on accidentally discovering another dead kinsman so soon after the first.

These were always unpleasant experiences, and occasionally dangerous ones, depending on the temperament of the informant. On one occasion I was planning to visit a village that had been raided about a week earlier. A woman whose name I had on my list had been killed by the raiders. I planned to check each individual on the list one by one to estimate ages, and I wanted to remove her name so that I would not say it aloud in the village. I knew that I would be in considerable difficulty if I said this name aloud so soon after her death. I called on my original informant and asked him to tell me the name of the woman who had been killed. He refused, explaining that she was a close relative of his. I then asked him if he would become angry if I read off all the names on the list. This way he did not have to say her name and could merely nod when I mentioned the right one. He was a fairly good friend of mine, and I thought I could predict his reaction. He assured me that this would be a good way of doing it. We were alone in my hut so that nobody could overhear us. I read the names softly, continuing to the next when he gave a negative reply. When I finally spoke the name of the dead woman he flew out of his chair, raised his arm to strike me, and shouted: "You son-of-a-bitch![2] If you ever say that name again, I'll kill you!" He was shaking with rage, but left my hut quietly. I shudder to think what might have happened if I had said the name unknowingly in the woman's village. I had other, similar experiences in different villages, but luckily the dead person had been dead for some time and was not closely related to the individual into whose ear I whispered the name. I was merely cautioned to desist from saying any more names, lest I get people angry with me.

I had been working on the genealogies for nearly a year when another individual came to my aid. It was Kaobawa, the headman of Upper Bisaasi-teri, the group in which I spent most of my time. He visited me one day after the others had left the hut and volunteered to help me on the genealogies. He was poor, he explained, and needed a machete. He would work only on the condition that I did not ask him about his own parents and other very close kinsmen who were dead. He also added that he would not lie to me as the others had done in the past. This was perhaps the most important single event in my fieldwork, for out of this meeting evolved a very warm friendship and a very profitable informant-fieldworker relationship.

Kaobawa's familiarity with his group's history and his candidness were remarkable. His knowledge of details was almost encyclopedic. More than that, he was enthusiastic and encouraged me to learn details that I might otherwise have ignored. If there were things he did not know intimately, he would advise me to wait until he could check things out with someone in the village. This he would do clandestinely, giving me a report the next day. As I was constrained by my part of the bargain to avoid discussing his close dead kinsmen, I had to rely on Rerebawa for this information. I got Rerebawa's genealogy from Kaobawa.

Once again I went over the genealogies with Kaobawa to recheck them, a considerable task by this time: they included about two thousand names, representing several generations of individuals from four different villages. Rerebawa's information was very accurate, and Kaobawa's contribution enabled me to trace the genealogies further back in time. Thus, after nearly a year of constant work on genealogies, Yanomamö demography and social organization began to fall into a pattern. Only then could I see how kin groups formed and exchanged women with each other over time, and only then did the fissioning of larger villages into smaller ones show a distinct pattern. At this point I was able to begin formulating more intelligent questions because there was now some sort of pattern to work with. Without the help of Rerebawa and Kaobawa, I could not have made very much sense of the plethora of details I had collected from dozens of other informants.

Kaobawa is about 40 years old. I say "about" because the Yanomamö numeration system has only three numbers: one, two, and more-than-two. He is the headman of Upper Bisaasi-teri. He has had five or six wives so far and temporary affairs with as many more women, one of which resulted in a child. At the present time he has just two wives, Bahimi and Koamashima. He has had a daughter and a son by Bahimi, his eldest and favorite wife. Koamashima, about 20 years old, recently had her first child, a boy. Kaobawa may give Koamashima to his youngest brother. Even now the brother shares in her sexual services. Kaobawa recently gave his third wife to another of his brothers because she was beshi: "horny." In fact, this girl had been married to two other men, both of whom discarded her because of her infidelity. Kaobawa had one daughter by her; she is being raised by his brother.

Kaobawa's eldest wife, Bahimi, is about thirty-five years old. She is his first cross-cousin. Bahimi was pregnant when I began my fieldwork, but she killed the new baby, a boy, at birth, explaining tearfully that it would have competed with

Ariwari, her nursing son, for milk. Rather than expose Ariwari to the dangers and uncertainty of an early weaning, she killed the new child instead. By Yanomamö standards, she and Kaobawa have a very tranquil household. He only beats her once in a while, and never very hard. She never has affairs with other men.

Kaobawa is quiet, intense, wise, and unobtrusive. He leads more by example than by threats and coercion. He can afford to be this way as he established his reputation for being fierce long ago, and other men respect him. He also has five mature brothers who support him, and he has given a number of his sisters to other men in the village, thereby putting them under some obligation to him. In short, his "natural" following (kinsmen) is large, and he does not have to constantly display his ferocity. People already respect him and take his suggestions seriously.

Rerebawa is much younger, only about twenty-two years old. He has just one wife by whom he has had three children. He is from Karohi-teri, one of the villages to which Kaobawa is allied. Rerebawa left his village to seek a wife in Kaobawa's group because there were no eligible women there for him to marry.

Rerebawa is perhaps more typical than Kaobawa in the sense that he is concerned about his reputation for ferocity and goes out of his way to act tough. He is, however, much braver than the other men his age and backs up his threats with action. Moreover, he is concerned about politics and knows the details of intervillage relationships over a large area. In this respect he shows all the attributes of a headman, although he is still too young and has too many competent older brothers in his own village to expect to move easily into the position of leadership there.

He does not intend to stay in Kaobawa's group and has not made a garden. He feels that he has adequately discharged his obligations to his wife's parents by providing them with fresh game for three years. They should let him take the wife and return to his own village with her, but they refuse and try to entice him to remain permanently in Bisaasi-teri to provide them with game when they are old. They have even promised to give him their second daughter if he will stay permanently.

Although he has displayed his ferocity in many ways, one incident in particular shows what his character is like. Before he left his own village to seek a wife, he had an affair with the wife of an older brother. When he was discovered, his brother attacked him with a club. Rerebawa was infuriated so he grabbed an axe and drove his brother out of the village after soundly beating him with the flat of the blade. The brother was so afraid that he did not return to the village for several days. I recently visited his village with him. He made a point to introduce me to this brother. Rerebawa dragged him out of his hammock by the arm and told me, "This is the brother whose wife I had an affair with," a deadly insult. His brother did nothing and slunk back into his hammock, shamed, but relieved to have Rerebawa release the vise-grip on his arm.

Despite the fact that he admires Kaobawa, he has a low opinion of the others in Bisaasi-teri. He admitted confidentially that he thought Bisaasi-teri was an abominable group: "This is a terrible neighborhood! All the young men are lazy and cowards and everybody is committing incest! I'll be glad to get back home." He also admired Kaobawa's brother, the headman of Monou-teri. This man was killed by raiders while I was doing my fieldwork. Rerebawa was disgusted that the others did not chase the raiders when they discovered the shooting: "He was the only fierce one in the whole group; he was my close friend. The cowardly Monou-teri hid like women in the jungle and didn't even chase the raiders!"

Even though Rerebawa is fierce and capable of being quite nasty, he has a good side as well. He has a very biting sense of humor and can entertain the group for hours on end with jokes and witty comments. And, he is one of few Yanomamö that I feel I can trust. When I returned to Bisaasi-teri after having been away for a year, Rerebawa was in his own village visiting his kinsmen. Word reached him that I had returned, and he immediately came to see me. He greeted me with an immense bear hug and exclaimed, "Shaki! Why did you stay away so long? Did you know that my will was so cold while you were gone that at times I could not eat for want of seeing you?" I had to admit that I missed him, too.

Of all the Yanomamö I know, he is the most genuine and the most devoted to his culture's ways and values. I admire him for that, although I can't say that I subscribe to or endorse these same values. By contrast, Kaobawa is older and wiser. He sees his own culture in a different light and criticizes aspects of it he does not like. While many of his peers accept some of the superstitions and explanatory myths as truth and as the way things ought to be, Kaobawa questions them and privately pokes fun at some of them. Probably, more of the Yanomamö are like Rerebawa, or at least try to be.

NOTES

1. "Shaki," or, rather, "Shakiwa," is the name they gave me because they could not pronounce "Chagnon." They like to name people for some distinctive feature when possible. *Shaki* is the name of a species of noisome bees; they accumulate in large numbers around ripening bananas and make pests of themselves by eating into the fruit, showering the people below with the debris. They probably adopted this name for me because I was also a nuisance, continuously prying into their business, taking pictures of them, and, in general, being where they did not want me.

2. This is the closest English translation of his actual statement, the literal translation of which would be nonsensical in our language.

Anybody's Son Will Do

Gwynne Dyer

introduction

To understand the term *socialization*, substitute the word learning. Socialization does not refer only to children. All of us are being socialized all of the time. Each time we are exposed to something new, we are being socialized. If we learn how to use a new computer program, play a new (or old) video game, listen to the radio, watch a movie, read a book, or listen to a college lecture, we are being socialized. Even when we talk to a friend, socialization is taking place, for ideas and perspectives are being exchanged, some of which become part of the way we view the world. And socialization doesn't stop when we reach a certain age. Even when we are old, we will be exposed to experiences that influence our perspectives. Socialization, then, is a lifelong process, one in which people become more and more a part of their culture—or of their subculture.

From these examples, you might conclude that socialization is usually gentle, subtle, and gradual. And you would be right. The shaping process usually is like this. But there are remarkable exceptions. Anyone who has been thrown into jail for the first time can attest to an exceptional socialization. So can people who have gone through a hazing ritual in a fraternity or sorority. One of these exceptions is analyzed by Dyer, who examines the techniques by which the U.S. Marine Corps turns young men into killers. Not only is it remarkable that this occurs, but also that this organization is able to accomplish this transformation in less than eleven weeks. As you will see, the Marines' techniques are brutal, swift, and effective.

Thinking Critically

As you read this article, ask yourself:

1. How do the U.S. Marines socialize their recruits?

2. How do the socialization techniques used by the Marines compare with the socialization techniques that were used to bring you to your current place in life?

3. Why are the socialization techniques of the Marines so effective?

You think about it and you know you're going to have to kill but you don't under-
stand the implications of that, because in the society in which you've lived murder
is the most heinous of crimes . . . and you are in a situation in which it's turned
the other way round. . . . When you do actually kill someone the experience, my
experience, was one of revulsion and disgust. . . .

I was utterly terrified—petrified—but I knew there had to be a Japanese sniper
in a small fishing shack near the shore. He was firing in the other direction at
Marines in another battalion, but I knew as soon as he picked off the people
there—there was a window on our side—that he would start picking us off. And
there was nobody else to go . . . and so I ran towards the shack and broke in and
found myself in an empty room. . . .

There was a door which meant there was another room and the sniper was in
that—and I just broke that down. I was just absolutely gripped by the fear that
this man would expect me and would shoot me. But as it turned out he was in a
sniper harness and he couldn't turn around fast enough. He was entangled in the
harness so I shot him with a .45, and I felt remorse and shame. I can remember
whispering foolishly, "I'm sorry" and then just throwing up. . . . I threw up all
over myself. It was a betrayal of what I'd been taught since a child.

—William Manchester

Yet he did kill the Japanese soldier, just as he had been trained to—the revulsion
only came afterward. And even after Manchester knew what it was like to kill another human being, a young man like himself, he went on trying to kill his "enemies"
until the war was over. Like all the other tens of millions of soldiers who had been
taught from infancy that killing was wrong, and had then been sent off to kill for
their countries, he was almost helpless to disobey, for he had fallen into the hands
of an institution so powerful and so subtle that it could quickly reverse the moral
training of a lifetime.

The whole vast edifice of the military institution rests on its ability to obtain
obedience from its members even unto death—and the killing of others. It has enormous powers of compulsion at its command, of course, but all authority must be
based ultimately on consent. The task of extracting that consent from its members
has probably grown harder in recent times, for the gulf between the military and
the civilian worlds has undoubtedly widened: Civilians no longer perceive the threat
of violent death as an everyday hazard of existence, and the categories of people
whom it is not morally permissible to kill have broadened to include (in peacetime)
the entire human race. Yet the armed forces of every country can still take almost
any young male civilian and turn him into a soldier with all the right reflexes and
attitudes in only a few weeks. Their recruits usually have no more than twenty years'
experience of the world, most of it as children, while the armies have had all of history to practice and perfect their techniques.

Just think of how the soldier is treated. While still a child he is shut up in the bar-
racks. During his training he is always being knocked about. If he makes the least
mistake he is beaten, a burning blow on his body, another on his eye, perhaps his

head is laid open with a wound. He is battered and bruised with flogging. On the march . . . they hang heavy loads round his neck like that of an ass.

—Egyptian, ca. 1500 B.C.

The moment I talk to the new conscripts about the homeland I strike a land mine. So I kept quiet. Instead, I try to make soldiers of them. I give them hell from morning to sunset. They begin to curse me, curse the army, curse the state. Then they begin to curse together, and become a truly cohesive group, a unit, a fighting unit.

—Israeli, ca. A.D. 1970

All soldiers belong to the same profession, no matter what country they serve, and it makes them different from everybody else. They have to be different, for their job is ultimately about killing and dying, and those things are not a natural vocation for any human being. Yet all soldiers are born civilians. The method for turning young men into soldiers—people who kill other people and expose themselves to death—is basic training. It's essentially the same all over the world, and it always has been, because young men everywhere are pretty much alike.

Human beings are fairly malleable, especially when they are young, and in every young man there are attitudes for any army to work with: the inherited values and postures, more or less dimly recalled, of the tribal warriors who were once the model for every young boy to emulate. Civilization did not involve a sudden clean break in the way people behave, but merely the progressive distortion and redirection of all the ways in which people in the old tribal societies used to behave, and modern definitions of maleness still contain a great deal of the old warrior ethic. The anarchic machismo of the primitive warrior is not what modern armies really need in their soldiers, but it does provide them with promising raw material for the transformation they must work in their recruits.

Just how this transformation is wrought varies from time to time and from country to country. In totally militarized societies—ancient Sparta, the samurai class of medieval Japan, the areas controlled by organizations like the Eritrean People's Liberation Front today—it begins at puberty or before, when the young boy is immersed in a disciplined society in which only the military values are allowed to penetrate. In more sophisticated modern societies, the process is briefer and more concentrated, and the way it works is much more visible. It is, essentially, a conversion process in an almost religious sense—and as in all conversion phenomena, the emotions are far more important than the specific ideas. . . .

Armies know this. It is their business to get men to fight, and they have had a long time to work out the best way of doing it. All of them pay lip service to the symbols and slogans of their political masters, though the amount of time they must devote to this activity varies from country to country. . . . Nor should it be thought that the armies are hypocritical—most of their members really do believe in their particular national symbols and slogans. But their secret is that they know these are not the things that sustain men in combat.

What really enables men to fight is their own self-respect, and a special kind of love that has nothing to do with sex or idealism. Very few men have died in battle, when the moment actually arrived, for the United States of America or for the sacred cause of Communism, or even for their homes and families; if they had any choice in the matter at all, they chose to die for each other and for their own vision of themselves. . . .

The way armies produce this sense of brotherhood in a peacetime environment is basic training: a feat of psychological manipulation on the grand scale which has been so consistently successful and so universal that we fail to notice it as remarkable. In countries where the army must extract its recruits in their late teens, whether voluntarily or by conscription, from a civilian environment that does not share the military values, basic training involves a brief but intense period of indoctrination whose purpose is not really to teach the recruits basic military skills, but rather to change their values and their loyalties. "I guess you could say we brainwash them a little bit," admitted a U.S. Marine drill instructor, "but you know they're good people."

The duration and intensity of basic training, and even its major emphases, depend on what kind of society the recruits are coming from, and on what sort of military organization they are going to. It is obviously quicker to train men from a martial culture than from one in which the dominant values are civilian and commercial, and easier to deal with volunteers than with reluctant conscripts. Conscripts are not always unwilling, however; there are many instances in which the army is popular for economic reasons. . . .

It's easier if you catch them young. You can train older men to be soldiers; it's done in every major war. But you can never get them to believe that they like it, which is the major reason armies try to get their recruits before they are 20. There are other reasons too, of course, like the physical fitness, lack of dependents, and economic dispensability of teenagers, that make armies prefer them, but the most important qualities teenagers bring to basic training are enthusiasm and naiveté. Many of them actively want the discipline and the closely structured environment that the armed forces will provide, so there is no need for the recruiters to deceive the kids about what will happen to them after they join.

> *There is discipline. There is drill. . . . When you are relying on your mates and they are relying on you, there's no room for slackness or sloppiness. If you're not prepared to accept the rules, you're better off where you are.*
> —British army recruiting advertisement, 1976

> *People are not born soldiers, they become soldiers. . . . And it should not begin at the moment when a new recruit is enlisted into the ranks, but rather much earlier, at the time of the first signs of maturity, during the time of adolescent dreams.*
> —Red Star (Soviet army newspaper), 1973

Young civilians who have volunteered and have been accepted by the Marine Corps arrive at Parris Island, the Corps's East Coast facility for basic training, in a state of considerable excitement and apprehension: Most are aware that they are about to undergo an extraordinary and very difficult experience. But they do not make their own way to the base; rather, they trickle in to Charleston airport on various flights throughout the day on which their training platoon is due to form, and are held there, in a state of suppressed but mounting nervous tension, until late in the evening. When the buses finally come to carry them the seventy-six miles to Parris Island, it is often after midnight—and this is not an administrative oversight. The shock treatment they are about to receive will work most efficiently if they are worn out and somewhat disoriented when they arrive.

The basic training organization is a machine, processing several thousand young men every month, and every facet and gear of it has been designed with the sole purpose of turning civilians into Marines as efficiently as possible. Provided it can have total control over their bodies and their environment for approximately three months, it can practically guarantee converts. Parris Island provides that controlled environment, and the recruits do not set foot outside it again until they graduate as Marine privates eleven weeks later.

> They're allowed to call home, so long as it doesn't get out of hand—every three weeks or so they can call home and make sure everything's all right, if they haven't gotten a letter or there's a particular set of circumstances. If it's a case of an emergency call coming in, then they're allowed to accept that call; if not, one of my staff will take the message. . . .
> In some cases I'll get calls from parents who haven't quite gotten adjusted to the idea that their son had cut the strings—and in a lot of cases that's what they're doing. The military provides them with an opportunity to leave home but they're still in a rather secure environment.
>
> —Captain Brassington, USMC

For the young recruits, basic training is the closest thing their society can offer to a formal rite of passage, and the institution probably stands in an unbroken line of descent from the lengthy ordeals by which young males in precivilized groups were initiated into the adult community of warriors. But in civilized societies it is a highly functional institution whose product is not anarchic warriors, but trained soldiers.

Basic training is not really about teaching people skills; it's about changing them, so that they can do things they wouldn't have dreamt of otherwise. It works by applying enormous physical and mental pressure to men who have been isolated from their normal civilian environment and placed in one where the only right way to think and behave is the way the Marine Corps wants them to. The key word the men who run the machine use to describe this process is *motivation*.

> I can motivate a recruit and in third phase, if I tell him to jump off the third deck, he'll jump off the third deck. Like I said before, it's a captive audience and I can train that guy; I can get him to do anything I want him to do. . . . They're good kids and they're out to do the right thing. We get some bad kids, but you know, we weed those out. But as far as motivation—here, we can motivate them to do anything you want, in recruit training.
>
> —USMC drill instructor, Parris Island

The first three days the raw recruits spend at Parris Island are actually relatively easy, though they are hustled and shouted at continuously. It is during this time that they are documented and inoculated, receive uniforms, and learn the basic orders of drill that will enable young Americans (who are not very accustomed to this aspect of life) to do everything simultaneously in large groups. But the most important thing that happens in "forming" is the surrender of the recruits' own clothes, their hair—all the physical evidence of their individual civilian identities.

During a period of only 72 hours, in which they are allowed little sleep, the recruits lay aside their former lives in a series of hasty rituals (like being shaven to the scalp) whose symbolic significance is quite clear to them even though they are quite deliberately given absolutely no time for reflection, or any hint that they might have the option of turning back from their commitment. The men in charge of them know how delicate a tightrope they are walking, though, because at this stage the recruits are still newly caught civilians who have not yet made their ultimate inward submission to the discipline of the Corps.

> *Forming Day One makes me nervous. You've got a whole new mob of recruits, you know, 60 or 70 depending, and they don't know anything. You don't know what kind of a reaction you're going to get from the stress you're going to lay on them, and it just worries me the first day. . . .*
>
> *Things could happen, I'm not going to lie to you. Something might happen. A recruit might decide he doesn't want any part of this stuff and maybe take a poke at you or something like that. In a situation like that it's going to be a spur-of-the-moment thing and that worries me.*
>
> —USMC drill instructor

But it rarely happens. The frantic bustle of forming is designed to give the recruit no time to think about resisting what is happening to him. And so the recruits emerge from their initiation into the system, stripped of their civilian clothes, shorn of their hair, and deprived of whatever confidence in their own identity they may previously have had as 18-year-olds, like so many blanks ready to have the Marine identity impressed upon them.

The first stage in any conversion process is the destruction of an individual's former beliefs and confidence, and his reduction to a position of helplessness and need. It isn't really as drastic as all that, of course, for three days cannot cancel out 18 years; the inner thoughts and the basic character are not erased. But the recruits have already learned that the only acceptable behavior is to repress any unorthodox thoughts and to mimic the character the Marine Corps wants. Nor are they, on the whole, reluctant to do so, for they *want* to be Marines. From the moment they arrive at Parris Island, the vague notion that has been passed down for a thousand generations that masculinity means being a warrior becomes an explicit article of faith, relentlessly preached: To be a man means to be a Marine.

There are very few 18-year-old boys who do not have highly romanticized ideas of what it means to be a man, so the Marine Corps has plenty of buttons to push. And it starts pushing them on the first day of real training: The officer in charge of the formation appears before them for the first time, in full dress uniform with medals, and tells them how to become men.

The United States Marine Corps has 205 years of illustrious history to speak for itself. You have made the most important decision in your life . . . by signing your name, your life, pledge to the Government of the United States, and even more importantly, to the United States Marine Corps—a brotherhood, an elite unit. In 10.3 weeks you are going to become a member of that history, those traditions, this organization—if you have what it takes. . . .

All of you want to do that by virtue of your signing your name as a man. The Marine Corps says that we build men. Well, I'll go a little bit further. We develop the tools that you have—and everybody has those tools to a certain extent right now. We're going to give you the blueprints, and we are going to show you how to build a Marine. You've got to build a Marine—you understand?

—Captain Pingree, USMC

The recruits, gazing at him with awe and adoration, shout in unison, "Yes, sir!" just as they have been taught. They do it willingly, because they are volunteers—but even conscripts tend to have the romantic fervor of volunteers if they are only 18 years old. Basic training, whatever its hardships, is a quick way to become a man among men, with an undeniable status, and beyond the initial consent to undergo it, it doesn't even require any decisions.

I had just dropped out of high school and I wasn't doing much on the street except hanging out, as most teenagers would be doing. So they gave me an opportunity— a recruiter picked me up, gave me a good line, and said that I could make it in the Marines, that I have a future ahead of me. And since I was living with my parents, I figured that I could start my own life here and grow up a little.

—USMC recruit

I like the hand-to-hand combat and . . . things like that. It's a little rough going on me, and since I have a small frame I would like to become deadly, as I would put it. I like to have them words, especially the way they've been teaching me here.

—USMC recruit (from Brooklyn), Parris Island

The training, when it starts, seems impossibly demanding physically for most of the recruits—and then it gets harder week by week. There is a constant barrage of abuse and insults aimed at the recruits, with the deliberate purpose of breaking down their pride and so destroying their ability to resist the transformation of values and attitudes that the Corps intends them to undergo. At the same time the demands for constant alertness and for instant obedience are continuously stepped up, and the standards by which the dress and behavior of the recruits are judged become steadily more unforgiving. But it is all carefully calculated by the men who run the machine, who think and talk in terms of the stress they are placing on the recruits: "We take so many c.c.'s of stress and we administer it to each man—they should be a little bit scared and they should be unsure, but they're adjusting." The aim is to keep the training arduous but just within most of the recruits' capability to withstand. One of the most striking achievements of the drill instructors is to create and maintain the illusion that basic training is an extraordinary challenge, one that will set those who graduate apart from others, when in fact almost everyone can succeed.

There has been some preliminary weeding out of potential recruits even before they begin training, to eliminate the obviously unsuitable minority, and some people do "fail" basic training and get sent home, at least in peacetime. The standards of acceptable performance in the U.S. armed forces, for example, tend to rise and fall in inverse proportion to the number and quality of recruits available to fill the forces to the authorized manpower levels. But there are very few young men who cannot be turned into passable soldiers if the forces are willing to invest enough effort in it.

Not even physical violence is necessary to effect the transformation, though it has been used by most armies at most times.

> *It's not what it was 15 years ago down here. The Marine Corps still occupies the position of a tool which the society uses when it feels like that is a resort that they have to fall to. Our society changes as all societies do, and our society felt that through enlightened training methods we could still produce the same product—and when you examine it, they're right. . . . Our 100 c.c.'s of stress is really all we need, not two gallons of it, which is what used to be. . . . In some cases with some of the younger drill instructors it was more an initiation than it was an acute test, and so we introduced extra officers and we select our drill instructors to "fine-tune" it.*
>
> —Captain Brassington, USMC

There is, indeed, a good deal of fine-tuning in the roles that the men in charge of training any specific group of recruits assume. At the simplest level, there is a sort of "good cop–bad cop" manipulation of the recruits' attitudes toward those applying the stress. The three younger drill instructors with a particular serial are quite close to them in age and unremittingly harsh in their demands for ever higher performance, but the senior drill instructor, a man almost old enough to be their father, plays a more benevolent and understanding part and is available for individual counseling. And generally offstage, but always looming in the background, is the company commander, an impossibly austere and almost godlike personage.

At least these are the images conveyed to the recruits, although of course all these men cooperate closely with an identical goal in view. It works: In the end they become not just role models and authority figures, but the focus of the recruits' developing loyalty to the organization.

> *I imagine there's some fear, especially in the beginning, because they don't know what to expect. . . . I think they hate you at first, at least for a week or two, but it turns to respect. . . . They're seeking discipline, they're seeking someone to take charge, 'cause at home they never got it. . . . They're looking to be told what to do and then someone is standing there enforcing what they tell them to do, and it's kind of like the father-and-son game, all the way through. They form a fatherly image of the DI whether they want to or not.*
>
> —Sergeant Carrington, USMC

Just the sheer physical exercise, administered in massive doses, soon has the recruits feeling stronger and more competent than ever before. Inspections, often several times daily, quickly build up their ability to wear the uniform and carry themselves like real Marines, which is a considerable source of pride. The inspections also help to set up the pattern in the recruits of unquestioning submission to military authority: Standing stock-still, staring straight ahead, while somebody else examines you closely for faults is about as extreme a ritual act of submission as you can make with your clothes on.

But they are not submitting themselves merely to the abusive sergeant making unpleasant remarks about the hair in their nostrils. All around them are deliberate reminders—the flags and insignia displayed on parade, the military music, the marching formations and drill instructors' cadenced calls—of the idealized organization, the "brotherhood" to which they will be admitted as full members if they submit and conform. Nowhere in the armed forces are the military courtesies so elaborately observed, the staffs' uniforms so immaculate (some DIs change several times a day), and the ritual aspects of military life so highly visible as on a basic training establishment.

Even the seeming inanity of close-order drill has a practical role in the conversion process. It has been over a century since mass formations of men were of any use on the battlefield, but every army in the world still drills its troops, especially during basic training, because marching in formation, with every man moving his body in the same way at the same moment, is a direct physical way of learning two things a soldier must believe: that orders have to be obeyed automatically and instantly, and that you are no longer an individual, but part of a group.

The recruits' total identification with the other members of their unit is the most important lesson of all, and everything possible is done to foster it. They spend almost every waking moment together—a recruit alone is an anomaly to be looked into at once—and during most of that time they are enduring shared hardships. They also undergo collective punishments, often for the misdeed or omission of a single individual (talking in the ranks, a bed not swept under during barracks inspection), which is a highly effective way of suppressing any tendencies toward individualism. And, of course, the DIs place relentless emphasis on competition with other "serials" in training: there may be something infinitely pathetic to outsiders about a marching group of anonymous recruits chanting, "Lift your heads and hold them high, 3313 is a-passin' by," but it doesn't seem like that to the men in the ranks.

Nothing is quite so effective in building up a group's morale and solidarity, though, as a steady diet of small triumphs. Quite early in basic training, the recruits begin to do things that seem, at first sight, quite dangerous: descend by ropes from fifty-foot towers, cross yawning gaps hand-over-hand on high wires (known as the Slide for Life, of course), and the like. The common denominator is that these activities are daunting but not really dangerous: the ropes will prevent anyone from falling to his death off the rappelling tower, and there is a pond of just the right depth—deep enough to cushion a falling man, but not deep enough that he is likely to drown—under the Slide for Life. The goal is not to kill recruits, but to build up their confidence as individuals and as a group by allowing them to overcome apparently frightening obstacles.

You have an enemy here at Parris Island. The enemy that you're going to have at Parris Island is in every one of us. It's in the form of cowardice. The most rewarding experience you're going to have in recruit training is standing on line every evening, and you'll be able to look into each other's eyes, and you'll be able to say to each other with your eyes: "By God, we've made it one more day! We've defeated the coward."

—Captain Pingree

Number on deck, sir, 45 . . . highly motivated, truly dedicated, rompin', stompin', bloodthirsty, kill-crazy United States Marine Corps recruits, SIR!

—Marine chant, Parris Island

If somebody does fail a particular test, he tends to be alone, for the hurdles are deliberately set low enough that most recruits can clear them if they try. In any large group of people there is usually a goat: someone whose intelligence or manner or lack of physical stamina marks him for failure and contempt. The competent drill instructor, without deliberately setting up this unfortunate individual for disgrace, will use his failure to strengthen the solidarity and confidence of the rest. When one hapless young man fell off the Slide for Life into the pond, for example, his drill instructor shouted the usual invective—"Well, get out of the water. Don't contaminate it all day"—and then delivered the payoff line: "Go back and change your clothes. You're useless to your unit now."

"Useless to your unit" is the key phrase, and all the recruits know that what it means is "useless in *battle*." The Marine drill instructors at Parris Island know exactly what they are doing to the recruits, and why. They are not rear-echelon people filling comfortable jobs, but the most dedicated and intelligent NCOs the Marine Corps can find; even now, many of them have combat experience. The Corps has a clear-eyed understanding of precisely what it is training its recruits for—combat—and it ensures that those who do the training keep that objective constantly in sight.

The DIs "stress" the recruits, feed them their daily ration of synthetic triumphs over apparent obstacles, and bear in mind all the time that the goal is to instill the foundations for the instinctive, selfless reactions and the fierce group loyalty that is what the recruits will need if they ever see combat. They are arch-manipulators, fully conscious of it, and utterly unashamed. These kids have signed up as Marines, and they could well see combat; this is the way they have to think if they want to live.

I've seen guys come to Vietnam from all over. They were all sorts of people that had been scared—some of them had been scared all their life and still scared. Some of them had been a country boy, city boys—you know, all different kinds of people—but when they got in combat they all reacted the same—99 percent of them reacted the same. . . . A lot of it is training here at Parris Island, but the other part of it is survival. They know if they don't conform—conform I call it, but if they don't react in the same way other people are reacting, they won't survive. That's just it. You know, if you don't react together, then nobody survives.

—USMC drill instructor, Parris Island

When I went to boot camp and did individual combat training they said if you walk into an ambush what you want to do is just do a right face—you just turn right or left, whichever way the fire is coming from, and assault. I said, "Man, that's crazy. I'd never do anything like that. It's stupid.". . . .

The first time we came under fire, on Hill 1044 in Operation Beauty Canyon in Laos, we did it automatically. Just like you look at your watch to see what time it is. We done a right face, assaulted the hill—a fortified position with concrete bunkers emplaced, machine guns, automatic weapons—and we took it. And we killed—I'd estimate probably 35 North Vietnamese soldiers in the assault, and we only lost three killed. I think it was about two or three, and about eight or ten wounded. . . . .

But you know, what they teach you, it doesn't faze you until it comes down to the time to use it, but it's in the back of your head, like, What do you do when you come to a stop sign? It's in the back of your head, and you react automatically.

—USMC sergeant

Combat is the ultimate reality that Marines—or any other soldiers, under any flag—have to deal with. Physical fitness, weapons training, battle drills, are all indispensable elements of basic training, and it is absolutely essential that the recruits learn the attitudes of group loyalty and interdependency which will be their sole hope of survival and success in combat. The training inculcates or fosters all of those things, and even by the halfway point in the 11-week course, the recruits are generally responding with enthusiasm to their tasks. . . .

In basic training establishments, . . . the malleability is all one way: in the direction of submission to military authority and the internalization of military values. What a place like Parris Island produces when it is successful, as it usually is, is a soldier who will kill because that is his job.

Hooking Up on the Internet

Helene M. Lawson and Kira Leck

introduction

The meaning of dating changes with geography, from one society to another, and with time, from one historical period to another. In some societies, dating is forbidden. Among traditional people in India and Arab countries, for example, to date would be an explicit violation of norms, a repudiation of the background assumptions that underlie morality. For a woman to see a man alone, unless he is her husband or a close relative, is taboo. Breaking this taboo brings swift and severe censure upon the transgressor. If something sexual took place—or even the suspicion that it did—the sanction can be death, with the father, brothers, or uncles carrying out the punishment.

In early United States, also a traditional society, dating as we know it was not practiced. Among the middle class, a young man "courted" a young woman in whom he became interested. He had to make his "intentions," as they were called, known to the girl's parents—and his "intentions" had better be good. Good meant marriage. To seek the girl's and parents' approval for marriage, the suitor, as he was called, would begin formal courtship. He would visit the parents' house, bringing flowers or candy, and sit stiffly in the parlor, the formal living room reserved for visitors. The parents would check out his manners and especially his potential for supporting their daughter. Only after the parents had approved of the young man was the couple allowed to sit in the parlor alone, and that for only limited periods of time with adults hovering in the background.

As society industrialized and traditional relationships changed, so did the custom of courting. The automobile gave young people freedom unknown to previous genera-tions, freedom from the watchful eyes of parents, freedom to be alone in places where they weren't known, and, ultimately, freedom to have sex. We can trace the beginning of the "sexual revolution" to the invention of the automobile, not the invention of the birth control pill. The pill merely speeded things up.

Dating customs, then, like most social behavior, respond to technology, changing as technology bends society. Just as the automobile ushered in fundamental changes in courtship, followed by the pill, so the Internet is having its impact. In this selection, Helene Lawson and Kira Leck examine some of these preliminary changes. You can be certain that the current influence of the Internet on dating is only the beginning of extensive change to come.

Thinking Critically

As you read this selection, ask yourself:

1. How would your life be different if you had been born and reared in one of the traditional societies described in the introduction to this article?

2. Have you done any Internet dating? Would you? Why or why not?

3. Do you think that meeting people online is risky? If so, how can you protect yourself?

The present research focused on the dynamics of Internet dating, a method of courting used by individuals who meet on the Internet and continue online correspondence in hopes of forming a supportive romantic relationship. It sought to determine why people choose to date online, what aspects of face-to-face relations are reproduced, and the rationales and strategies Internet daters use to negotiate and manage problems of risk accompanying the technology.

▪ ▪ ▪ ▪ A BRIEF HISTORY OF DATING PRACTICES

Although the practices of courting vary from culture to culture and change over time, technologies of communication have historically shaped courtship, making it freer and expanding possibilities. The timeless love letter notwithstanding, courtship interaction in the United States has been limited to supervised situations or contained within the bounds of engagement for marriage. This was especially true during the puritan, colonial, and Victorian eras (Hunt, 1959). Historians believe that freer dating practices, such as meeting privately and face-to-face for romantic interactions at scheduled times and places, emerged among middle-class teenagers in the 1920s. These practices developed alongside new technologies such as telephones, automobiles, and drive-in theaters, which allowed teenagers to become more independent from their parents. . . .

In the 1990s, the Internet became a major vehicle for social encounters. Through the Internet, people can interact over greater distances in a shorter period and at less expense than in the past. Theorists have debated the positive and negative effects this technology has on social interactions. Initially, theorists such as Zuboff (1991) believed "the Internet reduced face-to-face interaction" and created an "uncomfortable isolation" (pp. 479–482) for people at work. Conversely, Raney (2000) argued that online communication expands social networks. According to Raney, the Pew Internet and American Life Project found supporting evidence for this view in a study in which "more than half of Internet users reported that e-mail was strengthening their family ties. And Internet users reported far more offline social contact than non-users" (p. G7). . . . Today Internet video and sound communications are commonplace, and photographs, video, and sound clips can all be altered or fabricated entirely. These new technologies allow Internet daters enormous latitude to prepare their presentations of self.

USING THE INTERNET FOR DATING

The Internet is a new social institution that has the ability to connect people who have never met face to face and is thus likely to transform the dating process. Beginning with newsgroups such as Usenet and various bulletin boards that operated under the now-obsolete Gopher system, the Internet facilitated the formation of communities. . . .

We explored the phenomenology of Internet dating, which we defined as the pattern of periodic communication between potential partners using the Internet as a medium. We examined the respondents' concerns over the risk of being deceived, their anxieties about physical appearance, and the hazards of romantic involvement.

METHOD

Participants

Because we needed a sample of respondents who could be tracked over time and whose reliability could be verified, we began to investigate the phenomenon of Internet dating by interviewing people who were personally accessible, such as coworkers, acquaintances, and students. Soon the sample expanded because respondents told us about people they knew who dated online, which resulted in a snowball sample. . . . It was composed of 32% students, 24% business and clerical workers, 14% trade workers, and 14% professionals and semiprofessionals. The sample also included unemployed persons, small business owners, and housewives.

Because we were interested in romantic dating relationships that could result in commitment, we did not include people interested only in pornography or online sexual encounters as their primary focus. We defined dating as setting up specific times to mutually disclose personal information with potential romantic partners on an ongoing basis. We did not place any other restrictions on whom we were willing to interview. Consequently, the sample included homosexuals and unhappily married persons. Romance was not necessarily the goal of online dating, but in our sample, three married persons changed partners as a result of Internet interactions.

Interview Questions

Interviews were open-ended and informal. We asked respondents to (a) describe their experiences with Internet dating, (b) state whether these experiences were positive or negative, (c) state how and why they entered the world of online dating, and (d) state whether they used online dating services or met incidentally through chat rooms, online games, or common interest groups. Respondents were eager to relate their experiences, and many interviews lasted an hour or longer.

Interviews were conducted during lunch in restaurants, at respondents' homes, at the home of the first author, in the university cafeteria, and on walks in various neighborhoods. All respondents had ready access to computers in their homes, dorm rooms, or places of work. We watched while they talked back and forth online. In addition, the first author invited three newly paired couples to her home for dinner. Follow-up data were collected in person, on the phone, by e-mail, and by mail. Interviews were later transcribed and coded by keywords according to concepts that emerged through the dialogue, such as trust, time, risk, and need satisfaction.

We limited the number of respondents to 25 men and 25 women because we wanted to compare gender variables in a balanced sample. The men ranged in age from 18 to 58 with a mean age of 32.6. The women ranged in age from 15 to 48 with a mean age of 33. In all, 17 men and 11 women were single (never married), 7 men and 10 women were divorced, and 1 man and 4 women were married. Two men and one woman were gay. Two women and one man were African American. One man was Indian. Six men and seven women were the parents of young children, and as previously stated, five respondents were married when they began to interact romantically online.

■ ■ ■ RESULTS

Companionship

Lonely people tend to report being dissatisfied with their relationships and are often cynical, rejecting, bored, and depressed. They also have difficulty making friends, engaging in conversations, getting involved in social activities, and dating (Chelune, Sultan, & Williams, 1980; W. H. Jones, Hobbs, & Hockenbury, 1982). Their tendency to engage in minimal self-disclosure and be unresponsive to conversational partners often results in poor interactions that are unrewarding for both partners, which leads lonely individuals to feel dissatisfied with their relationships (McAdams, 1989). Both relationship dissatisfaction and difficulty with social behavior may lead lonely people to seek online relationships.

Regardless of their marital status, respondents of all ages tended to report being lonely. They all talked about needing more communication, emotional support, and companionship. Fred, a 19-year-old student who had never been married, said, "I hate being alone. You want to know someone out there at least cares."

Greta, a 43-year-old, unhappily married mother of a 9-year-old, worked a night shift. Her husband worked during the day, and they both dated others online through chat rooms. Chat rooms often require only token (username) identification. The face presented is largely cloaked, but marital status is usually not hidden. Rather, it is explained:

> I guess the big problem is that my husband works 6 days a week, is gone all day long, and doesn't spend time with me. It is like we are strangers living in the same house. We haven't actually gone out with anyone.

Kelly, a 48-year-old, unhappily married student also blamed her lack of communication with her husband for why she dated online:

> I think I qualify for this interview because I date someone online. In our house there is no communication. That is no way to be. It's two people living in the same house like roommates that have totally different lives. We never talk. That is how my life was before I met George [online]. . . .

Regardless of their marital status, . . . individuals seemed to perceive their social lives as incomplete. This may be a reflection of the separation of family and friends because of current societal structure. Thus, it is not surprising that they were highly motivated to become involved in online relationships with people who were willing to talk, listen, and serve a supportive function. . . .

Comfort After a Life Crisis

. . . [S]everal respondents in the present sample reported seeking comfort after a life crisis, such as the loss of a job, a divorce, or a death in the family. Robin, a 32-year-old, never married woman, said,

> I had suffered such a great loss when my grandpa died. We were very close and he raised me. I guess at that particular point in time in my life I needed someone in my life. One night I was searching for someone to talk with. There is a button you can hit to find a random chat partner. I must have gone through about 10 to 15 different people until his name popped up. I read his details that he provided about himself, and I sent him a message. The first night we talked for about 5 to 6 hours straight, nonstop.

Anna, a 39-year-old, divorced woman, also got online because of her recent divorce: "After my divorce, I cried all the time. My friends were tired of listening to me. I wanted a support group so I went into this chat room.". . .

Our society's lack of support structure for individuals who experience life crises may lead them to seek out comfort from online sources. . . . The online setting allows them to select which aspects of themselves to reveal to their online companions, which lessens the probability of unfavorable judgment that may be leveled by real-life friends and family members.

Control Over Presentation and Environment

The Internet provides a medium for people to present themselves in a way that they think is flattering. Clark (1998) reports that girls describe themselves as "thinner and taller" and otherwise prettier in Internet communications than they actually are. Because contact is mediated, individuals do not have to expose themselves directly on the Internet. In general, "the surest way for a person to prevent threats to his face is to avoid contacts in which these threats are likely to occur" (Goffman, 1967, p. 15).

Jean, a 35-year-old, never married woman, said if you were heavy, you could get to know someone who might like you instead of having to attract people with your looks before they wanted to know you:

> Many of the women I met from my chat room were way overweight. It's easy to sit at home and talk online, say things, and be appealing. I mean it's safe. It's totally safe if you don't ever plan on ever meeting anyone [face to face]. Later on, you do meet them, maybe they will like you anyway. By that time it's worth the risk. . . .

Reid, a 37-year-old, divorced father with two children, said,

> The Internet is a place where people can take risks without consequences. You can experiment with people you wouldn't normally meet or get involved with. You can grocery shop. There are more people to meet. You can play games for a long time. You can look at so many pictures; it's fun like a candy store.

. . . For people who are shy, anxious, and deficient in social skills, use of the Internet may facilitate social interaction because it requires different skills that are necessary for initiating heterosocial interaction in a face-to-face setting. In one study, college students reported using the Internet to meet people because they found it reduced their anxiety about social interaction (Knox, Daniels, Sturdivant, & Zusman, 2001).

Some respondents of both sexes claimed they found it difficult to talk to strangers in social situations such as parties or even in places such as the school cafeteria or a classroom. Rick, a 32-year-old, never married man, said he liked using the Internet because "I'm shy. That is why I went into a chat room. I can say things online that I can't say in person. I am so quiet. But, I can talk on the telephone too."

Pete, a 22-year-old, never married man, did not trust dating in general, but he liked the Internet better than bars:

> Bars are a meat market, and I feel that everybody there is putting on more of a show than actuality. I mean when you meet them [women] in a bar, it's like they are a different person than in real life. And it's the same thing with the Internet, you know, with a lot of women. So many haven't returned messages, or they just leave you hanging, or they pretend to be someone they are not. I'm too shy, too afraid of getting turned down. It's easier, less painful getting turned down on type than it is in person.

Men and women respondents complained that bars were not a good place to get to know prospective partner. Many argued that [they] did not trust the character of bar pickups:

> One thing I found with the bar is that most ladies who go there will say yes and say yes to about anybody given the time of night. Some ladies have propositioned me! Let's just say I don't like being in that situation.

Anna also said, "I don't want to go to bars to meet people. This is a lot safer."

Societal expectations for appearance and behavior can result in individuals who do not fit the norm and perceive themselves as deviants who will not be accepted. Furthermore, they may fear negative reprisals from more mainstream members of society and thus may retreat into an online setting where they feel safer and have control.

Freedom from Commitment and Stereotypes

Clark (1998) found that Internet dating is particularly appealing to teenage girls because it allows them to be aggressive while remaining sheltered. Clark argued that "Internet dating affords teenage girls in particular the opportunity to experiment with and claim power within heterosexual relationships," but she questioned whether the resulting relationships were any more emancipative than those found in the real-life experiences of teenagers. She suggested that "power afforded through self-construction on the Internet does not translate into changed gender roles and expectations in the social world beyond cyberspace." The teenage girls in Clark's study were "not interested in meeting the boys with whom they conversed as they might undermine (their) attractive and aggressive online persona" (pp. 160–169).

. . . Traditional gender norms that dictate that women wait for men to ask them out and men be assertive leaders are still common today (Mongeau, Hale, Johnson, & Hillis, 1993; Simmel, 1911). However, some research (e.g., Cooper & Sportolan, 1997) and responses from the interviewees suggest that these norms may not operate online.

Cathryn, a 15-year-old girl, stated:

> I like to play but not really be there. I met this boy and we talked about school and movies, but we didn't meet. We live in different states. I don't know much about him really. He's just fun to talk to. I tease him a lot. Sometimes my friends pretend they are older or even guys instead of girls.

This online interaction is free from commitment.

Five of the respondents, both men and women, talked about freedom from commitment and stereotypic sex roles. Anna said,

> We agreed that there would be no expectations and if we didn't like each other, we'd have a few laughs, go to a baseball game or two, have a few beers, who cares. Since

I like to travel, I also felt if the guy was a jerk, I had a credit card and would go to a different hotel and stay in San Diego and have a nice vacation. . . .

Ross, a 40-year-old, divorced father who had custody of his 10-year-old son, said,

There is such a difference between actually talking to somebody and putting things in print. You can make yourself sound like I could be Joe Big Stud or whatever on the Internet. Then when we met, we'd see if we got along.

Greg, a 21-year-old, never married student, said,

Every few weeks we'd say "Hey, how's it going?" I told her from day one we'd never know each other's real names, where we lived, or anything about it. She didn't know how old I was or if I was married or single or anything. But we loved talking, and we talked about meeting.

Although many respondents initially wanted freedom from commitment, they liked spending a lot of time online getting to know each other. Often after a period of months, they decided to meet face to face. Some changed their minds about having no commitment and increased their involvement, whereas others concluded that they had too little in common to justify continuing the relationship. Thus, as with traditional dating, online daters seemed to want to get to know their partners better before committing. . . .

Trust, Risk, and Lying Online

Trust may not be important in an interaction when compared to that of opening an opportunity for taking a gamble. Goffman (1967) believed, "Chance lies in the attitude of the individual himself—his creative capacity to redefine the world around him into its decisional potentialities" (p. 201). Goffman saw all forms of action as gambling. Similarly, Simmel (1911) argued that when a person is offered a token of trust, the recipient is expected to respond in kind. When people place online personals ads, those who respond may be perceived as offering a gift; the implication is made that "I trust you enough to treat me well.". . .

The Internet has been described as a "revolutionary social space" (Hardey, 2002, p. 577) in which old rules for social interaction are discarded in favor of new ones that may be better suited to the technology. However, Hardey (2002) found that Internet daters' interactions are often guided by "rituals and norms that protect the self" (p. 577), which was originally suggested by Goffman (1967). The technology of the Internet may present new challenges to building intimacy and avoiding rejection, but the basic motivations for protecting the self remain. New risks inspire new coping strategies to maintain an environment of trust. Such an environment is necessary to maintain the solidarity of society, according to Simmel (1978). Giddens (1990) emphasized a need to establish trust among individuals and observed that the alternative to trust is inaction, which in itself may be risky because if we do not take the risk of interacting, we will not develop a supportive friendship network. He saw relationships as "ties based upon trust, where trust is not pre-given but worked upon, and where the work involved means a mutual process of self-disclosure" (p. 121).

To establish close relationships within the constraints of the Internet, people use creative methods to identify themselves as cool and trustworthy. Emoticons, abbreviations, unconventional spellings, and specialized grammar are used to weed out people who do not share others' realities or ways of being (Waskul, 2003). Turkle (1995) observed that through photographs, profiles, and narratives, "people create and cycle through a sometimes surprising range of online identities" (p. 10). . . .

Online, people commonly misrepresent their appearance, making it more flattering (Clark, 1998). One sample of college students reported lying about their age, weight, and marital status (Knox et al., 2001). They may also misrepresent their gender (Danet, 1998; Knox et al., 2001). Misrepresentation in online social interactions seems so natural that few seem to give much thought to what usually could be dismissed as a makeover of one's persona. Given the limited amount of information available to respondents about each other in Internet interactions and their transitory nature, deception is common.

Most respondents said they had been lied to more than once, and some reported surprise when this happened. Robin, the 32-year-old, single woman, wanted to trust people:

> I was raised to believe and trust in people when they tell you things. So it was very hard for me to believe that someone could play on another person's feelings the way he did with me [a previous Internet relationship had not worked, and Robin believes he had not told her the truth about being truly interested in meeting her and being there for her]. But I have accepted the fact that it happened, and I have moved on with my life and met [also online] someone better. The only advice I have for people who are thinking of Internet dating is just be careful. There is a Web site out there where you can have someone's background checked out to see if they are telling you the truth. In the back of my mind I had a feeling he [her previous online date] was lying, but for some reason I didn't want to face the reality of it. . . .

Most men and women in this study took physical and emotional risks to gain risks and were willing to continue seeking online relationships even after others had lied to them. A few teenagers and adults who did not want committed relationships took fewer risks by taking on unrealistic roles, not being open, and postponing face-to-face meetings. Others developed symbolic trust indicators to lessen the consequential risks of interacting.

Indicators of Trust

Berger and Luckmann (1967) believed people decide to trust based on intuitive impressions that we refer to as "trust indicators." This research uncovered the presence of early and late trust indicators as part of early and late negotiating strategies that serve to minimize harm to the self.

The development of trust in an online dating relationship requires not only the assurance that the other means no physical harm but also that the other will treat the online persona with ritual deference. A remark such as, "I did not know you were so large; do you use Photoshop?" would be a devastating blow. This is one of the reasons some Internet daters postpone or evade face-to-face meetings. . . .

Younger respondents were concerned with the hermeneutics of keystrokes and codes. Arlene, a 17-year-old interviewed by the first author, used *LOL* (laughing out loud), *BRB* (be right back), and other abbreviations when chatting. We found younger people used this coded language more frequently than did older individuals. Respondents who were not adept in the use of such codes exposed their lack of grace in social interaction and were weeded out. Participants selected for interactions of usually only a few minutes duration were chosen many times based on one word or the speed of their typing. More mature respondents had different early indicators. Lisa, a 41-year-old, divorced woman, said,

> I don't use chat rooms much anymore. They are filled with a vast bastion of people looking for absolutely nothing. They are "players." They are talking to you while having cybersex with someone else and talking with a third person in another room at the same time. If you get serious, they don't like it. They use romance and dating rooms, sex cams, interest and game rooms, and they chat on the side at the same time. . . .

Chet, a 28-year-old, divorced man, said chat rooms were for mindless, immature people. He used dating services also:

> I look for women who are funny, sarcastic, you know, intellectual, sharp-witted. I can't start a conversation with someone who says she wants to come over and have sex the next day. Or the stereotypic interaction with emphasis on age, hobbies. . . . It's mindless, immature.

Janet, an 18-year-old, female student, said she could tell right away if it was going to work:

> You talk to them. If they answer with one-word sentences. . . . if the [online] conversation is really unbalanced, I look and see how much I have said and how much they have said. If I tell them what my field of study is and they don't understand anything at all about it. . . . Most people in chat rooms are uneducated, working class, and just plain dumb. You need to weed them out.

Respondents used indicators contained in e-mailed or posted pictures to help evaluate their potential mates and attempted to determine their age and degree of affluence. Clothing, hairstyle, and projected lifestyle were augured from photographs.

Jessie, a 24-year-old woman, focused on economic status:

> I met this man online in a church chat room. He was from South Africa, and he sent me e-mail pictures where he was standing in front of a very expensive car. His clothes were expensive-looking, too, and his house was like a mansion. He said he was a professional businessman with lots of money. He said he wanted to come over here to meet me and my family. He had never been in the States before. I told my mother about him.

Other indicators deal with time. Through face-to-face relating, we have come to expect a certain pattern of flow through which a relationship develops. This pattern is reflected through the timing of conversation and self-disclosure. Often on the Internet there is a pressure to disclose much in a short time to establish trust and kinship quickly. Some respondents dislike this pressure. Julian, 25-year-old salesman, observed,

> Internet people are more desperate; things move fast in weird ways. People put pictures up for everyone to see, but you don't know their personal mannerisms. Do they smell bad? Have a funny laugh? Do they bite their nails? The beginning is different. It [meeting online] sets you off on a weird path. You get way too intense too soon. There's like a speed to get to know each other. All you have is conversation that becomes exaggerated and magnified. It becomes drama. People attach deep meaning and feeling prematurely. Feelings get hurt. Self-revelation leads to distortion of the picture. One woman I met online said, "I think I am ready for a relationship now." This scared me. I wanted to just maybe have at least one date in person and get to know her better before committing to a relationship.

Although this respondent felt it was not a good practice to discuss personal matters too soon, we observed him doing just that in his second e-mail to a woman he had just recently met online.

To develop intimacy to create a bond with an online partner, Internet daters felt pressed to self-disclose as much information as they could in the shortest possible time, though letting people know one's shortcomings begs rejection. Furthermore, disclosing too much too fast violates social conventions and norms. The woman who told Julian, "I think I am ready for a relationship now," scared her potential partner away. . . .

Once Internet daters find each other compatible, they move on to the next step of relationship building. This involves spending more time getting to know one another to build trust. Basic interpersonal trust is either contractual trust based on social contracts as in family relationships or trust based on time in relations (Govier, 1992). Most respondents liked the time they spent getting to know each other. They said this time helped develop trust and intimacy. Robin said it seemed safer to get to know people over time:

> I guess I chose the Internet over meeting someone in a bar or on a blind date because to me it felt a little safer. In a bar you are meeting someone and you get the impression that they want just a one-night stand and that is it. That is not how I was raised. On the Internet you could talk to this person for as long as you wanted to before you went ahead and met that person.

Josh, a 56-year-old, never married man, also felt he had developed trust during time spent online:

> I felt I knew her even though we had not met yet. She was not a stranger. We had spoken over the phone and e-mailed over a period of 11 months. I was not afraid at all. It didn't even enter my mind. I didn't have any reason to believe she would be any different in person than she appeared to be. . . .

▪ ▪ ▪ DISCUSSION

The Internet has opened a new avenue for romantic interaction. In the present study, Internet daters reported being able to reach a larger pool of potential partners and experiencing increased freedom of choice among partners. The Internet also raises new issues of negotiating risk and establishing trust. Respondents said they were willing to take risks to take advantage of the new courting opportunities offered by this new technology. Some risks involved physical danger, and others involved loss of face and possible rejection, though interviewees developed rationales and strategies to deal with these risks to trust that they would have positive experiences.

Dating online modified gendered interactions by allowing women to behave more assertively and men to be more open. It also necessitated the development of new strategies based on keystrokes, codes interpreting online photographs, and reading user profiles to develop trust and confirm compatibility. In Internet interactions, gains and losses are only symbolic, and rejection by an online entity identified only as "suv4" can represent no great material loss. It is this very abstraction that motivates people to use the Internet for dating to avoid stereotyped gender roles and the pain of rejection.

The interrelating of Internet daters also reflects old patterns and problems common to all forms of courtship. Even if they do not find objectification and harassment online, meeting offline often brings objectification or harassment into a formerly nonjudgmental relationship. There is irony in seeking a way out of loneliness through a medium that ensures the insularity of participants and perpetuates gender stereotyping once participants meet.

Several old problems remain in Internet dating. It is easy for people to lie to each other, and appearance issues and shyness do not completely disappear when dating online. Rejection and its emotional pain are ultimately a part of Internet dating as much as of dating that is entirely face to face from the start. The fundamental issues of trust, self-presentation, and compatibility carry over from conventional courtship into its Internet variant.

The need to obtain companionship motivates people to seek out romantic relationships in a variety of ways, and the Internet is merely the latest technological development used by people to assist their romantic goals. Participants in the current study reported reducing their loneliness, obtaining comfort, and finding fun and excitement. These benefits appeared to outweigh the risks.

REFERENCES

Berger, P. L., & Luckmann, T. (1967). *The social construction of reality: A treatise in the sociology of knowledge.* New York: Anchor.

Chelune, G. J., Sultan, F. E., & Williams, C. L. (1980). Loneliness, self-disclosure, and interpersonal effectiveness. *Journal of Counseling Psychology, 27,* 462–468.

Clark, L. S. (1998). Dating on the Net: Teens and the rise of "pure" relationships. In S. Jones (Ed.), *Cybersociety 2.0: Revisiting computer-mediated communication and community* (pp. 159–181). Thousand Oaks, CA: Sage.

Cooper, A., & Sportolari, L. (1997). Romance in cyberspace: Understanding online attraction. *Journal of Sex Education and Therapy, 22,* 7–14.

Danet, B. (1998). Text as mask: Gender, play, and performance on the Internet. In S. Jones (Ed.), *Cybersociety 2.0: Revisiting computer-mediated communication and community* (pp. 129–157). Thousand Oaks, CA: Sage.

Giddens, A. (1990). *The consequences of modernity.* Stanford, CA: Stanford University Press.

Goffman, E. (1959). *The presentation of self in everyday life.* New York: Doubleday.

Goffman, E. (1967). *Interaction ritual: Essays on face-to-face behavior.* Doubleday.

Govier, T. (1992). Trust, distrust, and feminist theory. *Hypatia, 7,* NI.

Hardey, M. (2002). Life beyond the screen: Embodiment and identify through the Internet. *Sociological Review, 50,* 570–585.

Hunt, M. M. (1959). *The natural history of love.* New York: Knopf.

Jones, W. H., Hobbs, S. A., & Hockenbury, D. (1982). Loneliness and social skills deficits. *Journal of Personality and Social Psychology, 42,* 682–689.

Knox, D., Daniels, V., Sturdivant, L., & Zusman, M. (2001). College student use of the Internet for mate rejection. *College Student Journal, 35,* 158–160.

Mongeau, P. A., Hale, J. L., Johnson, K. L., & Hillis, J. D. (1993). Who's wooing whom? An investigation of female initiated dating. In P. J. Kalbfleisch (Ed.), *Interpersonal communication: Evolving interpersonal relationships* (pp. 51–68). Hillsdale, NJ: Lawrence Erlbaum.

Raney, R. F. (2000, May 11). Study finds Internet of social benefit to users. *New York Times.* p. G7.

Simmel, G. (1911). *Philosophische kultur: Gesammelte essays* [Philosophical culture: Collected essays] (2nd ed.). Leipzig, Germany: Alfred Kroner.

Turkle, S. (1995). *Life on the screen: Identity in the age of the Internet.* New York: Simon & Schuster.

Waskul, D. (2003). *Self-games and body-play: Personhood in online chat and cybersex.* New York: Peter Lang.

Zuboff, S. (1991). New worlds of computer-mediated work. In J. M. Hepslin (Ed.), *Down to earth sociology: Introductory readings* (6th ed., pp. 476–485). New York: Free Press.

Inside Organized Racism

Kathleen M. Blee

introduction ■ ■ ■ ■ ■

One of the most common research methods that sociologists use is interviewing, which becomes more powerful when it is combined with participant observation. These two methods, interviewing and participant observation, fit together very well. Participant observation gives the researcher insight into the social dynamics of group members (such as their motivations, the group's hierarchy, and what the group members find rewarding). This, in turn, suggests areas to investigate, even specific questions that should be asked. Similarly, what people talk about in response to open-ended questions cues the researcher into what to look for during participant observation.

In this selection, Blee reports on her research with women who are members of the organized hate movement. As she discusses how she did this study, she takes us behind-the-scenes of research. You will see, for example, how fearful she became. You will also see how her fears sharpened her research skills, how they even helped her gain a better understanding of racist women.

As I stated in the text, I admire the research that my fellow sociologists do, especially research that takes us behind the scenes of human groups to give us insight into why people in those groups think and behave as they do. I have special admiration for sociologists who do creative, risk-taking research, for it gives us understandings that cannot be gained in any other way. This research is one such example. I think you will enjoy this account.

Thinking Critically

As you read this selection, ask yourself:

1. Why would a sociologist risk her life to do this kind of research? Why would people who lead such subterranean lives even talk to a researcher?

2. Blee used participant observation and interviews to study women in hate groups. What types of information was she able to get that she could not have collected by other research methods?

3. Why do women (or men) join organized hate movements?

At a racist gathering on the West Coast, Frank, a skinhead from Texas, sidled up to me to share his disgust at an event so mild it was "something you could see on the family channel." At his side, Liz echoed his sentiment, complaining that she felt trapped in a "Baptist church social." We chatted some more. Frank boasted that this was nothing like he expected. He made the long trip to "get his juices going," not to be part of something concocted by "wimps." Liz agreed, pointing with disdain to a group of women hauling boxes of hamburger buns over to a large grill.

I found their reactions baffling. To me, the scene was horrifying, anything but mundane. Frank's arms were covered with swastika tattoos. On his head was a baseball cap with a comic-like depiction of an African American man being lynched. Liz's black skirt, hose, and boots accentuated the small Klan cross embroidered on her white tailored shirt. The rituals of historical hatred being enacted in front of us seemed far from disappointingly "tame," as Frank and Liz's complaints suggested. A cross was doused with gasoline and set ablaze. People spoke casually of the need to "get rid" of African Americans, immigrants, Jews, gay men and lesbians, and Asian Americans, or exchanged historical trivia purporting to expose the Holocaust as a Zionist hoax. . . .

Only much later did I understand how Frank and Liz could compare a racist rally to a community social gathering. It was years before I could bring myself to read my notes on this rally, written on sheets of paper to which faint scents of smoke and kerosene still seemed to cling. Yet with time and psychic distance from my encounters with Frank, Liz, and others like them, I came to see that aspects of racist gatherings do mirror church socials or neighborhood picnics, albeit in a distorted, perverse fashion. I remember a card table piled high with racist children's books, bumper stickers, and index cards of "white power recipes"; sessions on self-help for disgruntled or substance-addicted members; hymns sung as background to speeches about strengthening the "racialist movement"; and the pancake breakfast and "social hour."

It was with an eerie sense of the familiar colliding with the bizarre that I crossed the boundary that divides the racist underground from the mainstream to write this book. Much about racist groups appears disturbingly ordinary, especially their evocation of community, family, and social ties. One woman gushed that a Ku Klux Klan rally "was a blast. I had fun. And it was just like a big family get-together. We played volleyball. And you had your little church thing on Sunday. For the longest time I thought I would be bored. But I wasn't bored at all.". . .

Some of the ideas voiced by racist groups can seem unremarkable, as evident in the scary similarity to mainstream right-wing stands on such issues as gun control. Still, the watershed that divides racist activism from the rest of society is striking. The beliefs of racist groups are not just extreme variants of mainstream racism, xenophobia, or anti-Semitism. Rather, their conspiratorial logic and zeal for activism separate members of racist groups from those on "the outside," as racist activists call it. By combining the aberrant with the ordinary, the peculiar with the prosaic, modern racist groups gain strength. To design effective strategies to combat racist groups, we must understand this combination. . . .

Women are the newest recruiting targets of racist groups, and they provide a key to these groups' campaign for racial supremacy. "We are very picky when we come to girls," one woman told me. "We don't like sluts. The girls must know their place but take care of business and contribute a lot too. Our girls have a clean slate. Nobody could disrespect us if they tried. We want girls [who are] well educated, the whole bit. And tough. . . ."

The groups and networks that espouse and promote openly racist and anti-Semitic, and often xenophobic and homophobic, views and actions are what I call "organized racism." Organized racism is more than the aggregation of individual racist sentiments. It is a social milieu in which venomous ideas—about African Americans, Jews, Hispanics, Asians, gay men and lesbians, and others—take shape. Through networks of groups and activists, it channels personal sentiments of hatred into collective racist acts. . . .

Today, organized racism in the United States is rife with paradox. While racist groups are becoming more visible, their messages of racial hatred and white supremacy find little support in the rest of society. Racist groups increasingly have anti-Semitism as their core belief, though anti-Semitic attitudes in America as a whole are at their lowest ebb. Despite proclaiming bizarre and illogical views of race and religion, racist groups attract not only those who are ignorant, irrational, socially isolated, or marginal, but also intelligent, educated people, those with resources and social connections, those with something to lose. Organized racists trade in a currency of racist stereotyping little changed from the views of the nineteenth-century Klan and of anti-Semitism recycled from World War II–era Nazi propaganda, yet they recruit successfully among the young who have little or no knowledge of that history. They seize on racist rituals from the past to foment rage about the conditions of the present, appealing to teenagers whose lives are scarred by familial abuse and terror as well as the sons and daughters of stable and loving families, the offspring of privilege and the beneficiaries of parental attention. Racist groups project a sense of hypermasculinity in their militaristic swagger and tactics of bullying and intimidation, but they increasingly are able to bring women into their ranks.

When I began my research, I wanted to understand the paradoxes of organized racism. Were, I wondered, the increased numbers of women changing the masculine cast of racist groups? Why, I asked myself, did racist activists continue to see Jews, African Americans, and others as enemies, and why did they regard violence as a racial solution? Convinced that we can defeat organized racism only if we know how it recruits and retains its members, I also wanted to learn why people join organized racism and how being in racist groups affects them. . . .

■ ■ ■ ■ FOCUSING ON RACIST WOMEN

To understand organized racism from the inside—from the experiences and beliefs of its members—I decided that I needed to talk with racist activists. I chose to interview women for a variety of reasons. On a practical level, I found that I could get access to women racists and develop some measure of rapport with them. More substantively, I wanted to study women racists because we know so little about them. Since 1980 women have been actively recruited by U.S. racist groups both because racist leaders see them as unlikely to have criminal records that would draw the attention of police and because they help augment membership rolls. Today, women are estimated to constitute nearly 50 percent of new members in some racist groups, leading some antiracist monitoring groups to claim that they are the "fastest growing part of the racist movement." Yet this new group of racist activists has been ignored, as researchers have tended to view racism as male-dominated and racist women as more interested in domestic and personal concerns than in its politics.

Eventually, I persuaded thirty-four women from a variety of racist and anti-Semitic groups across the country to talk to me at length about themselves and their racist activities. Fourteen women were in neo-Nazi but not skinhead groups, six were members of Ku Klux Klans, eight were white power skinheads, and six were in Christian Identity or related groups. What they told me shatters many common ideas about what racist activists are like.

Among the women I interviewed there was no single racist *type*. The media depict unkempt, surly women in faded T-shirts, but the reality is different. One of my first interviews was with Mary, a vivacious Klanswoman who met me at her door with a big smile and ushered me into her large, inviting kitchen. Her blond hair was pulled back into a long ponytail and tied with a large green bow. She wore dangling gold hoop earrings, blue jeans, a modest flowered blouse, and no visible tattoos or other racist insignia. Her only other jewelry was a simple gold-colored necklace. Perhaps sensing my surprise at her unremarkable appearance, she joked that her suburban appearance was her "undercover uniform."

Trudy, an elderly Nazi activist I interviewed somewhat later, lived in a one-story, almost shabby ranch house on a lower-middle-class street in a small town in the Midwest. Her house was furnished plainly. Moving cautiously with the aid of a walker, she brought out tea and cookies prepared for my visit. Meeting her reminded me of the phrase "old country women," which I had once heard from a southern policeman characterizing the rural Klanswomen in his area. . . .

My encounters with skinhead women were more guarded, although some were quite animated and articulate. Not one invited me into her home—all I got was a quick glance when I picked her up for an interview in some other location. Most seemed to live at or barely above the level of squatters, in dirty, poorly equipped spaces that were nearly uninhabitable. Their appearance varied. Molly sported five ear piercings that held silver hoops and a silver female sign, an attractive and professionally cut punk hairstyle, fine features, and intense eyes. Others were ghostly figures, with empty eyes and visible scars poorly hidden behind heavy makeup and garish lipstick.

Over a two-year period I spent considerable time with these women, talking to them about their racist commitments and getting them to tell me their life stories. Listening to them describe their backgrounds, I realized that many did not fit common stereotypes about racist women as uneducated, marginal members of society raised in terrible families and lured into racist groups by boyfriends and husbands. . . .

Why were these racist women willing to talk to me? They had a variety of reasons. Some hoped to generate publicity for their groups or themselves—a common motivation for granting interviews to the media. Many saw an opportunity to explain their racial politics to a white outsider, even one decidedly unsympathetic to their arguments. In a racist variant on the religious imperative to "bear witness" to the unconverted, they wanted the outside world to have an accurate (even if negative) account to counter superficial media reports. As one young woman put it, "I don't know what your political affiliations are, but I trust that you'll try to be as objective as possible." Others wished to support or challenge what they imagined I had been told in earlier interviews with racist comrades or competitors. And, despite their deep antagonism toward authority figures, some young women were flattered to have their opinions solicited by a university professor. They had rarely encountered someone older who talked with them without being patronizing, threatening, or directive.

From the beginning, when I asked women if I could interview them, I made it clear that I did not share the racial convictions of these groups. I explicitly said that my views were quite opposed to theirs, that they should not hope to convert me to their views, but that I would try to depict women racist activists accurately. I revealed my critical stance but made it clear that I had no intent to portray them as crazy and did not plan to turn them over to law enforcement or mental health agencies.

I was prepared to elaborate on my disagreements with organized racism in my interviews, but in nearly every case the women cut me short, eager to talk about themselves. Recognizing the extreme marginalization of the racist movement in the American political landscape, these women had no doubt that an ideological gulf divided them from me—it separates their beliefs from nearly all political ideas deemed acceptable in modern public life. They were accustomed to having people disagree with them, and they rarely tried to sway those who openly opposed their opinions. They were interested in me not as a potential convert, but rather as a recorder of their lives and thoughts. Their desire, at once personal and politically evangelical, was that someone outside the small racist groups to which they belong hear and record their words.

Indeed, such eagerness to talk underscores the ethical dilemma of inadvertently providing a platform for racist propaganda. Studies on racist extremists have the power to publicize even as they scrutinize. The problem was brought to the fore as I considered the issue of anonymity for my interviewees. Although the inclusion of more biographical details about the racist women activists I interviewed would be useful, I decided that doing so would unavoidably reveal their identities and thus give further publicity to them and their groups. For this reason, I have used pseudonyms for interviewees and their groups and changed all identifying details, while rendering quotations verbatim. Most people interviewed by scholars desire to remain anonymous, but these women wanted to be known. Some tried to demand that I use their names or the names of their groups. When an older Ku Klux Klan woman thanked me "for writing an article that might inspire others," however, I was convinced that my decision to disguise identities was correct. . . .

Walking a tightrope in my interviews, I kept a balance between maintaining enough distance to make it clear that I rejected their ideas and creating sufficient rapport to encourage women to talk to me. A successful interview needs some conversational common ground. Each party needs to feel understood, if not entirely accepted, by the other. These racist women were unlikely to reveal much about themselves if they did not have some trust in me, if I could not manage to express interest in their lives and refrain from repeatedly condemning them.

Usually a researcher can establish rapport with interviewees by proffering details of his or her personal life or expressing agreement with their choices and beliefs. Because I was unwilling to do either, I was forced to rely on more indirect and fragile measures. Like those at family gatherings and office parties who strain toward congeniality across known lines of disagreement, I seized on any experiences or values that we shared, no matter how trivial. When they expressed dissatisfaction with their bodies, I let them know that I had the same concerns. I commented positively when they talked of their children in parental rather than political terms—for example, when they worried about having enough time to be good mothers—and hoped that my sympathy would lead them to overlook my silence when they discussed such things as the "racial education" they planned for their children. . . .

A researcher can be simultaneously an "insider" and an "outsider" to the culture of those being studied. As a white person I had access that no nonwhite researcher could enjoy. As a woman, I had a store of shared experiences that could support a stream of conversational banter about bodies, men, food, and clothing in which a male researcher would be unlikely to engage. Certainly, both I and the women I interviewed realized that I was an outsider to the world of organized racism. But even the obvious barriers between us gave me insight into their convoluted racial beliefs. For example, my contradictory status as both a racial outsider (to their politics) and an apparent racial insider (as white) helped me understand their ambivalent descriptions of their racial and racist identities.

Yet a reliance on rapport is problematic when scholars do not share a worldview with those they study. Trying to understand the world through the eyes of someone for whom you have even a little sympathy is one thing, but the prospect of developing empathy for a racist activist whose life is given meaning and purpose by the desire to annihilate you or others like you is a very different matter. . . .

There are uncomfortable emotional complexities to this kind of research. Interviewing members of racist groups is dangerous but also intriguing, even offering a voyeuristic thrill. Though I'm embarrassed to admit it, I found meeting racist activists to be exciting as well as horrifying. The ethnographer Barrie Thorne captures this sense of fieldwork as adventure: it consists of "venturing into exciting, taboo, dangerous, perhaps enticing social circumstances; getting the flavor of participation, living out moments of high drama; but in some ultimate way having a cop-out, a built-in escape, a point of outside leverage that full participants lack."[1]

Fieldwork with "unloved groups" also poses the problem of seduction. As Antonius Robben, an anthropologist of Argentinean fascism, notes, even when researchers and interviewees begin as wary opponents, scholars can be drawn into "trad[ing] our critical stance as observers for an illusion of congeniality with cultural insiders."[2] Indeed, others who study loathsome political groups cite the pain of discovering that participants in some of history's most dreadful social movements can be charming and engaging in interviews.[3]

My time with Linda, a white power skinhead from the West, illustrates one instance of emotional seduction. Before our formal interview, our relationship was tense. With every phone call Linda insisted on changing the place and conditions of the interview, demanding ever more evidence that I was not with the police. She repeatedly threatened to bring her boyfriend and a gun to the interview, in violation of our agreement. Each of her demands required more negotiation and gave Linda another opportunity to remind me that she would not hesitate to hurt anyone who betrayed her or her group. Indeed, I had ample reason to take her threats seriously: both Linda and her boyfriend had served prison sentences for assault, selling drugs, and other offenses. I came to the interview frightened and prepared for hostile confrontation. In person, however, Linda confounded my expectations. She was charming, soft-spoken, and concerned for my comfort during the interview. Although quite willing to express appalling attitudes, Linda prefaced many of her statements by apologizing for what I might find offensive. My fear eased, replaced by a seductive, false rapport as Linda set the parameters of our interaction and I responded to her. Off-guard, I pressed Linda less aggressively than the other women to explain contradictions in the chronology and logic of her story. In retrospect, the field notes that I taped immediately after the interview make me uneasy. They show how disarming emotional manipulation can be, even when one is on guard against it:

> I found the [negotiation and preparation for the] interview with Linda to be the most emotionally stressful, maybe with the exception of [another] interview during which I was fearing for my life. Actually with Linda and [her boyfriend] there was no indication that they might try to harm me at all. In fact, quite the contrary. I actually was afraid of that before they came because they both have very violent reputations, but in person they were extremely cordial and very friendly, not trying to intimidate me in any way. Perhaps trying to cultivate me.

Researchers often talk informally about the emotional side of doing fieldwork, but it is a subject rarely discussed in print. Pondering one's own emotional state may seem narcissistic—yet it also can be analytically revealing. In the early stages of this research, I experienced a great deal of fear. The violent reputations of some of the women I wanted to interview, including the skinhead organizer whose comrades referred to her as "Ms. Icepick," did little to dispel my concerns. As I got to know some people in the racist world, I became somewhat less afraid. As I began to see them in more complicated, less stereotyped ways, I no longer worried that every interaction would end in disaster. It also became clear that as a woman in that male-dominated world I was safer because I seemed to pose little threat: male researchers were seen as more personally challenging to male racists and more likely to be covert police operatives.

But in other respects, I grew more afraid as I became less naive. For one thing, I came to realize that my white skin color would provide me little protection. Many racist activists who have faced criminal charges were turned in by other whites, sometimes even members of their own groups. Moreover . . . some racists see race as determined by commitment to white power politics rather than by genetics. I could not assume that those I interviewed would view me either as white or as nonhostile. I could not count on racial immunity from violence.

As I was contacting and interviewing racist women, the structure of the racist movement also changed in two ways that increased my risk. First, the 1995 bombing of the Alfred P. Murrah Federal Building in Oklahoma City occurred midway through my interviewing. In its wake, the racist movement went further underground. Racist groups were subject to investigation and members became increasingly sensitive to the possibility of police informants and infiltrators. Second, as a result of the heightened scrutiny of hate groups after the Oklahoma City bombing, the racist movement became less organized. Some adopted a strategy known as "leaderless resistance," which was designed to make the racist movement less vulnerable to investigation and prosecution. Racist activists began to operate in small units or cells, sometimes in pairs or even alone, to avoid detection by authorities. While adhering to a common agenda of Aryan supremacism, they were able to develop their own strategies, even select enemies, without answering to formal leaders; they used the Internet or other anonymous means to disseminate their ideas rather than relying on organized groups.

Leaderless resistance makes studying the racist movement scarier because it reduces the accountability of individual racists. When I attended a racist rally in the later stages of my research, I came with the permission of the rally's leader. I felt, or at least hoped, that his invitation would ensure my safety. Yet a significant number of those in attendance felt no allegiance to him; they did not care whether their words or actions might reflect on the group or implicate its leader. The *organization* of organized racism, I realized, was double-pronged. It channeled the racist beliefs of members into collective strategies of terrorism, building an agenda of racist practices that could be catastrophic. But it could also curb the violence of particular individuals, unruly members whose actions could bring the collective and its leaders to the attention of the authorities. Without leaders, such restraints do not exist.

My fear was caused by more than simple proximity to racist groups. It was deliberately fed by the women I interviewed, who hoped to limit the scope of my study and shape my analysis. . . . The racist women constantly drew attention to my vulnerability to them, asking whether I was afraid to come see them, whether I was afraid to be in their homes. . . . Even a woman in prison on death row, who was brought to our interview in handcuffs, found a way to undermine any power I had over her by noting that she could call on gangs of allies in and outside the prison walls. "I'm not scared of anybody," she told me, "so I'm not gonna worry about it. I'll say what I got to say . . . 'cause I got the Jamaican Posse and the Cuban Posse all behind me, they gonna kick ass."

Some women were more indirect in their intimidation. Many bragged of their group's violence, making it clear that they treated enemies harshly. An Aryan supremacist boasted that the racist movement attracted people who were "totally messed up and totally mindless," people who were prone to "fight and kill, rip off armored cars, get guns.". . . Even now, years after completing the interviews, I receive signed and anonymous letters warning that they "are watching" me, that I had better tell "the truth" about them and their movement.

Often the women saw even the selection of where we would conduct the interview as an opening to use intimidation. Usually, I asked each woman to choose a place where she would feel comfortable, although I reminded her that I did not want to be interrupted by family members or racist group comrades. Several suggested their homes, saying that they would be most at ease there but also warning that their houses contained weapons and that other comrades (presumably less trustworthy than themselves) might appear at the house during the interview. Others picked a public place but indicated that they would station armed comrades nearby in case the interview did not "proceed as planned." On only two occasions did I refuse a suggestion for an interview site, both for safety reasons. One woman wanted me to be blindfolded and transported to an unknown destination in the back of a truck. Another proposed a meeting in a very remote racist compound to which I would have to be driven by a racist group member. And even in these cases, when my concerns for personal safety denied them their choice, they continued the implicit threats. For example, after the woman who had wanted me to be blindfolded agreed on a more visible site, she assured me that I should not be concerned for my safety there because "men with guns" would be hidden along the street "in case of a police raid.". . .

But fear went both ways. These women were afraid of me. I could betray their confidences to the police, to enemies, or to family members who were not aware of their activities. Telling me about their journey into organized racism could feel empowering to them, but it could also expose them to retribution. One Washington racist skinhead worried that I might secretly funnel information to violent gangs of antiracist skinheads about buildings occupied by racist skinheads: "[After you leave], well, uh, I wonder if some skin's house is gonna get Molotov-cocktailed and the [antiracist skinheads] are doing this in retaliation." An older neo-Nazi was concerned that my tape recording of her interview "could be used against me in a court of law." Many expressed suspicions about how I had found them at all. Throughout the interview a woman from the East repeatedly asked, "Just how did you become aware of the group that I'm in?" Worried that such fears could derail the interview, I assured each woman that her interview would be confidential and that I would not ask questions about illegal activities. . . . [Yet] I had to interrupt several of these women to keep them from telling me about their illegal activities or plans. A young Nazi activist in California, for example, deflected nearly all my inquiries about her family by saying that she was being constantly watched by the police, who could use such information against her, yet she repeatedly returned to an unsolicited story about her friends who "buried their guns in oil drums up in the hills for when the race war comes."

Racists also used their own fear to create rapport to keep the interview moving. Usually the task of creating rapport falls to the researcher, who generally has the most to gain from a successful interview. But many of these women were highly motivated to have me hear their stories. Thus, even as they tried to make me more afraid, they often pointed to their vulnerability to me; a woman might emphasize my exposure in the well-guarded living room of a racist leader, and at the same time observe that I probably had "really good connections to the police." At times, this tempering became nearly comical; one interviewee repeatedly made note of the guns and sketches of lynchings that lay around her living room but then sought to assure me that although "the average person has an idea that the Klan is very military [violent] and they're afraid," she was no threat, because she "wasn't aware of [that reputation] until just recently." But fear did help bring our sense of risk to the same level, making plain the stalemate in which we at least seemed to be equally unsafe.

Although the danger of engaging with racist activists actually increased while I was interviewing these women, I became less afraid over time, for reasons that are disturbing. The first interviews, conducted largely with members of the Ku Klux Klan, left me nearly paralyzed with fear. My field journal is full of notes on how to increase my own safety. Before each interview, I made elaborate preparations, giving friends instructions on what to do if I did not return on schedule. Yet my field notes on the last interviews, conducted largely with neo-Nazis and white power skinheads—members of groups that in recent years have been more likely than the Klan to engage in overt violence—show that my fears had largely abated. I took personal risks that earlier I would have found unthinkable. I had become more numb to tales of assaults and boasts of preparing for "race war."

It is terrifying to realize that you find it difficult to be shocked. But gradually my dealings with racist women became like a business transaction, with both parties parrying for favorable terms. I was not unafraid, but I took fewer precautions based on fear. Perhaps this change in attitude explains why my later interviews were less productive. In the earlier interviews, the tension created by fear made me think hard. As it subsided, some of my analytical edge slipped away as well. I was becoming anesthetized to the horrors of organized racism, a numbness that was personally dismaying and that also signaled my need to regain emotional distance from this research before writing about it—a process that took years. . . .

My experience suggests something about what it must feel to be inside a racist group: how the bizarre begins to feel normal, taken-for-granted, both unquestioned and unquestionable; how Jews or African Americans or gay men might come to seem so demonic and so personally threatening that group members could be moved to actions that seem incomprehensible to those on the outside. This state of mind results from a perceptual contraction that is all but imperceptible to the actor.

My feelings of fear also provide insight into the internal workings of racist groups. Fear is highly salient in the racist movement. Since they are greatly outnumbered by the racial, sexual, religious, and political groups they seek to destroy, organized racists use physical intimidation and the threat of violence to gain power over their opponents. Demonstrations, marches, violent propaganda, cross burnings, and terroristic actions are meant to demonstrate the strength of the racial movement and induce fear among enemies. So are the shocking cartoons and graphics that are the mainstay of racist propaganda. Racists pay close attention to their opponents' reactions, noting with glee any indication that they are feared by other groups or by the public. And fear is wielded within their groups as well. Members are warned repeatedly of the dire consequences that might befall them if they defect, particularly if they betray the group to the outside. These are not idle threats, as those who leave racist groups often risk violence at the hands of their former comrades. While I was doing these interviews, police on the East Coast were investigating the chilling abduction, assault, and near-murder of a young girl by a mixed-sex gang of skinheads who feared that she would defect from the group. . . .

The emotional world of organized racism becomes clearer when I consider the emotional work I needed to do to study racist groups. In the course of interviewing, I constantly sensed the need to display certain feelings. Sometimes I mimicked what I did not feel, forcing myself to laugh along with the more innocuous comments, hoping to establish rapport and fend off anecdotes that might be more offensive. At other times I withheld the emotions I did feel, maintaining a blank and studied expression when confronted with cross burnings or propaganda that glorified Nazi atrocities or even the interviewee's warped take on current events. In an interview done right after the Oklahoma City bombing, as the sickening images of the bombing were still in the newspapers and fresh in my mind, a woman told me that the people in her group "were happy about what happened in Oklahoma. There's a lot of anger out there. The people, some felt sorry for the [white] children but the rest of them got what they deserved, the government deserved. The government provoked this. . . . It's like in Germany when the skinheads went on the streets and burned down the refugee centers and the townspeople poured out and applauded. It could reach that point here." Throughout, I had to feign interest in the women's intricate stories of hatred, to ask questions in a neutral tone, and to be responsive when I wanted to flee or scream. But by examining my emotional work, I gained some insight into how the racist movement manipulates the emotions of its members, evoking not just fear but also awe.

Individual and political needs collide in writing about racism. As we acknowledge the rationality of racist women, we must never forget the evil they do. Yet writing from, and about, the stories of racist women runs the risk of personalizing them too much, making their ideas more sympathetic or less odious. It may subtly lend an academic gloss to the importance of racist activists, empowering them to work harder on behalf of their beliefs. These are dangerous outcomes—but the consequences of not learning from and about racists are worse.

If we stand too far back from racist groups and fail to look carefully at the women and men in organized racism, we are likely to draw politically misleading conclusions. Superficial studies simply caricature racist activists and make organized racism a foil against which we see ourselves as righteous and tolerant. We cannot simply comb the backgrounds of racist activists in search of a flaw—an absent parent, childhood victimization, or economic hard times—that "explains" their racist commitment. Moreover, we cannot use Germany in the 1930s as a prototype for all movements of the extreme right. Economic distress and social dislocation may explain the rise of such large-scale, powerful movements as the German Nazis or earlier American racist organizations, but such factors play only a small role in the tiny and politically marginal racist movement in the United States today.

We gain far more by taking a direct, hard look at the members of modern racist groups, acknowledging the commonalities between them and mainstream groups as well as the differences. In this book I tell the story of modern organized racism from the inside, focusing on how racist activists understand themselves and their worldviews. . . .

REFERENCES

1. Barrie Thorne, "Political Activist as Participant Observer: Conflicts of Commitment in a Study of the Draft Resistance Movement of the 1960s." In *Contemporary Field Research: A Collection of Readings,* Robert M. Emerson, ed. Prospect Heights, Ill: Waveland Press, 1983:235–252.

2. Antonius C. G. M. Robben, "The Politics of Truth and Emotion among Victims and Perpetrators of Violence." In *Fieldwork Under Fire: Contemporary Studies of Violence and Survival,* Carolyn Nordstrom and Antonius C. G. M. Robben, eds. Berkeley: University of California Press, 1995:81–104.

3. See Claudia Koonz, *Mothers in the Fatherland: Women, Family Life, and Nazi Politics.* New York: St. Martin's Press, 1987; and Robben, "Politics of Truth and Emotion."

II Social Groups and Social Control

It is easy to lose sight of the significance that our birth ushers us into a world that already exists. For the most part, we yawn at such a statement. It seems to be one of those "of course we all know that" types of observation, and we ordinarily fail to grasp its profound implications for our lives. That the world we enter is already constructed means that we join a human group that has established ways of "doing social life." Our group lays out for us an arbitrary system of norms that it expects us to follow. Although these norms (along with statuses and roles) may pinch, we are expected to conform to them. In effect, the expectations that the group sets out for us form a structure within which we are supposed to live our lives.

Social life is like a game, for it consists of rules and penalties for violating those rules. The game is already in progress when we are born, and because it is the only game in town, we have little choice but to play it. Our life consists of learning how to play the game set out for us and also of learning that there are subgames and how we can escape into them.

For social life to exist, there is no question that rules are necessary. If you can't depend on people to do things, everything falls apart. For social groups to function, they must be able to depend on their members to fulfill the tasks assigned them. This applies to all social groups, whether they be as small as our family or as large as a multinational corporation. It applies both to groups that are part of the mainstream society and to those that are part of the underworld.

As inevitable as norms are, so is deviance. Where there are rules, there will be rule breakers. All of us violate some of our group's many rules; that is, all of us fail to meet some of the expectations that others have of us. In sociological terms, we all become deviants. Deviant, in sociology, simply means someone who has deviated from the rules, someone who has wandered from the path that they were expected to follow. Deviant does not necessarily mean a horrible person—although horrible people are included in the term. Deviant is an inclusive term. It refers not only to killers and rapists, but also to people who tell "white" lies and to drivers who go over the speed limit.

As Berger said in our first reading, "The first wisdom of sociology is that things are not what they seem." In other words, a hidden reality lies behind the scenes that people (groups and organizations) put forward for others to view. A goal of sociology is to peer beneath the surface and expose this hidden reality. Sociologists do not to take for granted the views that groups put forward for public consumption, but rather they look under the hood so they can analyze what lies behind the images that people so carefully construct.

Sociologists have found that participant observation (see Reading 5) is a good way of peering behind the scenes. This method helps us to explore the reality that is usually open only to insiders. In the first article in this part, Steve Striffler does just this. As he takes us behind the scenes of a "chicken factory," we catch a glimpse of what it is like to work under the demeaning conditions that these workers experience. In the second selection, William Thompson takes us behind the scenes of mortuaries. Not only do we look over the shoulder of morticians as they sell caskets, but also we get to see how morticians handle the stigma of handling the dead, and how, despite this stigma attached to their work, they construct and maintain highly positive views of the self. In the third and concluding selection, in the only research by a sociologist on this topic, Ken Levi explores the experiences of a hit man, focusing on the ways by which he neutralizes his extreme deviance.

Working in a Chicken Factory

Steve Striffler

introduction

Few of us are born so wealthy that we do not have to work for a living. Some jobs seem to be of little importance, as with those we take during high school and college. We look at these jobs as temporary activities to help us get by for the time being. We discard them as we would an out–of–fashion shirt or blouse. In contrast, the jobs we take after we complete our education–those full–time endeavors at which we labor so long and hard–we invest much of ourselves in these. As our schedules–and even our lives–come to revolve around their demands, we become aware of how central these jobs are to our self–concept. All jobs, however, whether full time and permanent or temporary and discarded, contribute to our thinking and attitudes and basically to who we become in life. They become part of the general stockpile of experiences that culminates in our basic orientations.

Because of the significance of the conditions under which people work, then, so-ciologists pay a great deal of attention to the work setting. From my own experience working at a GE plant, I can say that one of the most demanding, demeaning, and de-moralizing jobs is that of the assembly line. Those of us who have served our time in this form of wage slavery–being controlled by objects moving in front of us at a pace set by "managers" who don't have to suffer the consequences of their decisions–have shared a work experience unlike any other. As Striffler examines the assembly line in a chicken factory, he makes evident how this job affects all aspects of the workers' lives. He also focuses on the immigrant experience, anticipating both the globalization of labor (Read-ing 9) and social class (Reading 10).

Thinking Critically

As you read this selection, ask yourself:

1. How does work at the chicken factory affect the lives of the workers? Why do they put up with such demanding, demoralizing, demeaning work? Why don't they just quit?

2. How have jobs influenced your orientations to life? How is the work that you are preparing for already influencing you?

3. How do you think that your worldview would be different if the assembly line were your fate in life?

Springdale, Arkansas, is an unremarkable working-class city at the center of the most productive poultry-producing region in the world. It is also home to the corporate headquarters of Tyson Foods. The company's Northwest Arkansas Job Center is a small building that resembles a government office. A sign in Spanish near the receptionist's desk says, "Do not leave children unattended." Another warns, "Thank you for your interest in our company, Tyson Foods, but please bring your own interpreter."

The receptionist seems surprised by my presence. "Sorry, hon, there are no openings for a mechanic." I assure her I'm not qualified to be a mechanic and that I want to work on a production line in one of the area's processing plants. She hands me a thick packet of forms and asks, "You want to work on the line?"

I can understand her confusion. The secretary and I are the only Americans, the only white folk, and the only English speakers in the room. Spanish predominates, but a couple in the corner converses in Lao and a threesome from the Marshall Islands in a micronesian language. In less than two decades, the poultry industry has drawn the "workers of the world" to the American South, a region that saw few foreign immigrants during the 20th century. As I know from my research as an anthropologist, Latin Americans first arrived in northwest Arkansas in the late 1980s seeking these jobs. Today, about three-quarters of the workers in the plant are Latin American, with Southeast Asians and Marshallese accounting for many of the rest. Workers born in the United States are few and far between.

Tyson processes job applicants like it processes poultry. The emphasis is on quantity not quality. No one at the Job Center spends more than a minute looking at my application, and no single person takes the time to review it all.

There are few pleasantries, but there is also no bullshit. I tell the interviewer I want a job at a processing plant, he makes a quick call, and five minutes later I have a job. Someone has already called my references, and I pass both the drug test and the physical. I'm Tyson material.

I arrive at the massive plant a few days later. At 3 P.M. sharp, the new recruits are escorted into a small classroom that contains a prominently displayed sign: "Democracies depend on the political participation of its citizens, but not in the workplace." Written in both English and Spanish, the message is clear in any language.

The nine (other) people in my orientation class are representative of the plant's second shift. Eight are Latin Americans, with six coming from Mexico and two from El Salvador. Six men, two women. As the younger men frequently lament, women in the plant tend to be slightly older than the men. In this respect, Maria (early 40s) and Carmen (early 50s) are quite typical. The six men vary in age from their early 20s to their 60s. Jorge, in his mid-30s, has lived in California for the past 13 years, mostly working in a textile factory. Like Jorge, the Mexican workers often come from rural areas in the state of Guanajuato, spend time in California working in factories or picking fruit, then find their way to the promised land of Arkansas. Not only is

From "Inside a Poultry Processing Plant: An Ethnographic Portrait," by Steve Striffler, Labor History, 43, pp. 305–313. Copyright 2002 by Taylor and Francis Informa UK Ltd., Journals. Reproduced with permission of Taylor and Francis Informa UK Ltd. via Copyright Clearance Center.

everything in Arkansas much cheaper, but Tyson Foods pays around eight dollars an hour, offers insurance, and consistently provides 40 hours of work a week. Poultry processing is a tough way to achieve upward mobility, but that is precisely what these jobs represent for most immigrants.

After putting on our smocks, aprons, earplugs, hairnets, beard nets, and boots, we're given a tour. Most have killed chickens on farms, but nobody is prepared for the overwhelming sounds, sights, and smells that await us. It doesn't help that the tour begins in "live hanging" (pollo vivo). Carmen says what we all are thinking: "My God! (¡Dios Mio!) How can one work here?" The answer turns out to be simple. Live hanging pays a bit more and there is actually a waiting list for the job. Chickens are flooding into a dark and hot room at about 200 a minute. The smell is indescribable, suffocating, and absolutely unforgettable. Five or six workers grab the flailing chickens, hooking them by their feet to an overhead rail system that transports the birds throughout the plant. Blood, shit, and feathers are flying everywhere.

Fortunately, I land a job on Saw Lines 1 and 2. It's not exactly pleasant, but it's a long way from live hanging. These "further" processing lines are at the heart of the revolution that has transformed the poultry industry and American diets over the past 25 years. Before then, most Americans bought chicken in one form: the whole bird. Today, Tyson produces thousands of "further processed/value-added" meat products. The poultry products include nuggets, patties, franks, pet food, and a range of parts in many shapes, sizes, textures, and flavors.

There are two identical processing lines where I work. Each takes a whole chicken, cuts it, marinates it, and breads it. With about 20 to 25 workers, each line processes what we've estimated to be about 80 birds a minute or 40,000 pounds of chicken a day. The lines are effectively divided into four sets of machinery: cut up, marinade, breading, and rebreading. Conveyer belts move the chicken from one section to the next. The birds are hung on the line, cut by rotating saws, injected with marinade (whose flavor changes depending on the day), and sent through a series of contraptions that lightly breads the parts. From there, the chicken is conveyed to another area to be cooked, packaged, and placed on tractor-trailers. Live birds enter the plant at one end; patties and nuggets depart from the other.

My coworkers are an interesting and diverse bunch. Of the 20 or so on the lines, two (excluding myself) are white Americans. Most white workers left the poultry plants during the region's economic boom in the 1990s, and those who remain tend to fall into two categories. An older group has been working at Tyson for more than 20 years, and they're hanging on to the benefits that seniority bestows. The few white workers who started more recently have few other options. Jane, for example, is well into her 60s. Factory work is all she knows. The language barrier keeps her from conversing with most of her coworkers, but she has a peculiar habit that endears her to nearly everyone. When the line stops, she often dances with an unsuspecting young man, embarrassing the victim but giving everyone else a much-needed laugh.

Most line workers are women, many in their 40s and 50s. In a plant where about two-thirds of the workers are male, this fact is telling. On-line jobs are the worst in the plant—monotonously, even dangerously, repetitive. These workers stand in the same place repeating the same motions for an entire shift. Women are concentrated in on-line jobs because they're excluded from all jobs that involve heavy lifting or running machinery. Mario, Alejandro, Roberto, Juan, Jeff, Carlo, and I come from all over the world, but in the plant we are "young" men who clean up waste, bring supplies, lift heavy objects, and operate hand carts and forklifts. As auxiliary workers, we do on-line work, but only intermittently.

I am to be the harinero, the breading operator, or as my 22-year-old supervisor Michael likes to call me, the little flour boy. Michael can't do the job himself and his instructions are simple: "Do what Roberto does." With five years on the job, Roberto can do every task on the line, fix the machines, and carry on a conversation at the same time. But he gives me little formal training, which makes learning my new job a bit tricky. Roberto is neither friendly nor cool at first; and unlike virtually everyone else in the plant, he is unimpressed that I speak Spanish. We would eventually talk about everything from his wife's struggles at a nearby turkey plant to his kids' achievements at school. I would even visit his parents in Mexico. In the beginning, however, I just watch, hoping to gain his respect and learn enough to survive the first week.

I learn quickly that "unskilled" labor requires immense skill. The job of harinero is extremely complicated. In a simple sense, the harinero empties 50-pound bags of flour all day. The work is backbreaking, but it takes less physical dexterity than many jobs on the line. At the same time, the job is multifaceted and cannot be quickly learned. The harinero constantly adjusts the breader and rebreader, monitors the marinade, turns the power on and off, and replaces old flour with fresh flour. All this would be relatively manageable if the lines ran well. They never do.

Problems with the rebreader are the main reason the line shuts down. It is here, with Roberto, that my education as both harinero and worker begins. One of the first things I learn is that I'll be doing the job of two people. There have always been two harineros, one for each line. However, Michael, the supervisor, recently decided to run both lines with only one harinero. He is essentially doing what he has done, or will do, with virtually all the on-line jobs. Two workers, not three, hang chicken; two, not three or four, arrange parts; one, not two, checks the marinade levels. This downsizing has been going on throughout the plant. About six months earlier, a generation of supervisors who had mostly come up through the production lines were more or less forced from their jobs by a new set of plant managers. The new managers ordered the older supervisors to push the workers harder and harder. Knowing how hard work on the line could be, many supervisors refused by simply leaving the plant. The managers were then free to replace them with younger, college-educated supervisors like Michael.

Michael is a working-class kid clawing his way into the middle class. One of the first in his family to attend college, he just graduated from the University of Arkansas with a degree in poultry science. Supervisors start at under $30,000 a year. Although he "never imagined" earning that much right out of college, the trade-off is considerable. Michael arrives every day at 12:30 P.M. and never leaves before 3:30 A.M. Unlike the workers, of course, he enjoys a job with some variety, almost never gets his hands dirty, and can hope to move up the corporate ladder. At least in the short term, however, he's as consumed by the plant as the rest of us.

Nevertheless, Michael is the focus of our anger. Michael (guided by his bosses) oversees the downsizing. One reason he succeeds—besides the lack of a labor union and binding job descriptions—is that cutting workers on the line doesn't necessarily halt it. The fewer workers just have to work faster. But as Roberto pointed out, the breading operator is different. When the breading operator falls behind, the entire line stops. And Michael would soon be replacing two experienced harineros, Roberto and Alejandro, with a single trainee—me.

When Michael told them there would soon be only one harinero, Roberto and Alejandro used their seniority to find other positions. Michael posted the job but no one in the plant wanted it, Roberto says. "It was too much work. So he had to get a new guy who couldn't say no—someone like you."

Roberto is right, but he's being less than candid. Giving up the position did matter to him. Alejandro is more blunt: "I had eight years as harinero. I like the job. It's like family here. It doesn't mean anything to Michael. For him it's just a job and we're just Mexicans. He doesn't know anything anyway. I wanted to stay, but why? Fuck that! Twice as much work for the same salary. I did my job well. I have nothing to be ashamed of."

During my first weeks, the line keeps shutting down. Few of the problems are tied to me, but the entire process is slowed by the fact that there is only one real harinero—Roberto. The harinero has to fix everything, but the main problem is that the rebreader apparatus simply doesn't have enough power to circulate the flour while pushing the chicken along the belt. In short, when enough flour flows through the valves to bread the chicken, the machine bogs down and the chicken piles up and falls on the floor. This results in loud shrieks from just about everyone. As breading operator, Roberto has to shut down the line and figure out which part of the rebreader isn't working.

The possible solutions to this problem shape an ongoing struggle between Michael, Roberto, and (now) me. First, the plant mechanics could feed enough power to the machine to handle both the chicken and the flour. This is clearly what Michael wants. Second, we could run less chicken, which, by reducing the weight on the belts, would allow the rebreader to operate properly at the current power level. This is simply unthinkable to Michael. His goal is to keep the line running at top speed and at full capacity all the time.

Roberto and I adopt two strategies to keep the rebreader running. First, we change the flour frequently. Fresh flour that's not yet wet and clumpy from the chicken circulates better. Michael, however, rejects this option because it costs more. Second, we try using only as much flour as the rebreader can support. But here again Michael insists that the rebreader can handle more (old) flour and that we're running it at levels that don't bread the chicken enough.

The difficulty for Roberto and me is that Michael is simply wrong. He passes by every hour and tells us to use more flour. He then leaves, and with remarkable precision the machine bogs down. We stop the line, clean up the mess, and lower the flour to a workable level. Michael then returns, calls for more flour, and the process begins again.

This uneasy and somewhat absurd tension continues all day. Only occasionally does Michael see the rebreader bog down because of his miscalculations. Roberto and I relish these moments. Roberto suddenly forgets how to fix the machine and simply watches as Michael frantically calls a mechanic on his walkie-talkie. After talking to Michael and staring at the machine for 10 minutes, the mechanic swallows his pride and asks Roberto what the problem is. Roberto then looks at Michael, smiles at me, and fixes it.

Looking back, it's hard to explain why this petty struggle seemed so damn important. The irony, of course, is that it was in our interests to follow Michael's (uninformed) directions and let the line stop. It was a pain to keep fixing the machine, but we got paid the same whether it ran or not. Finally, the shutdowns benefited all the workers by giving them a break.

Why, then, were so many of us profoundly irritated when the lines stopped? Several factors were at work. The first was Michael's attempt to use not only fewer harineros, but fewer workers in general. It confirmed our collective perception: Michael's inexperience led to decisions that made our lives intolerable. They were also economically unsound. We believed we could run the lines better. Second, and most important, by concentrating decision making in his own hands, Michael removed the very thing—control over the labor process—that gave the harinero job its meaning. Finally, almost all the workers took great pride in jobs that likewise had been largely degraded.

Despite our protests, Michael forges ahead, and in my fourth week I begin running both lines. What he does not tell us, however, is that he has finally gotten the mechanics to boost the power. Roberto and I quickly discover that Michael has won. With more power, the rebreader almost never bogs down. Running the lines no longer requires the expertise of someone like Roberto. But while the job demands less skill, it takes more work. I now fill the flour for two lines running at a faster pace. The intensity and monotony are almost unbearable. For the on-line workers the change is devastating. By the end of the week, Blanca, a Mexican woman in her 50s, is overwhelmed. She has been hanging chickens for too many years and her body can't keep up. Hoping to stay at Tyson until she retires, she quits within a week.

Noise, supervision, and the job's intensity limit communication on the plant floor. The break room is a different situation. Twice a shift, for 30 minutes, workers watch Spanish-language television, eat and exchange food, complain, and relax. Supervisors almost never enter the room, and they're uncomfortable when they do. I was often the only American present. The few other Americans on the second shift almost always gathered in a smaller room where smoking is permitted and the TV is in English.

A telling moment occurred in the break room only three weeks after I arrived. Although I'd eventually tell my new friends that I was an anthropologist, no one knew at the time. However else they viewed me—as a strange gringo who spoke Spanish, as a blanco who was too stupid to get a good job, or as an inept breading operator—I wasn't yet seen as an anthropologist or professor.

After pushing us hard that day, Michael gave us free boxes of fried chicken to thank us. He'd do this half a dozen other times while I worked there, and it always got the same reaction. After looking at the chicken, we'd stare at each other until someone said something like this in Spanish: "Pure asshole. I am not going to eat this shit." For an awkward moment we'd glance at each other, look away, and pretend not to know what was going on. Then someone would say: "We can't throw away good food and we're all hungry. Let's eat this shit." And so we would, more pissed off than ever.

Michael's gesture was insulting for many reasons. First, he wasn't just giving us food; he was giving us chicken. Second, it didn't come close to making up for what the workers had just gone through on the plant floor. As paternalism, it was pathetic and transparent. (Why Michael didn't see this is a different question.) Finally, it was insulting because even as we hesitated we knew we'd eat the chicken.

As we chewed the chicken that day, we had the following exchange. No one directly mentioned Michael's gesture, as if all of us had agreed not to relive the humiliation.

Roberto welcomes me into the group: "Ai, Steve, you are almost Mexican. All you need is a Mexican wife to cook you some decent lunch and you would be Mexican."

Alejandro, also from Mexico, chimes in: "Yes, Steve is a Mexican. He speaks Spanish, eats with Mexicans, and he works like a Mexican. It's pure Mexicans here. We all eat chicken."

Elisa, three years on the job, kindly protests: "Ai . . . I'm not Mexican. I'm Salvadoran."

Alejandro, gently explaining: "Look, we're all Mexicans here [in the plant]. Screwed-over Mexicans." He points at Li, an older woman from Laos. "Look, even she is a Mexican. Pure."

We laugh as Li, who's too far away to hear, quietly devours a chicken wing.

Ana, catching on to Alejandro's point, finally agrees: "Yes, it's the truth. We are Mexicans here in the plant."

I ask, somewhat interested: "And outside the plant, in Springdale, Fayetteville, and Rogers? Are we all Mexicans outside?" . . .

Alejandro . . . says to me: "Outside, you're a gringo. You are from here. Outside, we are Mexicans, but it is different. . . . We're still screwed, but in a different way. We are foreigners. We don't belong. At least here in the plant we belong even if we are exploited. Outside, we live better than in Mexico, but we do not belong, we are not from here and keep to ourselves."

I then ask: "And in Mexico? Who are we in Mexico?"

Roberto says to me: "In Mexico, you are a gringo. You are a foreigner, but not like we are here in Arkansas. You are more like a tourist, treated well. We are not tourists here. We are treated more like outsiders. In Mexico, we are normal people, Mexicans, just like everyone else. But in Mexico there is no future. My children were all born here, they are Americans. They have a future. Now, when I return to Mexico I feel like a tourist. I have money, travel, visit people. Our future is here now." . . .

When Alejandro looks around at people from Mexico, El Salvador, Honduras, Vietnam, Laos, and the Marshall Islands, and says we are all Mexicans, he is making a statement about class. He is not confused by the bright lights of the postmodern world, or unclear where he is located, socially, racially, and geographically. Rather, he is playing with the label, using it almost as a synonym for worker. "Yes, we are all Mexicans here" is almost the same as, "Yes, we are all workers here." And not any kind of worker—but those who do what society sees as the worst work. Shit work. In this respect, Li, from Laos, is not singled out by accident. She is Mexican, one of us, because she does the same crap; because she eats Michael's chicken; and because she is Mexican to Tyson's management.

We've yet to appreciate the full impact of transnational migration, especially on people like my coworkers at the plant. In the process of crossing borders in search of opportunity, their experiences may be leading them to question the national loyalties that borders reinforce. As they work together, both immigrants and the native-born may be developing new identities that run counter to old notions of citizenship. And some of these new identities are grounded in class. Could it be that globalization internationalizes not only capital, but also workers? It's worth considering. Poultry plants are, after all, one of the places where workers of the world come together.

Such sites will not automatically unite this diverse working class any more than factories did in 19th-century England. But if we really want to understand the global migrations that are reshaping today's world, we need to look at culture not just in terms of ethnic rituals and customs. We also have to confront the realities of class. The Mexicans, Salvadorans, Vietnamese, and Americans at the plant experience cultural differences every day when they exchange tortillas, tacos, rice, beans, and turkey sandwiches. But they also share—in different ways—the class experience of eating chicken that is as painful to swallow as it is to process.

Handling the Stigma
of Handling the Dead

William E. Thompson

introduction

Life expectancy used to be so much shorter. A hundred years ago, the average American died by the age of 40. Back then, death was also a family affair. Not only did people die at home, but also their mothers, wives, and sisters washed and dressed the body. Wakes (grieving ceremonies) were held at home, with the body put on display in the "parlor," where family, friends, and neighbors "paid their last respects." After the wake, the men transported the body in a coffin they had made and lowered it into a grave they had dug.

In today's world, formal organizations have replaced many family functions, including those of handling death. People die in hospitals, attended by strangers. Other strangers deliver the body to a funeral home. There, still more strangers prepare the body for burial by draining its blood and replacing it with embalming fluids. Afterward, strangers dress the body in clothing selected by relatives, comb the hair, put makeup on the face, and place the body on display in a room reserved for this purpose (sometimes called "the eternal slumber room"). The family participates by arranging a ceremony to be held in this room (or at a religious site) and by appointing friends to carry the body from this room to a vehicle whose only purpose is to transport dead bodies. Strangers drive this specialized vehicle to the graveyard. Who are these "death specialists" who handle dead bodies, and how do they handle the stigma that comes from handling the dead? This is the focus of Thompson's analysis.

Thinking Critically

As you read this selection, ask yourself:

1. Why have formal organizations taken over such a previously intimate function of the family as taking care of the dead? How would you feel about taking care of a dead family member? What is the origin of your feelings? (Don't say they are natural. They are not.)

2. How do "death specialists" handle the stigma of handling the dead?

3. If you have been to a funeral, compare what you experienced with what you read in this selection.

In a complex, industrialized society a person's occupation or profession is central to his or her personal and social identity. As Pavalko (1988) pointed out, two strangers are quite ". . . likely to 'break the ice' by indicating the kind of work they do." As a result, individuals often made a number of initial judgments about others based on preconceived notions about particular occupations.

This study examines how morticians and funeral directors handle the stigma associated with their work. Historically, stigma has been attached to those responsible for caring for the dead, and the job typically was assigned to the lower classes (e.g., the Eta of Japan and the Untouchables in India), and in some cases, those who handled the dead were forbidden from touching the living.

Morticians and funeral directors are fully aware of the stigma associated with their work, so they continually strive to enhance their public image and promote their social credibility. They must work to shift the emphasis on their work from the dead to the living, and away from sales and toward service. As Aries (1976, 99) noted:

> In order to sell death, it had to be made friendly . . . since 1885 . . . [funeral directors have] presented themselves not as simple sellers of services, but as "doctors of grief" who have a mission . . . [which] consists in aiding the mourning survivors to return to normalcy.

Couched within the general theoretical framework of symbolic interactionism, there are a variety of symbolic and dramaturgical methods whereby morticians and funeral directors attempt to redefine their occupations and minimize and/or neutralize negative attitudes toward them and what they do.

■ ■ ■ METHOD

This study reflects over 2 years of qualitative fieldwork. Extensive ethnographic interviews were conducted with 19 morticians and funeral directors in four states: Kansas, Missouri, Oklahoma, and Texas. The funeral homes included both privately owned businesses and branches of large franchise operations.

Interviewees included people from different age groups, both sexes, and both whites and nonwhites. There were 16 males and 3 females interviewed for this study, ranging in age from 26 to 64 years.

■ ■ ■ THE STIGMA OF HANDLING THE DEAD

Until [about 1900] in this country, people died at home and friends and family members prepared the bodies for burial (Lesy, 1987). As medical knowledge and technology progressed and became more specialized, more and more deaths occurred outside the home—usually in hospitals. Death became something to be handled by a select group of highly trained professionals—doctors, nurses, and hospital staff. As fewer people witnessed death firsthand, it became surrounded with more mystery, and physically handling the dead became the domain of only a few.

Members or friends of the family relinquished their role in preparing bodies for disposal to an *undertaker,* ". . . a special person who would 'undertake' responsibility for the care and burial of the dead" (Amos, 1983, 2). Most states began licensing embalmers around the end of the nineteenth century (Amos, 1983). These licensed embalmers were viewed as unusual, if not downright weird. They were not family members or friends of the deceased faced with the unsavory but necessary responsibility for disposing of a loved one's body, but strangers who *chose* to work with dead bodies—for compensation. Although most welcomed the opportunity to relinquish this chore they also viewed those who willingly assumed it with some skepticism and even disdain.

Sudnow (1967, 51–64) underscored the negative attitudes toward people who work with the dead in describing how those who work in a morgue, for example, are "death-tainted" and work very hard to rid themselves of the social stigma associated with their jobs. Morticians and funeral directors cannot escape from this "taint of death" and they must constantly work to "counteract the stigma" directed at them and their occupations.

Are morticians and funeral directors really that stigmatized? After all, they generally are well-known and respected members of their communities. In small communities and even many large cities, local funeral homes have been owned and operated by the same family for several generations. These people usually are members of civic organizations, have substantial incomes, and live in nice homes and drive nice automobiles. Most often they are viewed as successful business people. On the other hand, their work is surrounded by mystery, taboos, and stigma, and they often are viewed as cold, detached, and downright morbid for doing it. All the respondents in this study openly acknowledged that stigma was associated with their work. Some indicated that they thought the stigma primarily came from the "misconception" that they were "getting rich" off other people's grief; others believed it simply came from working with the dead. Clearly these two aspects of their work—handling the dead and profiting from death and grief—emerged as the two most stigmatizing features of the funeral industry according to respondents.

■ ■ ■ MANAGING STIGMA

Erving Goffman wrote the most systematic analysis of how individuals manage a "spoiled" social identity in his classic work, *Stigma* (1963). He described several techniques, such as "passing," "dividing the social world," "mutual aid," "physical distance," "disclosure," and "covering," employed by the *discredited* and *discreditable* to manage information and conceal their stigmatizing attributes (41–104). Although these techniques work well for the physically scarred, blind, stammerers, bald, drug addicted, ex-convicts, and many other stigmatized categories of people, they are less likely to be used by morticians and funeral directors.

Except perhaps when on vacation, it is important for funeral directors to be known and recognized in their communities and to be associated with their work. Consequently, most of the morticians and funeral directors studied relied on other strategies for reducing the stigma associated with their work. Paramount among these strategies were: symbolic redefinition of their work, role distance, professionalism, emphasizing service, and enjoying socioeconomic status over occupational prestige. This was much less true for licensed embalmers who worked for funeral directors, especially in chain-owned funeral homes in large cities. In those cases the author found that many embalmers concealed their occupation from their neighbors and others with whom they were not intimately acquainted.

Symbolic Redefinition

One of the ways in which morticians and funeral directors handle the stigma of their occupations is through symbolically negating as much of it as possible. Woods and Delisle (1978, 98) revealed how sympathy cards avoid the use of the terms "dead" and "death" by substituting less harsh words such as "loss," "time of sorrow," and "hour of sadness." This technique is also used by morticians and funeral directors to reduce the stigma associated with their work.

Words that are most closely associated with death are rarely used, and the most harsh terms are replaced with less ominous ones. The term *death* is almost never used by funeral directors; rather, they talk of "passing on," "meeting an untimely end," or "eternal slumber." There are no *corpses* or *dead bodies*, they are referred to as "remains," "the deceased," "loved one," or more frequently, by name (e.g., "Mr. Jones"). Use of the term *body* is almost uniformly avoided around the family. Viewing rooms (where the embalmed body is displayed in the casket) usually are given serene names such as "the sunset room," "the eternal slumber room," or, in one case, "the guest room." Thus, when friends or family arrive to view the body, they are likely to be told that "Mr. Jones is lying in repose in the eternal slumber room." This language contrasts sharply with that used by morticians and funeral directors in "backstage" areas (Goffman, 1959, 112) such as the embalming room where drowning victims often are called "floaters," burn victims are called "crispy critters," and others are simply referred to as "bodies" (Turner and Edgley, 1976).

All the respondents indicated that there was less stigma attached to the term *funeral director* than *mortician* or *embalmer,* underscoring the notion that much of the stigma they experienced was attached to physically handling the dead. Consequently, when asked what they do for a living, those who acknowledge that they are in the funeral business (several indicated that they often do not) referred to themselves as "funeral directors" even if all they did was the embalming. *Embalming* is referred to as "preservation" or "restoration," and in order to be licensed, one must have studied "mortuary arts" or "mortuary science." Embalming no longer takes place in an *embalming room,* but in a "preparation room," or in some cases the "operating room."

Coffins are now "caskets," which are transported in "funeral coaches" (not *hearses*) to their "final resting place" rather than to the *cemetery* or worse yet, *graveyard,* for their "interment" rather than *burial.* Thus, linguistically, the symbolic redefinition is complete, with death verbally redefined during every phase, and the stigma associated with it markedly reduced.

All the morticians and funeral directors in this study emphasized the importance of using the "appropriate" terms in referring to their work. Knowledge of the stigma attached to certain words was readily acknowledged, and all indicated that the earlier terminology was stigma-laden, especially the term "undertaker," which they believed conjured up negative images in the mind of the public. For example, a 29-year-old male funeral director indicated that his father still insisted on calling himself an "undertaker." "He just hasn't caught up with [modern times]," the son remarked. Interestingly, when asked why he did not refer to himself as an undertaker, he replied "It just sounds so old-fashioned [pause] plus, it sounds so morbid."

In addition to using language to symbolically redefine their occupations, funeral directors carefully attempt to shift the focus of their work away from the care of the dead (especially handling the body), and redefine it primarily in terms of caring for the living. The dead are deemphasized as most of the funeral ritual is orchestrated for the benefit of the friends and family of the deceased (Turner and Edgley, 1976). By redefining themselves as "grief therapists" or "bereavement counselors" their primary duties are associated with making funeral arrangements, directing the services, and consoling the family in their time of need.

Role Distance

Because a person's sense of self is so strongly linked to occupation, it is common practice for people in undesirable or stigmatized occupations to practice role distance. Although the specific role-distancing techniques vary across different occupations and among different individuals within an occupation, they share the common function of allowing individuals to violate some of the role expectations associated with the occupation, and express their individuality within the confines of the occupational role. Although the funeral directors and morticians in this study used a variety of role-distancing techniques, three common patterns emerged: emotional detachment, humor, and countering the stereotype.

Emotional Detachment.   One of the ways that morticians and funeral directors overcome their socialization regarding death taboos and the stigma associated with handling the dead is to detach themselves from the body of the work. Charmaz (1980) pointed out that a common technique used by coroners and funeral directors to minimize the stigma associated with death work is to routinize the work as much as possible. When embalming, morticians focus on the technical aspects of the job rather than thinking about the person they are working on. One mortician explained:

> When I'm in the preparation I never think about the who *who* I'm working on, I only think about what has to be done next. When I picked up the body, it was a person. When I get done, clean and dress the body, and place it in the casket, it becomes a person again. But in here it's just something to be worked on. I treat it like a mechanic treats an automobile engine—with respect, but there's no emotion involved. It's just a job that has to be done.

Another mortician described his emotional detachment in the embalming room:

> You can't think too much about this process [embalming], or it'll really get to you. For example, one time we brought in this little girl. She was about four years old—the same age as my youngest daughter at the time. She had been killed in a wreck; had gone through the windshield; was really a mess.
>
> At first, I wasn't sure I could do this one—all I could think about was my little girl. But when I got her in the prep room, my whole attitude changed. I know this probably sounds cold, and hard I guess, but suddenly I began to think of the challenge involved. This was gonna be an open-casket service, and while the body was in pretty good shape, the head and face were practically gone. This was gonna take a lot of reconstruction. Also, the veins are so small on children that you have to be a lot more careful.
>
> Anyway, I got so caught up in the job, that I totally forgot about working on a little girl. I was in the room with her about six hours when—[his wife] came in and reminded me that we had dinner plans that night. I washed up and went out to dinner and had a great time. Later that night, I went right back to work on her without even thinking about it.
>
> It wasn't until the next day when my wife was dressing the body, and I came in, and she was crying, that it hit me. I looked at the little girl, and I began crying. We both just stood there crying and hugging. My wife kept saying "I know this was tough for you," and "yesterday must have been tough." I felt sorta guilty, because I knew what she meant, and it should've been tough for me, real tough emotionally, but it wasn't. The only "tough" part had been the actual work, especially the reconstruction—I had totally cut off the emotional part.
>
> It sometimes makes you wonder. Am I really just good at this, or am I losing something. I don't know. All I know is, if I'd thought about the little girl the way I did that next day, I never could have done her. It's just part of this job—you gotta just do what has to be done. If you think about it much, you'll never make it in this business.

Humor.   Many funeral directors and morticians use humor to detach themselves emotionally from their work. The humor, of course, must be carefully hidden from friends and relatives of the deceased, and takes place in backstage areas such as the embalming room, or in professional group settings such as at funeral directors' conventions.

The humor varies from impromptu comments while working on the body to standard jokes told over and over again. Not unexpectedly, all the respondents indicated a strong distaste for necrophilia jokes. One respondent commented, "I can think of nothing less funny—the jokes are sick, and have done a lot of damage to the image of our profession."

Humor is an effective technique of diffusing the stigma associated with handling a dead body, however, and when more than one person is present in the embalming room, it is common for a certain amount of banter to take place, and jokes or comments are often made about the amount of body fat or the overendowment, or lack thereof, of certain body parts. For example, one mortician indicated that a common remark made about the males with small genitalia is, "Well, at least he won't be missed."

As with any occupation, levels of humor varied among the respondents. During an interview one of the funeral directors spoke of some of the difficulties in advertising the business, indicating that because of attitudes toward death and the funeral business, he had to be sure that his newspaper advertisements did not offend anyone. He reached into his desk drawer and pulled out a pad with several "fake ads" written on it. They included:

"Shake and Bake Special—Cremation with No Embalming"
"Business Is Slow, Somebody's Gotta Go"
"Try Our Layaway Plan—Best in the Business"
"Count on Us, We'll Be the Last to Let You Down"
"People Are Dying to Use Our Services"
"Pay Now, Die Later"
"The Buck Really Does Stop Here"

He indicated that he and one of his friends had started making up these fake ads and slogans when they were doing their mortuary internships. Over the years, they occasionally corresponded by mail and saw each other at conventions, and they would always try to be one up on the other with the best ad. He said, "Hey, in this business, you have to look for your laughs where you can find them."

Countering the Stereotype.   Morticians and funeral directors are painfully aware of the common negative stereotype of people in their occupations. The women in this study were much less concerned about the stereotype, perhaps because simply being female shattered the stereotype anyway. The men, however, not only acknowledged that they were well aware of the public's stereotypical image of them, but also indicated that they made every effort *not* to conform to it.

One funeral director, for instance, said:

People think we're cold, unfriendly, and unfeeling. I always make it a point to be just the opposite. Naturally, when I'm dealing with a family I must be reserved and show the proper decorum, but when I am out socially, I always try to be very upbeat—very alive. No matter how tired I am, I try not to show it.

Another indicated that he absolutely never wore gray or black suits. Instead, he wore navy blue and usually with a small pinstripe. "I might be mistaken for the minister or a lawyer," he said, "but rarely for an undertaker."

The word *cold,* which often is associated with death came up in a number of interviews. One funeral director was so concerned about the stereotype of being "cold," that he kept a handwarmer in the drawer of his desk. He said, "My hands tend to be cold and clammy. It's just a physical trait of mine, but there's no way that I'm going to shake someone's hand and let them walk away thinking how cold it was." Even on the warmest of days, he indicated that during services, he carried the handwarmer in his right-hand coat pocket so that he could warm his hand before shaking hands with or touching someone.

Although everyone interviewed indicated that he or she violated the public stereotype, each one expressed a feeling of being atypical. In other words, although they believed that they did not conform to the stereotype, they felt that many of their colleagues did. One funeral director was wearing jeans, a short-sleeved sweatshirt and a pair of running shoes during the interview. He had just finished mowing the lawn at the funeral home. "Look at me," he said, "Do I look like a funeral director? Hell, _____ [the funeral director across the street] wears a suit and tie to mow his grass!—or, at least he would if he didn't hire it done."

Others insisted that very few funeral directors conform to the public stereotype when out of public view, but feel compelled to conform to it when handling funeral arrangements, because it is an occupational role requirement. "I always try to be warm and upbeat," one remarked, "But, let's face it, when I'm working with a family, they're experiencing a lot of grief—I have to respect that, and act accordingly." Another indicated that he always lowered his voice when talking with family and friends of the deceased, and that it had become such a habit, that he found himself speaking softly almost all the time. "One of the occupational hazards, I guess," he remarked.

The importance of countering the negative stereotype was evident, when time after time, persons being interviewed would pause and ask "I'm not what you expected, am I?" or something similar. It seemed very important for them to be reassured that they did not fit the stereotype of funeral director or mortician.

Professionalism

Another method used by morticians and funeral directors to reduce occupational stigma is to emphasize professionalism. Amos (1983, 3) described embalming as:

> . . . an example of a vocation in transition from an occupation to a profession. Until mid-nineteenth century, embalming was not considered a profession and this is still an issue debated in some circles today.

Most morticians readily admit that embalming is a very simple process and can be learned very easily. In all but two of the funeral homes studied, the interviewees admitted that people who were not licensed embalmers often helped with the embalming process. In one case, in which the funeral home was owned and operated by two brothers, one of the brothers was a licensed funeral director and licensed embalmer. The other brother had dropped out of high school and helped their father with the funeral business while his brother went to school to meet the educational requirements for licensure. The licensed brother said:

> By the time I got out of school and finished my apprenticeship, _____ [his brother] had been helping Dad embalm for over three years—and he was damned good at it. So when I joined the business, Dad thought it was best if I concentrated on handling the funeral arrangements and pre-service needs. After Dad died, I was the only licensed embalmer, so "officially" I do it all—all the embalming and the funeral arrangements. But, to tell you the truth, I only embalm every now and then when we have several to do, 'cause _____ usually handles most of it. He's one of the best—I'd match him against any in the business.

Despite the relative simplicity of the embalming process and the open admission by morticians and funeral directors that "almost anyone could do it with a little practice," most states require licensure and certification for embalming. The four states represented in this study (Kansas, Oklahoma, Missouri, and Texas) have similar requirements for becoming a licensed certified embalmer. They include a minimum of 60 college hours with a core of general college courses (English, mathematics, social studies, etc.) plus 1 year of courses in the "mortuary sciences" or "mortuary arts." These consist of several courses in physiology and biology, and a 1-year apprenticeship under a licensed embalmer. To become a licensed funeral director requires the passing of a state board examination, which primarily requires a knowledge of state laws related to burial, cremation, disposal of the body, and insurance.

Although the general consensus among them was that an individual did not need a college education to become a good embalmer, they all stressed the importance of a college education for being a successful funeral director. Most thought that some basic courses in business, psychology, death and dying, and "bereavement counseling" were valuable preparation for the field. Also, most of the funeral directors were licensed insurance agents, which allowed them to sell burial policies.

Other evidence of the professionalization of the funeral industry includes state, regional, and national professional organizations that hold annual conventions and sponsor other professional activities; professional journals; state, regional, and national governing and regulating boards; and a professional code of ethics. Although the funeral industry is highly competitive, like most other professions, its members demonstrate a strong sense of cohesiveness and in-group identification.

One of the married couples in this study indicated that it was reassuring to attend national conventions where they met and interacted with other people in the funeral industry because it helps to "reassure us that we're not weird." The wife went on to say:

> A lot of people ask us how we can stand to be in this business—especially because he does all of the embalming. They act like we must be strange or something. When we go to the conventions and meet with all of the other people there who are just like us—people who like helping other people—I feel normal again.

All these elements of professionalization—educational requirements, exams, boards, organizations, codes of ethics, and the rest—lend an air of credibility and dignity to the funeral business while diminishing the stigma associated with it. Although the requirements for licensure and certification are not highly exclusive, they still represent forms of boundary maintenance, and demand a certain level of commitment from those who enter the field. Thus, professionalization helped in the transition of the funeral business from a vocation that can be pursued by virtually anyone to a profession that can be entered only by those with the appropriate qualifications. As Pine (1975, 28) indicated:

> Because professionalization is highly respected in American society, the word . . . "profession". . . tends to be used as a symbol by occupations seeking to improve or enhance the lay public's conception of that occupation, and funeral directing is no exception. To some extent, this appears to be because the funeral director hopes to overcome the stigma of "doing death work."

By claiming professional status, funeral directors claim prestige and simultaneously seek to minimize the stigma they experience for being death workers involved in "dirty work."

The Shroud of Service

One of the most obvious ways in which morticians and funeral directors neutralize the stigma associated with their work is to wrap themselves in a "shroud of service." All the respondents emphasized their service role over all other aspects of their jobs. Although their services were not legally required in any of the four states included in this study, all the respondents insisted that people desperately needed them. As one funeral director summarized, "Service, that's what we're all about—we're there when people need us the most."

Unlike the humorous fantasy ads mentioned earlier, actual advertisements in the funeral industry focus on service. Typical ads for the companies in this study read:

> "Our Family Serving Yours for Over 60 Years"
> "Serving the Community for Four Generations"
> "Thoughtful Service in Your Time of Need"

The emphasis on service, especially on "grief counseling" and "bereavement therapy," shifts the focus away from the two most stigmatizing elements of funeral work: the handling and preparation of the body, which already has been discussed at length; and retail sales, which are widely interpreted as profiting from other people's grief. Many of the funeral directors indicated that they believed the major reason for negative public feelings toward their occupation was not only that they handled dead bodies, but the fact that they made their living off the dead, or at least, off the grief of the living.

All admitted that much of their profit came from the sale of caskets and vaults, where markup is usually a minimum of 100%, and often 400–500%, but all played down this aspect of their work. The Federal Trade Commission requires that funeral directors provide their customers with itemized lists of all charges. The author was provided with price lists for all merchandise and services by all the funeral directors in this study. When asked to estimate the "average price" of one of their funerals, respondents' answers ranged from $3,000 to $4,000. Typically, the casket accounted for approximately half of the total expense. Respondents indicated that less than 5% of their business involved cremations, but that even then they often encouraged the purchase of a casket. One said, "A lot of people ask about cremation, because they think it's cheaper, but I usually sell them caskets even for cremation; then, if you add the cost of cremation and urn, cremation becomes more profitable than burial."

Despite this denial of the retail aspects of the job, trade journals provide numerous helpful hints on the best techniques for displaying and selling caskets, and great care is given to this process. In all the funeral homes visited, one person was charged with the primary responsibility for helping with "casket selection." In smaller family-operated funeral homes, this person usually was the funeral director's wife. In the large chain-owned companies, it was one of the "associate funeral directors." In either case, the person was a skilled salesperson.

Nevertheless, the sales pitch is wrapped in the shroud of service. During each interview, the author asked to be shown the "selection room," and to be treated as if he were there to select a casket for a loved one. All the funeral directors willingly complied, and most treated the author as if he actually were there to select a casket. Interestingly, most perceived this as an actual sales opportunity and mentioned their "pre-need selection service" and said that if the author had not already made such arrangements, they would gladly assist him with the process. The words "sell," "sales," "buy," and "purchase" were carefully avoided.

Also, although by law the price for each casket must be displayed separately, most funeral homes also displayed a "package price" that included the casket and "full services." If purchased separately, the casket was always more expensive than if it was included in the package of services. This gave the impression that a much more expensive casket could be purchased for less money if bought as part of a service package. It also implied that the services provided by the firm were of more value than the merchandise.

The funeral directors rationalized the high costs of merchandise and funerals by emphasizing that they were a small price to pay for the services performed. One insisted, "We don't sell merchandise, we sell service!" Another asked "What is peace of mind worth?" and another "How do you put a price on relieving grief?"

Another rationalization for the high prices was the amount involved in arranging and conducting funeral services. When asked about the negative aspects of their jobs, most emphasized the hard work and long hours involved. In fact, all but two of the interviewees said that they did not want their children to follow in their footstep, because the work was largely misunderstood (stigmatized), too hard, the hours too long, and "the income not nearly as high as most people think."

In addition to emphasizing the service aspect of their work, funeral directors also tend to join a number of local philanthropic and service organizations (Pine, 1975, 49). Although many businessmen find that joining such organizations is advantageous for making contacts, Stephenson (1985, 223) contended that the small-town funeral director "may be able to counter the stigma of his or her occupation by being active in the community, thereby counteracting some of the negative images associated with the job of funeral directing."

Socioeconomic Status versus Occupational Prestige

It seems that what funeral directors lack in occupational prestige, they make up for in socioeconomic status. Although interviewees were very candid about the number of funerals they performed every year and the average costs per funeral, most were reluctant to disclose their annual incomes. One exception was a 37-year-old funeral home owner, funeral director, and licensed embalmer in a community of approximately 25,000 who indicated that in the previous year he had handled 211 funerals and had a gross income of just under $750,000. After deducting overhead (three licensed embalmers on staff, a receptionist, a gardener, a student employee, insurance costs, etc.), he estimated his net income to have been "close to $250,000." He quickly added, however, that he worked long hours, had his 5-day vacation cut to two (because of a "funeral call that he had to handle personally") and despite his relatively high income (probably one of the two or three highest incomes in the community), he felt morally, socially, and professionally obligated to hide his wealth in the community. "I have to walk a fine line," he said, "I can live in a nice home, drive a nice car, and wear nice suits, because people know that I am a successful businessman—but, I have to be careful not to flaunt it."

One of the ways he reconciles this dilemma was by enjoying "the finer things in life" outside the community. He owned a condominium in Vail where he took ski trips and kept his sports car. He also said that none of his friends or neighbors there knew that he was in the funeral business. In fact, when they inquired about his occupations he told them he was in insurance (which technically was true because he also was a licensed insurance agent who sold burial policies). When asked why he did not disclose his true occupational identity, he responded:

> When I tell people what I really do, they initially seem "put off," even repulsed. I have literally had people jerk their hands back during a handshake when somebody

introduces me and then tells them what I do for a living. Later, many of them become very curious and ask a lot of questions. If you tell people you sell insurance, they usually let the subject drop.

Although almost all the funeral directors in this study lived what they characterized as fairly "conservative lifestyles," most also indicated that they enjoyed many of the material things that their jobs offered them. One couple rationalized their recent purchase of a very expensive sailboat (which both contended they "really couldn't afford"), by saying, "Hey, if anybody knows that you can't take it with you, it's us—we figured we might as well enjoy it while we can." Another commented, "Most of the people in this community would never want to do what I do, but most of them would like to have my income."

■ ■ ■ SUMMARY AND CONCLUSION

This study describes and analyzes how people in the funeral industry attempt to reduce and neutralize the stigma associated with their occupations. Morticians and funeral directors are particularly stigmatized, not only because they perform work that few others would be willing to do (preparing dead bodies for burial), but also because they profit from death. Consequently, members of the funeral industry consciously work at stigma reduction.

Paramount among their strategies are symbolically redefining their work. This especially involves avoiding all language that reminds their customer of death, the body, and retail sales; morticians and funeral directors emphasize the need for their professional services of relieving family grief and bereavement counseling. They also practice role distance, emphasize their professionalism, wrap themselves in a "shroud of service," and enjoy their relatively high socioeconomic status rather than lament their lower occupational prestige.

REFERENCES

Amos, E. P. 1983. *Kansas Funeral Profession Through the Years.* Topeka: Kansas Funeral Directors' Association.

Aries, P. 1976. *Western Attitudes Toward Death: From the Middle Ages to the Present.* Trans. P. M. Ranum. Baltimore: Johns Hopkins University Press, p. 99.

Charmaz, K. 1980. *The Social Reality of Death: Death in Contemporary America.* Reading, MA: Addison-Wesley.

Goffman, E. 1959. *The Presentation of Self in Everyday Life.* Garden City, NY: Anchor Doubleday.

Lesy, M. 1987. *The Forbidden Zone.* New York: Farrar, Straus & Giroux.

Pavalko, R. M. 1988. *Sociology of Occupations and Profession,* 2nd ed. Itasca, IL: Peacock.

Pine, V. R. 1975. *Caretaker of the Dead: The American Funeral Director.* New York: Irvington.

Stephenson, J. S. 1985. *Death, Grief and Mourning: Individual and Social Realities.* New York: Free Press.

Sudnow, D. 1967. *Passing On: The Social Organization of Dying.* Englewood Cliffs, NJ: Prentice-Hall.

Turner, R. E., and D. Edgley. 1976. "Death as Theater: A Dramaturgical Analysis of the American Funeral." *Sociology and Social Research, 60* (July): 377–392.

Woods, A. S., and R. G. Delisle. 1978. "The Treatment of Death in Sympathy Cards." Pp. 95–103 in C. Winick (ed.), *Deviance and Mass Media.* Beverly Hills, CA: Sage.

Becoming a Hit Man

Ken Levi

introduction

There is no doubt that we all have deviant desires. We all feel hedged in at times, and we want to break loose, throwing aside some of the rules that constrain us. But there is more to our deviant desires than this. If we probe deeper, perhaps into some hidden recesses, we might even uncover a cesspool of feelings and impulses that we don't want to reveal to others or, at times, even to ourselves. If we were to give in to them, at a minimum we would be unwelcome in most places—or we might see our name and photo on some wanted poster. To get along in society, for the most part we accede to social norms and ignore or suppress our desires for deviance. Ignored or suppressed, however, these desires remain, sometimes hidden, sometimes cautiously entertained. Yet we—or I should say, some of us—are aware of our capacity for deviance. Even highly conforming people, those whose deviant desires are under tight control, can do appalling things when the conditions are right.

But killing people in cold blood? Shooting men and women because someone offers money for their deaths? Who would do such a thing? And those who do, how do they think of themselves—as monsters, the way we might think of them? On the contrary, as Levi shows, just as we have ways of neutralizing our deviances (telling a "white" lie or using the Internet to do a "little" cheating on a class paper), so hit men have ways of neutralizing what they do. After all, just like us, they have to live with themselves.

Thinking Critically

As you read this selection, ask yourself:

1. Under what conditions could I become a hit man or a hit woman?

2. How do hit men neutralize their murders?

3. How do you use neutralization techniques to neutralize your own deviances?

Our knowledge about deviance management is based primarily on behavior that is easily mitigated. The literature dwells on unwed fathers (Pfuhl, 1978), and childless mothers (Veevers, 1975), pilfering bread salesmen (Ditton, 1977), and conniving shoe salesmen (Freidman, 1974), bridge pros (Holtz, 1975), and poker pros

(Hayano, 1977), marijuana smokers (Langer, 1976), massage parlor prostitutes (Verlarde, 1975), and other minor offenders (see, for example, Berk, 1977; Farrell and Nelson, 1976; Gross, 1977). There is a dearth of deviance management articles on serious offenders, and no scholarly articles at all about one of the (legally) most serious offenders of all, the professional murderer. Drift may be possible for the minor offender exploiting society's *ambivalence* toward his relatively unserious behavior (Sykes and Matza, 1957). However, excuses for the more inexcusable forms of deviant behavior are, by definition, less easily come by, and the very serious offender may enter his career with few of the usual defenses.

This article will focus on ways that one type of serious offender, the professional hit man, neutralizes stigma in the early stages of his career. As we shall see, the social organization of the "profession" provides "neutralizers" which distance its members from the shameful aspects of their careers. But for the novice, without professional insulation, the problem is more acute. With very little outside help, he must negate his feelings, neutralize them, and adopt a "framework" (Goffman, 1974) appropriate to his chosen career. This process, called "reframing," is the main focus of the present article. Cognitively, the novice must *reframe his experience* in order to enter his profession.

■ ■ ■ ■ THE SOCIAL ORGANIZATION OF MURDER

Murder, the unlawful killing of a person, is considered a serious criminal offense in the United States, and it is punished by extreme penalties. In addition, most Americans do not feel that the penalties are extreme enough (Reid, 1976:482). In overcoming the intense stigma associated with murder, the hit man lacks the supports available to more ordinary types of killers.

Some cultures allow special circumstances or sanction special organizations wherein people who kill are insulated from the taint of murder. Soldiers at war, or police in the line of duty, or citizens protecting their property operate under what are considered justifiable or excusable conditions. They receive so much informal support from the general public and from members of their own group that it may protect even a sadistic member from blame (Westley, 1966).

Subcultures (Wolfgang and Ferracuti, 1967), organizations (Maas, 1968), and gangs (Yablonsky, 1962) that unlawfully promote killing can at least provide their members with an "appeal to higher loyalties" (Sykes and Matza, 1957), if not a fully developed set of deviance justifying norms.

Individuals acting on their own, who kill in a spontaneous "irrational" outburst of violence can also mitigate the stigma of their behavior.

> I mean, people will go ape for one minute and shoot, but there are very few people who are capable of thinking about, planning, and then doing it [Joey, 1974:56].

From "Becoming a Hit Man" by Ken Levi in *Journal of Contemporary Ethnography*, 10(1), pp. 47–63. Copyright 1981 by Sage Publications Inc., Journals. Reprinted with permission of Sage Publications, Inc. via Copyright Clearance Center.

Individuals who kill in a hot-blooded burst of passion can retrospectively draw comfort from the law which provides a lighter ban against killings performed without premeditation or malice or intent (Lester and Lester, 1975:35). At one extreme, the spontaneous killing may seem the result of a mental disease (Lester and Lester, 1975:39) or dissociative reaction (Tanay, 1972), and excused entirely as insanity.

But when an individual who generally shares society's ban against murder, is fully aware that his act of homicide is (1) unlawful, (2) self-serving, and (3) intentional, he does not have the usual defenses to fall back on. How does such an individual manage *to overcome his inhibitions and avoid serious damage to his self-image* (assuming that he does share society's ban)? This is the special dilemma of the professional hit man who hires himself out for murder.

■ ■ ■ RESEARCH METHODS

Information for this article comes primarily from a series of intensive interviews with one self-styled "hit man." The interviews were spread over seven, tape-recorded sessions during a four-month period. The respondent was one of fifty prison inmates randomly sampled from a population of people convicted of murder in Metropolitan Detroit. The respondent told about an "accidental" killing, involving a drunken bar patron who badgered the respondent and finally forced his hand by pulling a knife on him. In court he claimed self-defense, but the witnesses at the bar claimed otherwise, so they sent him to prison. During the first two interview sessions, the respondent acted progressively ashamed of this particular killing, not on moral ground, but because of its "sloppiness" or "amateurishness." Finally, he indicated there was more he would like to say. So, I stopped the tape recorder. I asked him if he was a hit man. He said he was.

He had already been given certain guarantees, including no names in the interview, a private conference room, and a signed contract promising his anonymity. Now, as a further guarantee, we agreed to talk about him in the third person, as a fictitious character named "Pete," so that none of his statements would sound like a personal confession. With these assurances, future interviews were devoted to his career as a professional murderer, with particular emphasis on his entry into the career and his orientation toward his victims.

Was he reliable? Since we did not use names, I had no way of checking the veracity of the individual cases he reported. Nevertheless, I was able to compare his account of the hit man's career with information from other convicted murderers, with police experts, and with accounts from the available literature (Gage, 1972; Joey, 1974; Maas, 1968). Pete's information was generally supported by these other sources. As to his motive for submitting to the interview, it is hard to gauge. He apparently was ashamed of the one "accidental" killing that had landed him in prison, and he desired to set the record straight concerning what he deemed an illustrious career, now that he had arrived, as he said, at the end of it. Hit men pride themselves on not "falling" (going to jail) for murder, and Pete's incarceration hastened a decision to retire—that he had already been contemplating, anyway.

A question might arise about the ethics of researching self-confessed "hit men" and granting them anonymity. Legally, since Pete never mentioned specific names or specific dates or possible future crimes, there does not seem to be a problem. Morally, if confidentiality is a necessary condition to obtaining information about serious offenders, then we have to ask: Is it worth it? Pete insisted that he had retired from the profession. Therefore, there seems to be no "clear and imminent danger" that would justify the violation of confidentiality, in the terms set forth by the American Psychological Association (1978:40). On the other hand, the *possibility* of danger does exist, and future researchers will have to exercise their judgment.

Finally, hit men are hard to come by. Unlike more lawful killers, such as judges or night watchmen, and unlike run-of-the-mill murderers, the hit man (usually) takes infinite care to conceal his identity. Therefore, while it is regrettable that this paper has only one case to report on, and while it would be ideal to perform a comparative analysis on a number of hit men, it would be very difficult to obtain such a sample. Instead, Pete's responses will be compared to similar accounts from the available literature. While such a method can never produce verified findings, it can point to suggestive hypotheses.

■ ■ ■ THE SOCIAL ORGANIZATION OF PROFESSIONAL MURDER

There are two types of professional murderers: the organized and the independent. The killer who belongs to an organized syndicate does not usually get paid on a contract basis, and performs his job out of loyalty and obedience to the organization (Maas, 1968:81). The independent professional killer is a freelance agent who hires himself out for a fee (Pete). It is the career organization of the second type of killer that will be discussed.

The organized killer can mitigate his behavior through an "appeal to higher loyalties" (Sykes and Matza, 1957). He also can view his victim as an enemy of the group and then choose from a variety of techniques available for neutralizing an offense against an enemy (see, for example, Hirschi, 1969; Rogers and Buffalo, 1974). But the independent professional murderer lacks most of these defenses. Nevertheless, built into his role are certain structural features that help him avoid deviance ascription. These features include:

(1) *Contract.* A contract is an unwritten agreement to provide a sum of money to a second party who agrees, in return, to commit a designated murder (Joey, 1974:9). It is most often arranged over the phone, between people who have never had personal contact. And the victim, or "hit," is usually unknown to the killer (Gage, 1972:57; Joey, 1974:61–62). This arrangement is meant to protect both parties from the law. But it also helps the killer "deny the victim" (Sykes and Matza, 1957) by keeping him relatively anonymous.

In arranging the contract, the hired killer will try to find out the difficulty of the hit and how much the customer wants the killing done. According to Pete, these considerations determine his price. He does not ask about the motive for the killing, treating it as none of his concern. Not knowing the motive may hamper the killer from morally justifying his behavior, but it also enables him to further deny the victim by maintaining his distance and reserve. Finally, the contract is backed up by a further understanding.

> Like this guy who left here (prison) last summer, he was out two months before he got killed. Made a mistake somewhere. The way I heard it, he didn't finish filling a contract [Pete].

If the killer fails to live up to his part of the bargain, the penalties could be extreme (Gage, 1972:53; Joey, 1974:9). This has the ironic effect that after the contract is arranged, the killer can somewhat "deny responsibility" (Sykes and Matza, 1957), by pleading self-defense.

(2) *Reputation and Money.* Reputation is especially important in an area where killers are unknown to their customers, and where the less written, the better (Joey, 1974:58). Reputation, in turn, reflects how much money the hit man has commanded in the past,

> And that was the first time that I ever got 30 grand . . . it's based on his reputation. . . . Yeah, how good he really is. To be so-so, you get so-so money. If you're good, you get good money [Pete].

Pete, who could not recall the exact number of people he had killed, did, like other hit men, keep an accounting of his highest fees (Joey, 1974:58, 62). To him big money meant not only a way to earn a living, but also a way to maintain his professional reputation.

People who accept low fees can also find work as hired killers. Heroin addicts are the usual example. But, as Pete says, they often receive a bullet for their pains. It is believed that people who would kill for so little would also require little persuasion to make them talk to the police (Joey, 1974:63). This further reinforces the single-minded emphasis on making big money. As a result, killing is conceptualized as a "business" or as "just a job." Framing the hit in a normal businesslike context enables the hit man to deny wrongfulness, or "deny injury" (Sykes and Matza, 1957).

In addition to the economic motive, Pete and hit men discussed by other authors, refer to excitement, fun, game-playing, power, and impressing women as incentives for murder (Joey, 1974:81–82). However, none of these motives are mentioned by all sources. None are as necessary to the career as money. And, after a while, these other motives diminish and killing becomes only "just a job" (Joey, 1974:20). The primacy of the economic motive has been aptly expressed in the case of another deviant profession.

> Women who enjoy sex with their customers do not make good prostitutes, according to those who are acquainted with this institution first hand. Instead of thinking about the most effective way of making money at the job, they would be doing things for their own pleasure and enjoyment [Goode, 1974:342].

(3) *Skill.* Most of the hit man's training focuses on acquiring skill in the use of weapons.

> Then, he met these two guys, these two white guys . . . them two, them two was the best. And but they stayed around over there and they got together, and Pete told [them] that he really wanted to be good. He said, if [I] got to do something, I want to be good at it. So, they got together, showed him, showed him *how to shoot.* . . . And gradually, he became good. . . . Like he told me, like when he shoots somebody, he always goes for the head; he said, that's about the best shot. I mean, if you want him dead then and there. . . . And these two guys showed him, and to him, I mean, hey, I mean, he don't believe nobody could really outshoot these two guys, you know what I mean. *They know everything you want to know about guns, knives, and stuff like that* [Pete].

The hit man's reputation, and the amount of money he makes depends on his skill, his effective ability serve as a means to someone else's ends. The result is a focus on technique.

> Like in anything you do, when you do it, you want to do it just right. . . . On your target and you hit it, how you feel: I hit it! I hit it! [Pete].

This focus on technique, on means, helps the hit man to "deny responsibility" and intent (Sykes and Matza, 1957). In frame-analytic terms, the hit man separates his morally responsible, or "principal" self from the rest of himself, and performs the killing mainly as a "strategist" (Goffman, 1974:523). In other words, he sees himself as a "hired gun." The saying, "If I didn't do it, they'd find someone else who would," reflects this narrowly technical orientation.

To sum up thus far, the contract, based as it is on the hit man's reputation for profit and skill, provides the hit man with opportunities for denying the victim, denying injury, and denying responsibility. But this is not enough. To point out the defenses of the professional hit man is one thing, but it is unlikely that the *novice* hit man would have a totally professional attitude so early in his career. The novice is at a point where he both lacks the conventional defense against the stigma of murder, *and* he has not yet fully acquired the exceptional defenses of the professional. How, then, does he cope?

■ ■ ■ THE FIRST TIME: NEGATIVE EXPERIENCE

Goffman defines "negative experience" as a feeling of disorientation.

> Expecting to take up a position in a well-framed realm, he finds that no particular frame is immediately applicable, or the frame that he thought was applicable no longer seems to be, or he cannot bind himself within the frame that does apparently apply. He loses command over the formulation of viable response. He flounders. Experience, the meld of what the current scene brings to him and what be brings to it— meant to settle into a form even while it is beginning, finds no form and is therefore no experience. Reality anomically flutters. He has a "negative experience"—negative in the sense that it takes its character from what it is not, and what it is not is an organized and organizationally affirmed response [1974:378–379].

Negative experience can occur when a person finds himself lapsing into an old understanding of the situation, only to suddenly awaken to the fact that it no longer applies. In this regard, we should expect negative experience to be a special problem for the novice. For example, the first time he killed a man for money, Pete supposedly became violently ill:

> When he [Pete], you know, hit the guy, when he shot the guy, the guy said, "You killed me". . . something like that, cause he struck him all up here. And what he said, it was just, I mean, *the look right in the guy's eye,* you know. I mean he looked like: *why me?* Yeah? And he [Pete] couldn't shake that. Cause he remembered a time or two when he got cut, and all he wanted to do was get back and cut this guy that cut him. And this here. . . . No, he just could not shake it. And then he said that at night-time he'll start thinking about the guy: like he shouldn't have looked at him like that. . . . I mean actually [Pete] was sick. . . . He couldn't keep his food down, I mean, or nothing like that. . . . [It lasted] I'd say about two months. . . . Like he said that he had feelings . . . that he never did kill nobody before [Pete].

Pete's account conforms to the definition of negative experience. He had never killed anyone for money before. It started when a member of the Detroit drug world had spotted Pete in a knife fight outside an inner city bar, was apparently impressed with the young man's style, and offered him fifty dollars to do a "job." Pete accepted. He wanted the money. But when the first hit came about, Pete of course knew that he was doing it for money, but yet his orientation was revenge. Thus, he stared his victim in the *face,* a characteristic gesture of people who kill enemies for revenge (Levi, 1975:190). Expecting to see defiance turn into a look of defeat, they attempt to gain "face" at the loser's expense.

But when Pete stared his victim in the face, he saw not an enemy, but an innocent man. He saw a look of: "Why me?" And this *discordant* image is what remained in his mind during the weeks and months to follow and made him sick. As Pete says, "He shouldn't have looked at him like that." The victim's look of innocence brought about what Goffman (1974:347) refers to as a "frame break":

> Given that the frame applied to an activity is expected to enable us to come to terms with all events in that activity (informing and regulating many of them), it is understandable that the unmanageable might occur, an occurrence which cannot be effectively ignored and to which the frame cannot be applied, with resulting bewilderment and chagrin on the part of the participants. In brief, a break can occur in the applicability of the frame, a break in its governance.

When such a frame break occurs, it produces negative experience. Pete's extremely uncomfortable disorientation may reflect the extreme dissonance between the revenge frame, that he expected to apply, and the unexpected look of innocence that he encountered and continued to recall.

■ ■ ■ SUBSEQUENT TIME: REFRAMING THE HIT

According to Goffman (1974:319), a structural feature of frames of experience is that they are divided into different "tracks" or types of information. These include, "a main track or story line and ancillary tracks of various kinds." The ancillary tracks are the directional track, the overlay track, the concealment tracks, and the disattend track. The disattend track contains the information that is perceived but supposed to be *ignored*. For example, the prostitute manages the distasteful necessity of having sex with "tricks" by remaining "absolutely . . . detached. Removed. Miles and miles away" (1974:344). The existence of different tracks allows an individual to define and redefine his experience by the strategic placement of information.

Sometimes, the individual receives outside help. For example, when Milgram in 1963 placed a barrier between people administering electric shocks, and the bogus "subjects" who were supposedly receiving the shocks, he made it easier for the shockers to "disattend" signs of human distress from their hapless victims. Surgeons provide another example. Having their patients completely covered, except for the part to be operated on, helps them work in a more impersonal manner. In both examples, certain crucial information is stored away in the "concealment track" (Goffman, 1974:218).

In other cases help can come from guides who direct the novice on what to experience and what to block out. Beginning marijuana smokers are cautioned to ignore feelings of nausea (Becker, 1953:240). On the other hand, novice hit men like Pete are reluctant to share their "experience" with anyone else. It would be a sign of weakness.

In still other cases, however, it is possible that the subject can do the reframing *on his own*. And this is what appears to have happened to Pete.

> And when the second one [the second hit] came up, [Pete] was still thinking about the first one. . . . Yeah, when he got ready to go, he was thinking about it. *Something changed. I* don't know how to put it right. Up to the moment that he killed the second guy now, he waited, you know. Going through his mind was the first guy he killed. He still seeing him, still see *the expression on his face.* Soon, the second guy walked up; I mean, it was like his mind just *blanked out* for a minute, everything just blanked out. . . . Next thing he know, he had killed the second guy. . . . *He knew what he was doing, but* what I mean, he just didn't have nothing on his mind. Everything was wiped out [Pete].

When the second victim approached, Pete says that he noticed the victim's approach, he was aware of the man's presence. But he noticed none of the victim's personal features. He did not see the victim's face or its expression. Thus, he did not see the very thing that gave him so much trouble the first time. It is as if Pete had *negatively conditioned* himself to avoid certain cues. Since he shot the victim in the head, it is probable that Pete saw him in one sense; this is not the same kind of experience as a "dissociative reaction," which has been likened to sleepwalking (Tanay, 1972). Pete says that, "he knew what he was doing." But he either did not pay attention to his victim's personal features at the time of the killing, or he blocked them out immediately afterward, so that now the only aspect of his victim he recalls is the victim's approach (if we are to believe him).

After that, Pete says that killing became *routine*. He learned to view his victims as "targets," rather than as people. Thus, he believes that the second experience is the crucial one, and that the disattendance of the victim's personal features made it so.

Support from other accounts of hit men is scant, due to a lack of data. Furthermore, not everything in Pete's account supports the "reframing" hypothesis. In talking about later killings, it is clear that he not only attends to his victims' personal features, on occasion, but he also derives a certain grim pleasure in doing so.

> [The victim was] a nice looking woman. . . . She started weeping, and [she cried], "I ain't did this, I ain't did that . . . and [Pete] said that he shot her. Like it wasn't nothing . . . he didn't feel nothing. It was just money [Pete].

In a parallel story, Joey, the narrator of the *Killer,* also observes his victim in personal terms.

> [The victim] began to beg. He even went so far as to tell us where he had stashed his money. Finally, he realized there was absolutely nothing he could do. He sat there quietly. Then, he started crying. I didn't feel a thing for him [1974:56].

It may be that this evidence contradicts what I have said about reframing; but perhaps another interpretation is possible. Reframing may play a more crucial role in the original redefinition of an experience than in the continued maintenance of that redefinition. Once Pete has accustomed himself to viewing his victims as merely targets, as "just money," then it may be less threatening to look upon them as persons, once again. Once the "main story line" has been established, discordant information can be presented in the "overlay track" (Goffman, 1974:215), without doing too much damage. Indeed, this seems to be the point that both hit men are trying to make in the above excerpts.

■ ■ ■ THE HEART OF THE HIT MAN

For what I have been referring to as "disattendance" Pete used the term "heart," which he defined as a "coldness." When asked what he would look for in an aspiring hit man, Peter replied,

> See if he's got a whole lot of heart . . . you got to be cold . . . you got to build a coldness in yourself. It's not something that comes automatically. Cause, see, I don't care who he is, first, you've got feelings [Pete].

In contrast to this view, Joey (1974:56) said,

> There are three things you need to kill a man: the gun, the bullets, and the balls. A lot of people will point a gun at you, but they haven't got the courage to pull the trigger. It's as simple as that.

It may be that some are born with "heart," while others acquire it in the way I have described.

However, the "made rather than born" thesis does explain one perplexing feature of hit men and other "evil" men whose banality has sometimes seemed discordant. In other aspects of their lives they all seem perfectly capable of feeling ordinary human emotions. Their inhumanity, their coldness, seems narrowly restricted to their jobs. Pete, for example, talked about his "love" for little children. Eddie "The Hawk" Ruppolo meekly allowed his mistress to openly insult him in a public bar (Gage, 1972). And Joey (1974:55) has this to say about himself:

> Believe it or not, I'm a human being. I laugh at funny jokes. I love children around the house, and I can spend hours playing with my mutt.

All of these examples of human warmth indicate that the cold heart of the bit man may be less a characteristic of the killer's individual personality, than a feature of the professional framework of experience which the hit man has learned to adapt himself to, when he is on the job.

■ ■ ■ DISCUSSION

This article is meant as a contribution to the study of deviance neutralization. The freelance hit man is an example of an individual who, relatively alone, must deal with a profound and unambiguous stigma in order to enter his career. Both Pete and Joey emphasize "heart" as a determining factor in becoming a professional. And Pete's experience, after the first hit, further indicates that the inhibitions against murder-for-money are real.

In this article "heart"—or the ability to adapt to a rationalized framework for killing—has been portrayed as the outcome of an initial process of reframing, in addition to other neutralization techniques established during the further stages of professionalization. As several theorists (see, for example, Becker, 1953; Douglas et al., 1977; Matza, 1969) have noted, people often enter into deviant acts first, and then develop rationales for their behavior later on. This was also the case with Pete, who began his career by first, (1) "being willing" (Matza, 1969), (2) encountering a frame break, (3) undergoing negative experience, (4) being willing to try again (also known as "getting back on the horse"), (5) reframing the experience, and (6) having future, routine experiences wherein his professionalization increasingly enabled him to "deny the victim," "deny injury," and "deny responsibility." Through the process of reframing, the experience of victim-as-target emerged as the "main story line," and the experience of victim-as-person was downgraded from the main track to the disattend track to the overlay track. Ironically, the intensity of the negative experience seemed to make the process all the more successful. Thus, it may be possible for a person with "ordinary human feelings" to both pass through the novice stage, and to continue "normal relations" thereafter. The reframing hypothesis has implications for other people who knowingly perform stigmatized behaviors. It may be particularly useful in explaining a personal conversion experience that occurs despite the relative absence of deviant peer groups, deviant norms, extenuating circumstances, and neutralization rationales.

REFERENCES

American Psychological Association (1978) Directory of the American Psychological Association, Washington, DC: Author.

Becker, H. (1953) "Becoming a marijuana user." Amer. J. of Sociology 59: 235–243.

Berk, B. (1977) "Face-saving at the singles dance." Social Problems 24, 5: 530–544.

Ditton, J. (1977) "Alibis and aliases: some notes on motives of fiddling bread salesmen." Sociology 11, 2: 233–255.

Douglas, J., P. Rasmussen, and C. Flanagan (1977) The Nude Beach. Beverly Hills: Sage.

Farrell, R. and J. Nelson (1976) "A causal model of secondary deviance; the case of homosexuality," Soc. Q 17: 109–120.

Friedman, N. L. (1974) "Cookies and contests: notes on ordinary occupational deviance and its neutralization." Soc. Symposium (Spring): 1–9.

Gage, N. (1972) Mafia, U.S.A. New York: Dell.

Goffman, E. (1974) Frame Analysis. Cambridge, MA: Harvard Univ. Press.

Goode, E. (1978) Deviant Behavior: An Interactionist Approach. Englewood Cliffs, NJ: Prentice-Hall.

Gross, H. (1977) "Micro and macro level implications for a sociology of virtue—case of draft protesters to Vietnam War." Soc. Q. 18, 3: 319–339.

Hayano, D. (1977) "The professional poker player: career identification and the problem of respectability." Social Problems 24 (June): 556–564.

Hirschi, T. (1969) Causes of Delinquency. Berkeley: Univ. of California Press.

Holtz, J. (1975) "The professional duplicate bridge player: conflict management in a free, legal, quasi-deviant occupation." Urban Life 4, 2: 131–160.

Joey (1974) Killer: Autobiography of a Mafia Hit Man. New York: Pocket Books.

Langer, J. (1976) "Drug entrepreneurs and the dealing culture." Australian and New Zealand J. of Sociology 12. 2: 82–90.

Lester, D. and G. Lester (1975) Crime of Passion: Murder and the Murderer. Chicago: Nelson-Hall.

Levi, K. (1975) Icemen. Ann Arbor, MI: University Microfilms.

Maas, P. (1968) The Valachi Papers. New York: G. P. Putnam.

Matza, D. (1969) Becoming Deviant. Englewood Cliffs, NJ: Prentice-Hall.

Pfuhl, E. (1978) "The unwed father: a non-deviant rule breaker." Soc. Q. 19: 113–128.

Reid, S. (1976) Crime and Criminology. Hinsdale, IL: Dryden Press.

Rogers, J. and M. Buffalo (1974) "Neutralization techniques: toward a simplified measurement scale." Pacific Soc. Rev. 17, 3: 313.

Sykes, G. and D. Matza (1957) "Techniques of neutralization: a theory of delinquency." Amer. Soc. Rev. 22: 664–670.

Tanay, E. (1972) "Psychiatric aspects of homicide prevention." Amer. J. of Psychology 128: 814–817.

Veevers, J. (1975) "The moral careers of voluntarily childless wives: notes on the defense of a variant world view." Family Coordinator 24, 4: 473–487.

Verlarde, A. (1975) "Becoming prostituted: the decline of the massage parlor profession and the masseuse." British J. of Criminology 15, 3: 251–263.

Westley, W. (1966) "The escalation of violence through legitimation." Annals of the American Association of Political and Social Science 364 (March) 120–126.

Wolfgang, M. and F. Ferracuti (1967) The Subculture of Violence. London: Tavistock.

Yablosnky, L. (1962) The Violent Gang. New York: Macmillan.

PART
III Social Inequality

■■■ ■

It is impossible to have a society of equals. Despite the dreams of some to build an egalitarian society, every society will be marked by inequality. Always there will be what sociologists call *social stratification*.

Each social group has a value system. That is, it values certain things above others. In a tribal group, this could be running, jumping, shooting arrows, throwing spears, or showing bravery. Some members of the tribe will have greater abilities to do the particular things that their group values—no matter what those things may be. Their abilities and accomplishments will set them apart. These people will be looked up to, and they will likely be treated differently.

By considering abilities and accomplishments, as in a tribal group, we can see why social distinctions are inevitable. Social stratification, however, is based on much more than ability and accomplishment. In fact, ability and accomplishment are seldom the bases of social stratification. Much more common are inherited social distinctions.

Every society stratifies its members according to whatever particular values it cherishes. That is, every human group divides its people into layers, and treats each layer differently. Once a society is stratified, birth ushers children into the various positions (statuses) that the society has laid out. By virtue of where their parents are located in their society's social structure, children inherit some of the social distinctions of their parents. These can be their religion (Christian, Jew, Muslim), social class (upper, middle, lower), caste (Brahmin, Shudra, Dalit), or any other distinction that their group makes.

Because their group has already set up rules about gender, children also inherit a set of wide-ranging expectations based on their sex. So it may be with their race-ethnicity. In addition, geopolitics come into play. Birth ushers children onto a world stage, where they inherit their country's position in what is known as *global stratification*. Their nation may be rich and powerful or poor and weak. Wherever it is located on the world scene, this, too, has fundamental consequences for people's world views and other vital aspects of their lives.

In this third part of the book, we look at some of the major aspects of social inequality. We begin with a broad view of global stratification. By tracking a job that was exported from the United States to Mexico, William Adler illustrates how the globalization of capitalism directly impacts people's lives. His analysis helps us to understand that where a nation is located in the global scheme of things makes fundamental differences for what happens to us in life. Herbert Gans, following with a functional analysis of poverty, analyzes why society *needs* poor people. Kevin Bales then gives us details on the lives of girls and women in a Bangkok brothel. This inside report exposes how the imbalance of power and gender separates people into considerably different fates in life. To turn our focus on race-ethnicity, Anthony Walton analyzes how his being classified as a black man in the United States has implications for almost all aspects of his life. With Cynthia Loucks' report on the treatment that her mother received in a nursing home, we close this third part with a focus on the social inequality of age.

Job on the Line

William M. Adler

introduction ▪ ▪ ▪ ▪

One of history's most significant changes is the *globalization of capitalism*. Because capitalism is based on competition and the pursuit of profits, capitalists are constantly trying to lower their production costs and find ways to expand their markets. The globalization of capitalism is helping them reach both of these goals. Not only do the workers in the Least Industrialized Nations work cheaply, but also, as their incomes increase, they become consumers. By lowering the costs of the goods we buy, this process increases our own standard of living. We all, for example, like to buy quality clothing at a fraction of what it would have cost years ago.

One of the downsides of the globalization of capitalism is *downsizing*, a fancy way of saying that a company is firing workers. In their frenetic pursuit of profits, U.S. firms, followed more reluctantly by the Europeans and the Japanese, have laid off millions of workers. Awaiting their jobs are deprived people in the Least Industrialized Nations, who eagerly seize any crumbs falling from the banquet table of the Most Industrialized Nations. This situation is a capitalist's dream—docile workers who are willing to accept peanuts for wages, and are glad to get them.

We don't have to go to Thailand or Indonesia to follow this process. We have an example much closer to home. Just south of the U.S. border are countries where millions of unemployed men and women are eager to take any kind of work, and to work for almost any wages in almost any conditions. Adler compares the experiences of two workers to explore implications of this aspect of the globalization of capitalism.

Thinking Critically

As you read this selection, ask yourself:

1. Is the employment of young workers in U.S. factories that have been relocated to Mexico an example of exploitation by capitalists or opportunity for these workers?

2. Besides a paycheck that doesn't bounce, what do you think employers owe workers?

3. What solutions do you see to the problems described in this selection?

At 3 o'clock on a warm June afternoon, the second of two wash-up bells rings for the final time. Mollie James stands hunched over the sink as she rinses her hands with industrial soap alongside her co-workers. She first came to work here, on the assembly line at Universal Manufacturing Company in Paterson, New Jersey, a few years after the factory opened in 1951. She was the first woman at the factory to run a stamping machine, the first to laminate steel. She was among the first female union stewards and among the first African American stewards; hers was a self-assured presence any grievant would want on their side. And now, after 34 years on the line—nearly two-thirds of her life—she is the last to go.

At the end of every other shift for more than three decades, Mollie and her fellow employees beat a quick path to the plant parking lot. On this day there is less sense of hurry. There are still children to feed, clothes to wash, bills to pay, errands to run, other jobs to race to. But as she and the others leave the washroom, no one seems pressed to leave. All about the plant entrance, and out in the lot, people stand in small clusters, like mourners at their own wake, talking, laughing, hugging, crying. Almost always Mollie James is outgoing and outspoken, her voice loud and assertive, her smile nicely lighted. At 59 she is a strong woman, her strength forged from a life of hard work and sacrifice, and faith in God. She is not one to betray her emotions, but this day is different. Her bearing has turned to reserve, her normally quick eyes dull and watery. Her working life is over, and that is the only life she has ever known.

Universal had always turned a tidy profit. Its signature product, ballasts that regulate the current in fluorescent lights, attracted attention only when the ballast failed—causing the light fixture to hum or flicker. In the mid-1980s, however, the locally owned company was twice swept up in the gale of winds of Wall Street's merger mania. Twice within eight months Universal was sold, both times to firms headed by disciples of Michael Milken, the Street's reigning evil genius. Not long after the second sale, to a Los Angeles-based electrical components conglomerate called MagneTek, Inc., movers began pulling up the plant's massive machinery, much of which had been bolted to the floor when the factory opened.

Mollie had sensed what was happening in January 1989, the morning she came to work and noticed a hole in the floor. It wasn't a hole, really, in the sense an opening; it was more of a void: a great yawning space of discolored concrete where just the afternoon before had sat a steel-stamping machine, a hulking piece of American industrial might. Before long, more holes appeared, each tracing the outline of the base of another machine, like chalk around a sidewalk corpse.

Now, on the last day, when there is no one left to say goodbye to, Mollie slumps behind the wheel of her rusting 1977 Dodge Charger and follows the procession out of the lot. It is not far, three miles or so from the plant in Paterson's industrial Bunker Hill neighborhood to the three-story, three-family house she owns on the near East Side. Upon pulling into her customary space in the driveway, Mollie sits in the car a good long while, letting the heat of the summer afternoon settle her. By the time she fits the key into the back-door lock and begins climbing the three flights of stairs to her bedroom, she has stopped crying.

The machine that Mollie used to stamp steel for three decades makes its way south, past factories that Universal opened in Mississippi and Arkansas during the 1960s and 1970s to take advantage of cheaper labor and taxes, before arriving in Matamoros, Mexico, a booming border city just across the Rio Grande from Browns-ville, Texas. On a blindingly blue morning, MagneTek executives from "corporate" in L.A. arrive for the gala ribbon cutting of the first MagneTek plant here. Plant man-ager Chuck Peeples, an affable Arkansas expatriate, leads the officials on a tour of the gleaming factory. Outfitted in natty going-native panama hats emblazoned with the company's royal-blue capital-M "power" logo, the MagneTek honchos parade past equipment ripped from the shopworn floor in Paterson, machinery now oper-ated by a young, almost entirely female workforce. These women, primarily in their teens and 20s, have come north to Matamoros in search of work and a better future than the bleakness promised in the jobless farming towns of the interior.

Balbina Duque Granados found a job at MagneTek in 1993, after leaving her family's home in a picturesque but poor mountain village of central Mexico. Just out of her teens, she has an easy, dimpled smile and long black hair worn in a ponytail. With its comparatively low wages, endless supply of labor, lack of regulation, and proximity to the United States, Matamoros is a magnet for *ma-quiladoras,* the foreign-owned assembly plants that wed First World engineering with Third World working conditions. Balbina's probationary pay is slightly less than $26 a week, or about 65 cents an hour. It is difficult work, winding coils, repetitive and tiring and mind numbing, but it is a job she is thrilled to have—her "answered prayer." And although Balbina doesn't know it, it is not just any job. It is Mollie's job. . . .

At a few minutes before 2 o'clock on a cold, pitch-black morning in November 1950, Mollie and her father, Lorenzo Brown, waited anxiously on the platform of the or-nate World War I-era train station in Richmond, Virginia. The Browns were from Cartersville, 45 miles west, in the rolling farmland of central Virginia. Mollie was headed to Penn Station in Newark, New Jersey, to meet her fiance, Sam James, who would take her home, to Paterson, to her new life. She was dressed in her finest: a new navy-blue suit, new shoes, new hairdo. She carried nearly everything she owned in a half-dozen sky-blue suitcases her father had given her for the trip.

Mollie was traveling alone, but the "colored" train cars of the Silver Meteor, and indeed those of the other great northbound coaches—the Champion, the Florida Sunbeam, the Silver Comet—were full of Mollie Browns: black southerners crossing the Mason-Dixon Line, heading for the promised land. Mollie's intended was wait-ing at the station in his new, yellow, two-door Ford to take her to Paterson, a city of 140,000 residents some 15 miles west of New York City. Sam drove her home to the one-room apartment he rented for $20 a week above the flat where his sister and brother-in-law lived. Although the accommodations were far from luxurious—Mollie and Sam shared a kitchen and bath with other upstairs tenants—her new life seemed as bright as Sam's shiny car.

Paterson at precisely the middle of the 20th century was absolutely humming, filled with vibrant neighborhoods, a bustling downtown retail and cultural district, and above all, factories small and large, producing everything from textiles to machine tools to electrical components. "There were so many places to work, I could have five jobs in the same day," Mollie recalled years later. "And if I didn't like one, I could leave and get another, sure."

Mollie's new hometown was born of entrepreneurial dreamers and schemers. The city had been founded on the 16th anniversary of the Declaration of Independence, July 4, 1792, not as a municipality but as a business: the home of the country's first industrial corporation, the Society for Useful Manufactures. The grand plans of the society and its guiding light, Alexander Hamilton, ultimately failed, but Paterson established itself as a cradle of American industry. The city became renowned for its textile mills—silk especially—and later for the union-busting tactics of its mill owners. During the 19th century, textile manufacturers in Paterson were responsible for what were probably the nation's first runaway shops, opening "annexes" in rural Pennsylvania to take advantage of workers who could be subjected to longer hours for half the wages paid in New Jersey. In 1913, the Industrial Workers of the World mobilized Paterson's 25,000 employees to walk away from their looms, effectively nailing shut the nation's silk-manufacturing center. Able to rely on their nonunion factories, mill owners refused to negotiate; starved into submission, the strikers were forced to return to work with neither gains in wages nor improved working conditions.

By the time the 19-year-old Mollie Brown arrived in Paterson, the economy was booming. Unemployment was low, wages high. In her first few years in town, Mollie ran through several jobs. "You'd just catch the bus and go from factory to factory and see who was hiring." Among her stops was a low-slung cement building in northeast Paterson. The sign out front said UNIVERSAL MANUFACTURING CO. The owner himself, a gregarious man named Archie Sergy, showed her through the plant, explaining that the company made a part for fluorescent lights called a ballast. "They showed me how it was made, the whole assembly line. I learned there's a lot to it, a *very* lot." The starting salary was 90 cents an hour, but the company was about to implement a second shift, from 3 P.M. to midnight, that would pay an extra dime an hour. Those hours were ideal for Mollie. She and Sam had three children under the age of five and another on the way, and if she were to work nights and he days, the couple could care for the children without hiring a sitter. She accepted the job. "I hope you'll be here a long time," Sergy told her. "I hope we'll all be here a long time!"

By the early 1960s, Universal employed a workforce of some 1,200. Archie Sergy and his top managers continued to demonstrate a sincere interest in the welfare of their employees. "They never treated you as inferior, regardless of whether you cleaned the toilets or whatever your job was," Mollie says. "They'd walk up and down the line and talk to us, joke with us, sometimes have their sandwiches with us right there on the line. . . . If you needed a home loan, they'd give it to you, and you could make arrangements to pay it back."

Sergy saw the world as an industrialist, not a financier, and he maintained a steely eyed focus on quality and customer service to the degree that it probably hurt profit margins. But his company was no social service agency; it venerated the bottom line as much as any self-respecting capitalist enterprise. Mollie and her co-workers enjoyed good wages and job security in large part because they belonged to Teamsters Local 945, which bargained for higher pay and better benefits. In 1963, determined to insulate Universal from threats of work stoppage, Sergy followed the tradition established by the early Paterson silk makers: He opened an annex, a Universal factory in the Deep South. The new plant was located in rural Mississippi, providing Sergy with a low-wage workforce as well as an ever-present threat of plant closing to quiet employees in Paterson.

That same year, strapped for operating capital and lacking a successor, Sergy also succumbed to the lure of Wall Street: He sold Universal to a New York-based conglomerate. Sergy remained as titular head of Universal, but outsiders controlled the economic destiny of the women and men who toiled there. This was most evidently revealed when Sergy announced to the employees in April 1968, seven months before his death, that the parent company itself had been swallowed whole by *another* conglomerate. "We're all working for a company out of Chicago," he said. "Who they are I have no idea."

Whether those who held the purse strings were faceless financiers from New York or Chicago or Los Angeles didn't matter much to Mollie James. Owners came and went, and the principal visible sign of each transition was a new company name on the payroll checks. So when word spread in early 1986 that an outfit called MagneTek was the new owner, Mollie took the news calmly. Surely some things would change—managers in, managers out, maybe—but she had no reason to question her job security. Although the company had added a second Southern plant, in Arkansas, Paterson was still the flagship. Mollie came to work for Universal—and stayed—because of the peace of mind that came from a secure job: a job she could raise a family on, buy a house, a car, borrow money against, count on for the future.

But right away Mollie could tell the future was darkening. Like the earlier owners, MagneTek was a faraway, far-flung holding company, but the previous management's hands-off, don't fix-it-if-it-ain't-broke page was missing from its corporate manual. "It started the day our name disappeared from the building," she says. "Poof, no more Universal."

By the end of 1988, not only had Universal's name vanished from the plant; its machines, too, were disappearing, torn from the floor like trees from their roots. "The movers came at night, like thieves, sometimes just taking one piece at a time," Mollie recalls. "We'd come in in the mornings and there'd be another hole in the floor."

The machinery had been used to make a large specialty ballast known as the HID, or High Intensity Discharge, the kind used in thousand-watt fixtures installed in outdoor stadiums. Paterson was the lone Universal plant manufacturing the HID; making its precision-wound coils required different training and equipment than the garden-variety 40-watt fluorescent ballast the two Southern plants pumped out by the tens of thousands daily.

If Paterson's workers were more sophisticated, they were also more costly, Mollie earned $7.91 an hour, 75 cents more than she would have earned in Mississippi and almost a dollar more than in Arkansas. But if the wages down South were low, they were not low enough. They were not the cheapest possible wages. They weren't as low as workers earned in Mexico, where the prevailing pay at the maquiladoras was less than $8 a day. And so, in the early months of 1988, the machines began disappearing, bound ultimately for Matamoros. "All we kept hearing was how good a job we were doing." Mollie says, "that we had nothing to worry about, that we'd always have work in Paterson."

The nightly bus to Matamoros would not roll through the depot nearest Balbina Duque's village until 9:15. It was only mid-morning, just a couple of hours since she'd said her goodbyes to the family, since she'd pressed her lips for the last time to her baby son's cheek and handed him to her mother. It was only mid-morning, and already Balbina could feel the tropical sun on her face, could feel her funds dwindling fast. She had started with 200 pesos, the equivalent of about $65, and now that she'd paid a man nearly $20 to taxi her the hour from Monte Bello, her mountain village—a place of clean and clear air, brilliant high-desert flowers, and almost surrealistically bright light—to the bus station in town, and now that she'd bought a couple of tamales from a sidewalk vendor and a one-way ticket to the border for $30, Balbina was down to less than $15.

Balbina had turned 20 only weeks earlier. She was leaving for Matamoros, 400 miles north, to look for work in the maquiladoras. She was torn about going, especially about having to leave behind her 18-month-old son, Iban. "If there were work here," Balbina said in Spanish during a visit home some years later, "everyone would stay."

There was nothing to keep them at home. Balbina's village comprised maybe 1,000 people living in a couple of hundred pastel-colored homes with thatched roofs. There was neither running water nor electricity. Much of Balbina's day was spent filling and refilling a water bucket from a central well down a hill and carrying it back on her head to use for bathing, laundry, washing dishes, cooking, and drinking. A typical day might require 24 trips to the well, a chore that claimed three to four hours beginning at first light.

The interminable, grueling days were not for Balbina. Monte Bello felt like a sentence from which she needed to escape. It was a place for "people too old to work or too young to work," she said. "For me there was nothing. If you do not work in the fields there is nothing else to do." She decided she would celebrate her 20th birthday with her family, and then, as soon as she had saved enough for the bus fare, would take off for the border, where the maquiladoras favor young women for their nimble fingers and compliant minds, and where a job in a *maquila* trumps any other employment options.

It was dark when Balbina finally boarded the bus. Heading north, through a vast valley of corn, Highway 85 was flat as a tortilla. With two seats to herself, Balbina was able to curl into a comfortable enough position, and sleep came at once. When the bus pulled into Matamoros at dawn, she had to rouse herself from a dream about her son. Meeting her at the central station on Canales Avenue was a distant aunt, who escorted her to a small dwelling in the liltingly named *Colonia Vista Hermosa*—Beautiful View. But there was little beauty in the *colonia;* it was wedged between a pungent, milky-white irrigation canal and the Finsa park, the massive industrial park where MagneTek and other foreign-owned maquiladoras employed most of the working-age residents of Vista Hermosa.

One morning, the second Friday of 1993, Balbina and her younger sister, Elsa, caught a ride downtown to the headquarters of the big maquiladora workers' union, the SJOI—the Spanish acronym for the Union of Industrial Workers and Day Laborers. Four times weekly, waves of several thousand applicants washed up at dawn at the SJOI offices, the de facto employment agency for the maquilas. All nonsalaried workers applied through its central hiring hall, women on Mondays and Fridays, men on Tuesdays and Thursdays.

It was not yet 7 o'clock, and Balbina and Elsa had already been in line for an hour, a line that snaked through the three-story building, past the armed guard at the door, and stretched outside for more than a block. By eight, they had squeezed and elbowed and prodded their way inside the assembly hall, a room roughly the size and ambience of a drafty old high-school gymnasium. Mounted fans whirred overhead, efficiently distributing the rank air and grime into all corners.

At 8:30, with no conspicuous signal that the cattle call was on the verge of starting, there was a near stampede toward the makeshift elevated stage at the front quadrant of the room. The entire room seemed like an aquarium, one rear corner of which had suddenly been tipped, causing its entire contents to flow into its diagonal. For the next few hours, Balbina, Elsa, and 1,600 other hopefuls would be crammed nose to shoulder, as close to the stage as possible, like groupies at a rock concert.

At 8:40, three union officials emerged from the anteroom beside the stage. Through a two-way mirror, they had been keeping an eye on the surging crowd while their clerks matched the day's maquila employment needs with the application forms on file. All morning long, the fax machines and phones in the union headquarters had been ringing with the day's specifications from the companies. One maquila, for instance, asked for 91 applicants, all of whom should be 16 (the legal minimum age) or older, with a secondary-school education and without "scheduling problems"— code for childless. All the maquilas favor youth, and some, MagneTek for one, insist on it. *"No mayores de 27 años"*—None older than 27—the company's director of industrial relations instructed in a faxed letter to the union. Women in their late teens and early 20s are considered in the prime of their working lives; a 31-year-old is unlikely to be hired, and a 35-year-old is considered a relic.

When the tally of the day's employment needs was deemed complete, the officials stepped onto the stage, and into the bedlam. Between them and the spirited throng were three steps cordoned by a thin chain, a flimsy plywood railing, and a bouncer the size of an offensive lineman, whose sartorial taste ran to late Elvis: a white shirt unbuttoned nearly the length of his heroic torso, a gold medallion dangling to his midsection, and a formidable, gleaming pompadour crowning a Frigidaire face and muttonchop sideburns.

Following a call to order on a tinny public-address system, a woman unceremoniously announced the day's available jobs. "We're calling workers for Deltronicos," she said, referring to the GM car-radio subsidiary, and then read a list of 50 names. The "lucky ones," as one disappointed applicant called them, made their way through a pair of swinging doors, where a fleet of old Loadstar school buses waited to transport them to the Finsa park for a job interview and medical screening with their prospective employer. If their luck held, they would then be hired for a 30-day probationary period at lower, "training" wages before attaining full-employee status.

The drill was repeated for each maquila until the day's hiring needs were met. Neither Balbina nor Elsa were among the lucky ones, but they knew that few are chosen on the first go-round; some they met had endured several months of twice-weekly trips to the hall. Each Monday and Friday over the next few weeks the Duques returned faithfully. In March, Balbina's prayers were finally answered. She was assigned to a third-shift coil-winding job at MagneTek. All she knew about the job was that her sister-in-law once worked in the same plant, a low-lying white building no more than 75 yards from her tiny house. What she did not know was that Mollie James once held that very job.

Balbina started work at MagneTek the same year President Clinton signed the North American Free Trade Agreement, designed in large part to hasten the spread of maquiladoras. The trade deal enables companies to take advantage of 700,000 workers at 1,800 plants all along the border in ways that would not be tolerated in the United States. When MagneTek first set up shop in Matamoros, employees worked six-day weeks in a stifling, poorly ventilated plant; speaking on the line or going to the bathroom was grounds for suspension.

Although the company has improved working conditions in the last few years, sexual harassment and discrimination remain a constant of factory life. Many female employees at MagneTek have firsthand stories to tell about sexism on the job. "When new girls come in," says a 31-year-old MagneTek retiree who asked not to be identified, "a supervisor gives them the eye and asks them to go for a walk." Balbina says she received similar propositions when she started work at Plant 1. "My supervisor asked if I wanted to work more overtime. I told him I did, but that I wouldn't go to a hotel with him to get it."

The other constant of factory life is low wages. Even when she works an eight-hour overtime shift, as she usually does two or three times a week, Balbina finds it impossible to make ends meet on a MagneTek salary. *"No alcance,"* she says. It doesn't reach. For years she surmounted her weekly shortfall by pooling her income and expenses with Elsa. The sisters lived, like nearly all of their co-workers, *"en montón"*—in a heap: two adults and five children in two small rooms, the kitchen in front, the bedroom in the rear. Their shared three-family flat was a cement structure

45 feet by 15 feet by 10 feet high. Its corrugated metal roof doubled as the ceiling. There were cinder-block walls between the three units that stopped about a foot short of the ceiling, making for a pungent stew of sound and aroma when all three families were home.

The shadeless yard—of mud or dust, depending on the season—was fenced by chicken wire and a rickety gate, and served as an extension of the kitchen. The residents shared a clothesline, an outhouse, and a single spigot—the lone source of water. Balbina believes the water flowed from an open canal running near plants in the industrial park that manufacture pesticides or use toxic solvents. The water had to be boiled, of course; sometimes there was propane to do so, sometimes not.

The neighborhood, Vista Hermosa, exists in a commercial and municipal twilight zone. It sprang up to serve the maquiladoras, not the residents. There are several high-priced convenience stores in the colonia, but no full-fledged grocers, no place to buy meat. Nor is there a pharmacy or medical clinic. There is no police presence, and vandalism and petty theft are rampant. There is one school, an overcrowded kindergarten. Older students catch the same bus to school that drops off first-shift workers at the industrial park. "You have to adapt to the maquilas' routine," says a neighbor with school-age children, "because they're not going to adapt to ours.". . .

Vista Hermosa breeds disease like it does mosquitoes. The lack of septic and sewage lines, potable water, and sanitation services puts the neighborhood at great risk for all manner of illnesses, from intestinal parasites to tuberculosis. But the gravest, most frightening threat comes not from the neighborhood, but from beyond the chain-link fence around the Finsa park. The fence, less than a football field away from Balbina's house, may divide the First and Third worlds, but it also unites them under a single toxic cloud. When the maquilas illegally dump toxic waste into irrigation canals, when a hot north wind blows the acrid smell of *chapapote*—pitch—from the MagneTek plant over its workers' homes, when runoff from a pesticide plant spills into a ditch, when chemical spills or leaks or explosions or fires erupt in the air, it doesn't take a Sierra Club member to understand the environmental wasteland the maquilas have created.

Nor does it take an epidemiologist to question the cause of an outbreak of anencephaly—babies born with either incomplete or missing brains and skulls. In one 36-hour period in the spring of 1991, three babies were born without brains at a single hospital across the river in Brownsville. Doctors soon learned of dozens of other anencephalic births in Brownsville and Matamoros. From 1989 to 1991, the rate of such defects for Brownsville was 10 times the U.S. average, or about 30 anencephalic births per 10,000 births. During the same years, there were 68 cases in Matamoros and 81 in Reynosa, a maquila site upriver.

Many who have studied the outbreak suspect it was due to industrial pollution unchecked by regulatory agencies in both countries. "These were atrocities committed by two uncaring governments," says Dr. Margaret Diaz, the occupational health specialist in Brownsville who detected the anencephaly cluster. "They are the product of years of neglect."

In a lawsuit filed in 1993, families of 28 children born with anencephaly or spina bifida—an incomplete closure of the spinal cord—blamed the outbreak on contamination from the Matamoros maquilas. The families sued 40 maquilas, including MagneTek, charging that the companies negligently handled "toxic compounds" and that the birth defects occurred after "exposure to toxins present in the local environment." The companies steadfastly denied wrongdoing, but internal memoranda documented that some plants released toxic emissions into the air in quantities impermissible in the United States. And trash sifted from the Matamoros city dump established that the maquilas were burning their industrial waste there, rather than disposing of it in the United States, as required by law. One videotape made by an investigator for the families portrays the charred but clearly visible remains of a MagneTek rapid-start ballast. The companies eventually paid a total of $17 million to the stricken families and cleaned up their worst excesses.

Although MagneTek and other companies insist they are improving conditions both inside and outside their plants, wages remain at poverty levels. Rolando Gonzalez Barron, a maquila owner and former president of the Matamoros Maquila Association, points to an advertising supplement in the *Brownsville Herald* lauding companies for their financial contributions to Matamoros schools. "Take 'Adopt-a-School,'" he says. "We put sewerage and bathrooms in schools where little girls had to do their necessities outside."

What about paying a living wage so that the parents of those little girls could afford indoor plumbing themselves? "Yes," Gonzalez replies, "housing needs to be developed, but our main goal is to create value for our customers."

What about your employees? What is your obligation to them? "If a worker is not eating," Gonzalez says, sounding every bit the farmer discussing a plow horse, "he's not going to work for you. We need to meet at least the basic needs."

But the basic needs—"eating, housing, clothing," as Gonzalez puts it—are unmet, and the evidence is as obvious and irrefutable as the colonia in MagneTek's backyard, where Balbina and her neighbors wrestle every single day with ferociously difficult decisions: Should I work overtime or huddle with my children to keep them warm? Buy meat or medicine? Pay the light bill or the gas bill? She makes those decisions based on a daily salary of 58 pesos, the equivalent of $7.43. That's an hourly wage of 92 cents—roughly the same starting wage Mollie James earned nearly half a century before. And Balbina often makes those decisions after working a grueling double shift—from 3:30 in the afternoon until six the following morning, after which she arrives home in time to fix breakfast for her children, accompany her oldest to school, and squeeze in a few hours of sleep before heading back to the plant in the afternoon.

No alcance. It doesn't reach. Over and over one hears this. No alcance, but we make it reach. They make it reach by taking odd jobs, or by scavenging for recyclables at the Matamoros city dump—an otherworldly metropolis of its own covering 50 acres—or peddling wares in the plant during breaks and shift changes. "It's prohibited," Balbina says, "but the company looks the other way and almost everybody does it." There are the ubiquitous Avon ladies, as well as sellers of homemade candy, tamales and gorditas, clothes, marijuana. And some sell their bodies, living la doble vida—the double life of coil-winder by day and prostitute by night.

Balbina has yet to resort to a second job. Instead, she works overtime as often as possible and recently moved into a government-subsized house; it is more comfortable than the one she shared with her sister, but it is hers only as long as she keeps her job. She is 29, an advanced age for a maquiladora worker. She lives with her boyfriend, a fellow MagneTek employee, and they stagger their shifts so that one provides child care while the other is working. Still, even the small necessities remain out of reach. "I need a lock for the door," Balbina says one afternoon. "I don't need it now, but soon I will."

Why not now?

"There is nothing worth locking now," she replies.

Mollie James never again found full-time work. She received a severance payment, after taxes, of $3,171.66—about $93 for each of the 34 years she worked. She collected unemployment benefits for six months and then enrolled in a computer-repair school, receiving a certificate of completion and numerous don't-call-us responses to job inquiries. Late last year, at the age of 68, she took a part-time job as an attendant at a nursing home. For the remainder of her income, she depends on Social Security and the rent she collects from the three-family house she owns, as well as a monthly pension of $71.23 from her Teamsters local. "That's nothing," she says. "That doesn't even pay your telephone bill. It's gone before you know it."

Although Paterson is a tenacious city, it seems defined by what is gone. Its last heyday was during and after World War II, when entrepreneurs like Archie Sergy and migrants like Mollie James helped sustain the city as a proud symbol of industrial might. But the old factory district near the Great Falls has been in ruins for decades, and although a number of the ancient brick mills have been splendidly restored—as a museum, a hospital clinic, and housing for artists—Paterson today is thought of as one of those discarded American places, a city so squalid, so defeated, that few people who do not live or work in Paterson venture there.

Mollie James has spent a half-century in Paterson. She married and divorced there, raised four children, bought a house. She sunk deep roots, and would like nothing better than to see the seeds of renewal take sprout, but she is fed up with high taxes, crime, the unstable economy. Like many "up-South" blacks of retirement age, she thinks often about going home, to rural central Virginia, to the land she left as a teenager. She still owns her childhood home amid three wooded acres.

During a trip back home not long ago, Mollie visited the cemetery where her parents are buried. It is where she wishes to be buried as well. "They better not put me in no dirt up there in New Jersey," she says. "Bring me back home, brother."

Balbina, too, dreams of returning to her ancestral home, to the quiet and clear air of Monte Bello, where she could raise her children in a calm, safe place. But there is no work around Monte Bello for her, no future there for her children. She is more concerned with the immediate future of her job. In the last couple of years, MagneTek closed the two old Universal plants in Arkansas and Mississippi and transferred the bulk of those operations not to Matamoros, but 60 miles upriver to Reynosa, where the union is even weaker, the wages lower still. Now the talk in Matamoros is that the company will once again use the threat of a move, as it did first in Paterson and then in the Southern plants, as a lever for lower wages.

Balbina scoffs at the notion of transferring to Reynosa if the company relocates her job there. "What if they were to move again?" she asks. "Maybe to Juárez or Tijuana? What then? Do I chase my job all over the world?"

The Uses of Poverty: The Poor Pay All

Herbert J. Gans

introduction

Of the several social classes in the United States, sociologists have concentrated their studies on the poor. For the most part, the wealthy are beyond the reach of researchers. Sociologists are not members of the wealthy classes or of the power elite, people who for the most part are beyond the reach of researchers. Those in these groups have the means to insulate themselves from the prying eyes (and tape recorders) of sociologists. Sociologists are members of the middle classes, and we could focus our research there. But like others, we sociologists generally take what is in plain sight for granted. Our own characteristics and orientations seldom strike us as scintilating topics for research. The characteristics and situations of the poor, in contrast, are different enough to strike our interests. And the poor are accessible. It is easy for us to get interviews from people in poverty. The poor are even a bit flattered that sociologists, for the most part members of the upper middle class, will take the time to talk to them. Hardly anyone else takes them seriously.

A couple thousand years ago, Jesus said, "The poor you'll always have with you." As Gans places the sociological lens yet again on people in poverty, he uses a functional-ist perspective to explain why we will always have people in poverty. Simply put, from a functionalist perspective, we *need* poor people.

Thinking Critically

As you read this selection, ask yourself:

1. What functions (or uses) of poverty does Gans identify?

2. Which two functions of poverty do you think are the most important? Which two are the least important? Why?

3. Do you think that Gans has gone overboard with his analysis? That is, do you think he has stretched the functionalist perspective beyond reason? Or do you agree with him? Why or why not?

Some years ago Robert K. Merton applied the notion of functional analysis to explain the continuing though maligned existence of the urban political machine: If it continued to exist, perhaps it fulfilled latent—unintended or unrecognized—positive functions. Clearly it did. Merton pointed out how the political machine provided central authority to get things done when a decentralized local government could not act, humanized the services of the impersonal bureaucracy for fearful citizens, offered concrete help (rather than abstract law or justice) to the poor, and otherwise performed services needed or demanded by many people but considered unconventional or even illegal by formal public agencies.

Today, poverty is more maligned than the political machine ever was; yet it, too, is a persistent social phenomenon. Consequently, there may be some merit in applying functional analysis to poverty, in asking whether it also has positive functions that explain its persistence.

Merton defined functions as "those observed consequences [of a phenomenon] which make for the adaptation or adjustment of a given [social] system." I shall use a slightly different definition; instead of identifying functions for an entire social system, I shall identify them for the interest groups, socioeconomic classes, and other population aggregates with shared values that "inhabit" a social system. I suspect that in a modern heterogeneous society, few phenomena are functional or dysfunctional for the society as a whole, and that most result in benefits to some groups and costs to others. Nor are any phenomena indispensable; in most instances, one can suggest what Merton calls "functional alternatives" or equivalents for them, i.e., other social patterns or policies that achieve the same positive functions but avoid the dysfunction. (In the following discussion, positive functions will be abbreviated as functions and negative functions as dysfunctions. Functions and dysfunctions, in the planner's terminology, will be described as benefits and costs.)

Associating poverty with positive functions seems at first glance to be unimaginable. Of course, the slumlord and the loan shark are commonly known to profit from the existence of poverty, but they are viewed as evil men, so their activities are classified among the dysfunctions of poverty. However, what is less often recognized, at least by the conventional wisdom, is that poverty also makes possible the existence or expansion of respectable professions and occupations, for example, penology, criminology, social work, and public health. More recently, the poor have provided jobs for professional and para-professional "poverty warriors," and for journalists and social scientists, this author included, who have supplied the information demanded by the revival of public interest in poverty.

Clearly, then, poverty and the poor may well satisfy a number of positive functions for many nonpoor groups in American society. I shall describe 13 such functions—economic, social and political—that seem to me most significant.

From Herbert J. Gans, "The Uses of Poverty: The Poor Pay All." *Social Policy,* July/August 1971. Copyright © 1971 by Social Policy Magazine. Reprinted by permission of the publisher.

■ ■ ■ ■ THE FUNCTIONS OF POVERTY

First, the existence of poverty ensures that society's "dirty work" will be done. Every society has such work: physically dirty or dangerous, temporary, dead-end and underpaid, undignified, and menial jobs. Society can fill these jobs by paying higher wages than for "clean" work, or it can force people who have no other choice to do the dirty work—and at low wages. In America, poverty functions to provide a low-wage labor pool that is willing—or rather, unable to be *un*willing—to perform dirty work at low cost. Indeed, this function of the poor is so important that in some Southern states, welfare payments have been cut off during the summer months when the poor are needed to work in the fields. Moreover, much of the debate about the Negative Income Tax and the Family Assistance Plan [welfare programs] has concerned their impact on the work incentive, by which is actually meant the incentive of the poor to do the needed dirty work if the wages therefrom are no larger than the income grant. Many economic activities that involve dirty work depend on the poor for their existence: restaurants, hospitals, parts of the garment industry, and "truck farming," among others, could not persist in their present form without the poor.

Second, because the poor are required to work at low wages, they subsidize a variety of economic activities that benefit the affluent. For example, domestics subsidize the upper-middle and upper classes, making life easier for their employers and freeing affluent women for a variety of professional, cultural, civic, and partying activities. Similarly, because the poor pay a higher proportion of their income in property and sales taxes, among others, they subsidize many state and local governmental services that benefit more affluent groups. In addition, the poor support innovation in medical practice as patients in teaching and research hospitals and as guinea pigs in medical experiments.

Third, poverty creates jobs for a number of occupations and professions that serve or "service" the poor, or protect the rest of society from them. As already noted, penology would be minuscule without the poor, as would the police. Other activities and groups that flourish because of the existence of poverty are the numbers game, the sale of heroin and cheap wines and liquors, Pentecostal ministers, faith healers, prostitutes, pawn shops, and the peacetime army, which recruits its enlisted men mainly from among the poor.

Fourth, the poor buy goods others do not want and thus prolong the economic usefulness of such goods—day-old bread, fruit and vegetables that otherwise would have to be thrown out, secondhand clothes, and deteriorating automobiles and buildings. They also provide incomes for doctors, lawyers, teachers, and others who are too old, poorly trained or incompetent to attract more affluent clients.

In addition to economic functions, the poor perform a number of social functions.

Fifth, the poor can be identified and punished as alleged or real deviants in order to uphold the legitimacy of conventional norms. To justify the desirability of hard work, thrift, honesty, and monogamy, for example, the defenders of these norms must be able to find people who can be accused of being lazy, spendthrift, dishonest, and promiscuous. Although there is some evidence that the poor are about as moral and law-abiding as anyone else, they are more likely than middle-class transgressors to be caught and punished when they participate in deviant acts. Moreover, they lack the political and cultural power to correct the stereotypes that other people hold of them and thus continue to be thought of as lazy, spendthrift, etc., by those who need living proof that moral deviance does not pay.

Sixth, and conversely, the poor offer vicarious participation to the rest of the population in the uninhibited sexual, alcoholic, and narcotic behavior in which they are alleged to participate and which, being freed from the constraints of affluence, they are often thought to enjoy more than the middle classes. Thus many people, some social scientists included, believe that the poor not only are more given to uninhibited behavior (which may be true, although it is often motivated by despair more than by lack of inhibition) but derive more pleasure from it than affluent people (which research by Lee Rainwater, Walter Miller and others shows to be patently untrue). However, whether the poor actually have more sex and enjoy it more is irrelevant; so long as middle-class people believe this to be true, they can participate in it vicariously when instances are reported in factual or fictional form.

Seventh, the poor also serve a direct cultural function when culture created by or for them is adopted by the more affluent. The rich often collect artifacts from extinct folk cultures of poor people; and almost all Americans listen to the blues, Negro spirituals, and country music, which originated among the Southern poor. Recently they have enjoyed the rock styles that were born, like the Beatles, in the slums, and in the last year, poetry written by ghetto children has become popular in literary circles. The poor also serve as culture heroes, particularly, of course, to the left; but the hobo, the cowboy, the hipster, and the mythical prostitute with a heart of gold have performed this function for a variety of groups.

Eighth, poverty helps to guarantee the status of those who are not poor. In every hierarchical society, someone has to be at the bottom; but in American society, in which social mobility is an important goal for many and people need to know where they stand, the poor function as a reliable and relatively permanent measuring rod for status comparisons. This is particularly true for the working class, whose politics is influenced by the need to maintain status distinctions between themselves and the poor, much as the aristocracy must find ways of distinguishing itself from the *nouveaux riches.*

Ninth, the poor also aid the upward mobility of groups just above them in the class hierarchy. Thus a goodly number of Americans have entered the middle class through the profits earned from the provision of goods and services in the slums, including illegal or nonrespectable ones that upper-class and upper-middle-class businessmen shun because of their low prestige. As a result, members of almost every immigrant group have financed their upward mobility by providing slum housing, entertainment, gambling, narcotics, etc., to later arrivals—most recently to blacks and Puerto Ricans.

Tenth, the poor help to keep the aristocracy busy, thus justifying its continued existence. "Society" uses the poor as clients of settlement houses and beneficiaries of charity affairs; indeed, the aristocracy must have the poor to demonstrate its superiority over other elites who devote themselves to earning money.

Eleventh, the poor, being powerless, can be made to absorb the costs of change and growth in American society. During the nineteenth century, they did the backbreaking work that built the cities; today, they are pushed out of their neighborhoods to make room for "progress." Urban renewal projects to hold middle-class taxpayers in the city and expressways to enable suburbanites to commute downtown have typically been located in poor neighborhoods, since no other group will allow itself to be displaced. For the same reason, universities, hospitals, and civic centers also expand into land occupied by the poor. The major costs of the industrialization of agriculture have been borne by the poor, who are pushed off the land without recompense; and they have paid a large share of the human cost of the growth of American power overseas, for they have provided many of the foot soldiers for Vietnam and other wars.

Twelfth, the poor facilitate and stabilize the American political process. Because they vote and participate in politics less than other groups, the political system is often free to ignore them. Moreover, since they can rarely support Republicans, they often provide the Democrats with a captive constituency that has no other place to go. As a result, the Democrats can count on their votes, and be more responsive to voters—for example, the white working class—who might otherwise switch to the Republicans.

Thirteenth, the role of the poor in upholding conventional norms (see the *fifth* point, above) also has a significant political function. An economy based on the ideology of laissez-faire requires a deprived population that is allegedly unwilling to work or that can be considered inferior because it must accept charity or welfare in order to survive. Not only does the alleged moral deviancy of the poor reduce the moral pressure on the present political economy to eliminate poverty but socialist alternatives can be made to look quite unattractive if those who will benefit most from them can be described as lazy, spendthrift, dishonest and promiscuous.

■ ■ ■ THE ALTERNATIVES

I have described 13 of the more important functions poverty and the poor satisfy in American society, enough to support the functionalist thesis that poverty, like any other social phenomenon, survives in part because it is useful to society or some of its parts. This analysis is not intended to suggest that because it is often functional, poverty *should* exist, or that it *must* exist. For one thing, poverty has many more dysfunctions than functions; for another, it is possible to suggest functional alternatives.

For example, society's dirty work could be done without poverty, either by automation or by paying "dirty workers" decent wages. Nor is it necessary for the poor to subsidize the many activities they support through their low-wage jobs. This would, however, drive up the costs of these activities, which would result in higher prices to their customers and clients. Similarly, many of the professionals who flourish because of the poor could be given other roles. Social workers could provide counseling to the affluent, as they prefer to do anyway; and the police could devote themselves to traffic and organized crime. Other roles would have to be found for badly trained or incompetent professionals now relegated to serving the poor, and someone else would have to pay their salaries. Fewer penologists would be employable, however. And Pentecostal religion could probably not survive without the poor—nor would parts of the second- and third-hand-goods market. And in many cities, "used" housing that no one else wants would then have to be torn down at public expense.

Alternatives for the cultural functions of the poor could be found more easily and cheaply. Indeed, entertainers and adolescents are already serving as the deviants needed to uphold traditional morality and as devotees of orgies to "staff" the fantasies of vicarious participation.

The status functions of the poor are another matter. In a hierarchical society, some people must be defined as inferior to everyone else with respect to a variety of attributes, but they need not be poor in the absolute sense. One could conceive of a society in which the "lower class," though last in the pecking order, received 75 percent of the median income, rather than 15–40 percent, as is now the case. Needless to say, this would require considerable income redistribution.

The contribution the poor make to the upward mobility of the groups that provide them with goods and services could also be maintained without the poor's having such low incomes. However, it is true that if the poor were more affluent, they would have access to enough capital to take over the provider role, thus competing with, and perhaps rejecting, the "outsiders.". . . Similarly, if the poor were more affluent, they would make less willing clients for upper-class philanthropy, although some would still use settlement houses to achieve upward mobility, as they do now. Thus "Society" could continue to run its philanthropic activities.

The political functions of the poor would be more difficult to replace. With increased affluence the poor would probably obtain more political power and be more active politically. With higher incomes and more political power, the poor would be likely to resist paying the costs of growth and change. Of course, it is possible to imagine urban renewal and highway projects that properly reimbursed the displaced people, but such projects would then become considerably more expensive, and many might never be built. This, in turn, would reduce the comfort and convenience of those who now benefit from urban renewal and expressways.

In sum, then, many of the functions served by the poor could be replaced if poverty were eliminated, but almost always at higher costs to others, particularly more affluent others. Consequently, a functional analysis must conclude that poverty persists not only because it fulfills a number of positive functions but also because many of the functional alternatives to poverty would be quite dysfunctional for the affluent members of society. A functional analysis thus ultimately arrives at much the same conclusion as radical sociology, except that radical thinkers treat as manifest what I describe as latent: that social phenomena that are functional for affluent or powerful groups and dysfunctional for poor or powerless ones persist; that when the elimination of such phenomena through functional alternatives would generate dysfunctions for the affluent or powerful, they will continue to persist; and that phenomena like poverty can be eliminated only when they become dysfunctional for the affluent or powerful, or when the powerless can obtain enough power to change society.

■ ■ ■ POSTSCRIPT*

Over the years, this article has been interpreted as either a direct attack on functionalism or a tongue-in-cheek satirical comment on it. Neither interpretation is true. I wrote the article for two reasons. First and foremost, I wanted to point out that there are, unfortunately, positive functions of poverty which have to be dealt with by antipoverty policy. Second, I was trying to show that functionalism is not the inherently conservative approach for which it has often been criticized, but that it can be employed in liberal and radical analyses.

*A note from the author to the editor.

Because She Looks Like a Child

Kevin Bales

introduction ■ ■ ■ ■ ■

You might think that an article on prostitution is an unusual choice for a reading on gender. It certainly is, but as you read the details of life in this brothel in Bangkok, Thailand, you will see *gender* throughout. In this form of slavery, which occurs throughout the world, young women are the victims. While these girls and women are bought and sold like cattle, those who grow wealthy from this trade in human bodies are primarily men. It is men who control Thai society—from the politicians to the local policeman who helps control "the girls." Underlying what you are about to read are their views of what a "woman's place" is in society.

It is also men who are the customers, demanding ever-changing human objects to satisfy their sexual desires. To satisfy both pedophiliac interest and the desire to avoid sexually transmitted diseases, men continue to sell customers the bodies of young women, some of them just girls. The difference in power between men and women is essential to understand what is occurring in this form of modem slavery.

It is also important to grasp that routine, ordinary, and calculated decisions underlie the misery you are about to enter through this reading. Behind closed doors—the privacy and privilege that their wealth brings—men make rational, profit-based decisions. Should they buy another girl? Should they open another brothel? Should they hire another enforcer to control their "girls"? Or should they save money by making do with the ones they already employ (control)? As you'll notice, these are similar to the deliberations that underlay the slave trade that used to exist in North and South America.

Thinking Critically

As you read this selection, ask yourself:

1. How is gender central to the events in this reading?

2. Why do country girls become prostitutes in Bangkok?

3. Why don't girls who dislike life in the brothel just leave and go home?

*W*hen Siri wakes it is about noon.[1] In the instant of waking she knows exactly who and what she has become. As she explained to me, the soreness in her genitals reminds her of the fifteen men she had sex with the night before. Siri is fifteen years old. Sold by her parents a year ago, she finds that her resistance and her desire to escape the brothel are breaking down and acceptance and resignation are taking their place.

In the provincial city of Ubon Ratchathani, in northeastern Thailand, Siri works and lives in a brothel. About ten brothels and bars, dilapidated and dusty buildings, line the side street just around the corner from a new Western-style shopping mall. Food and noodle vendors are scattered between the brothels. The woman behind the noodle stall outside the brothel where Siri works is also a spy, warder, watchdog, procurer, and dinner lady to Siri and the other twenty-four girls and women in the brothel.

The brothel is surrounded by a wall, with iron gates that meet the street. Within the wall is a dusty yard, a concrete picnic table, and the ubiquitous spirit house, a small shrine that stands outside all Thai buildings. A low door leads into a windowless concrete room that is thick with the smell of cigarettes, stale beer, vomit, and sweat. This is the "selection" room *(hong du)*. On one side of the room are stained and collapsing tables and booths; on the other side is a narrow elevated platform with a bench that runs the length of the room. Spotlights pick out this bench, and at night the girls and women sit here under the glare while the men at the tables drink and choose the one they want.

Passing through another door, at the far end of the bench, the man follows the girl past a window, where a bookkeeper takes his money and records which girl he has selected. From there he is led to the girl's room. Behind its concrete front room, the brothel degenerates even further, into a haphazard shanty warren of tiny cubicles where the girls live and work. A makeshift ladder leads up to what may have once been a barn. The upper level is now lined with doors about five feet apart, which open into rooms of about five by seven feet that hold a bed and little else.

Scraps of wood and cardboard separate one room from the next, and Siri has plastered her walls with pictures of teenage pop stars cut from magazines. Over her bed, as in most rooms, there also hangs a framed portrait of the king of Thailand; a single bare lightbulb dangles from the ceiling. Next to the bed a large tin can holds water; there is a hook nearby for rags and towels. At the foot of the bed, next to the door, some clothes are folded on a ledge. The walls are very thin, and everything can be heard from the surrounding rooms; a shout from the bookkeeper echoes through all of them, whether their doors are open or closed.

After rising at midday, Siri washes herself in cold water from the single concrete trough that serves the brothel's twenty-five women. Then, dressed in a T-shirt and skirt, she goes to the noodle stand for the hot soup that is a Thai breakfast. Through the afternoon, if she does not have any clients, she chats with the other girls and women as they drink beer and play cards or make decorative handicrafts together. If the pimp is away the girls will joke around, but if not they must be constantly deferential and aware of his presence, for he can harm them or use them as he pleases. Few men visit in the afternoon, but those who do tend to have more money and can buy a girl for several hours if they like. Some will even make appointments a few days in advance.

At about five, Siri and the other girls are told to dress, put on their makeup, and prepare for the night's work. By seven the men will be coming in, purchasing drinks, and choosing girls; Siri will be chosen by the first of the ten to eighteen men who will buy her that night. Many men choose Siri because she looks much younger than her fifteen years. Slight and round faced, dressed to accentuate her youth, she could pass for eleven or twelve. Because she looks like a child, she can be sold as a "new" girl at a higher price, about $15, which is more than twice that charged for the other girls.

Siri is very frightened that she will get AIDS. Long before she understood prostitution she knew about HIV, as many girls from her village returned home to die from AIDS after being sold into the brothels. Every day she prays to Buddha, trying to earn the merit that will preserve her from the disease. She also tries to insist that her clients use condoms, and in most cases she is successful, because the pimp backs her up. But when policemen use her, or the pimp himself, they will do as they please; if she tries to insist, she will be beaten and raped. She also fears pregnancy, but like the other girls she receives injections of the contraceptive drug Depo-Provera. Once a month she has an HIV test. So far it has been negative. She knows that if she tests positive she will be thrown out to starve.

Though she is only fifteen, Siri is now resigned to being a prostitute. The work is not what she had thought it would be. Her first client hurt her; and at the first opportunity she ran away. She was quickly caught, dragged back, beaten, and raped. That night she was forced to take on a chain of clients until the early morning. The beatings and the work continued night after night, until her will was broken. Now she is sure that she is a very bad person to have deserved what has happened to her. When I comment on how pretty she looks in a photograph, how like a pop star, she replies, "I'm no star; I'm just a whore, that's all." She copes as best she can. She takes a dark pride in her higher price and the large number of men who choose her. It is the adjustment of the concentration camp, an effort to make sense of horror.

In Thailand prostitution is illegal, yet girls like Siri are sold into sex slavery by the thousands. The brothels that hold these girls are but a small part of a much wider sex industry. How can this wholesale trade in girls continue? What keeps it working? The answer is more complicated than we might think. Thailand's economic boom and its social acceptance of prostitution contribute to the pressures that enslave girls like Siri.

▪ ▪ ▪ RICE IN THE FIELD. FISH IN THE RIVER. DAUGHTERS IN THE BROTHEL.

Thailand is blessed with natural resources and sufficient food. The climate is mild to hot, there is dependable rain, and most of the country is a great plain, well watered and fertile. The reliable production of rice has for centuries made Thailand a large exporter of grains, as it is today. Starvation is exceedingly rare in its history, and social stability very much the norm. An old and often-repeated saying in Thai is "There is always rice in the fields and fish in the river." And anyone who has tried the imaginative Thai cuisine knows the remarkable things that can be done with those two ingredients and the local chili peppers.

One part of Thailand that is not so rich in necessities of life is the mountainous north. In fact, that area is not Thailand proper; originally the kingdom of Lanna, it was integrated into Thailand only in the late nineteenth century. The influence of Burma here is very strong—as are the cultures of the seven main hill tribes, which are distinctly foreign to the dominant Thai society. Only about a tenth of the land of the north can be used for agriculture, though what can be used is the most fertile in the country. The result is that those who control good land are well-off; those who live in the higher elevations, in the forest, are not. In another part of the world this last group might be called hillbillies, and they share the hardscrabble life of mountain dwellers everywhere.

The harshness of this life stands in sharp contrast to that on the great plain of rice and fish. Customs and culture differ markedly as well, and one of those differences is a key to the sexual slavery practiced throughout Thailand today. For hundreds of years many people in the north, struggling for life, have been forced to view their own children as commodities. A failed harvest, the death of a key breadwinner, or any serious debt incurred by a family might lead to the sale of a daughter (never a son) as a slave or servant. In the culture of the north it was a life choice not preferred but acceptable and one that was used regularly. In the past these sales fed a small, steady flow of servants, workers, and prostitutes south into Thai society.

▪ ▪ ▪ ONE GIRL EQUALS ONE TELEVISION

The small number of children sold into slavery in the past has become a flood today. This increase reflects the enormous changes in Thailand over the past fifty years as the country has gone through the great transformation of industrialization—the same process that tore Europe apart over a century ago. If we are to understand slavery in Thailand, we must understand these changes as well, for like so many other parts of the world, Thailand has always had slavery, but never before on this scale.

The economic boom of 1977 to 1997 had a dramatic impact on the northern villages. While the center of the country, around Bangkok, rapidly industrialized, the north was left behind. Prices of food, land, and tools all increased as the economy grew, but the returns for rice and other agriculture were stagnant, held down by government policies guaranteeing cheap food for factory workers in Bangkok. Yet visible everywhere in the north is a flood of consumer goods—refrigerators, televisions, cars and trucks, rice cookers, air conditioners—all of which are extremely tempting. Demand for these goods is high as families try to join the ranks of the prosperous. As it happens, the cost of participating in this consumer boom can be met from an old source that has become much more profitable: the sale of children.

In the past, daughters were sold in response to serious family financial crises. Under threat of losing its mortgaged rice fields and facing destitution, a family might sell a daughter to redeem its debt, but for the most part daughters were worth about as much at home as workers as they would realize when sold. Modernization and economic growth have changed all that. Now parents feel a great pressure to buy consumer goods that were unknown even twenty years ago; the sale of a daughter might easily finance a new television set. A recent survey in the northern provinces found that of the families who sold their daughters, two-thirds could afford not to do so but instead preferred to buy color televisions and video equipment.[2] And from the perspective of parents who are willing to sell their children, there has never been a better market.

The brothels' demand for prostitutes is rapidly increasing. The same economic boom that feeds consumer demand in the northern villages lines the pockets of laborers and workers in the central plain. Poor economic migrants from the rice fields now work on building sites or in new factories earning many times what they did on the land. Possibly for the first time in their lives, these laborers can do what more well-off Thai men have always done: go to a brothel. The purchasing power of this increasing number of brothel users strengthens the call for northern girls and supports a growing business in their procurement and trafficking.

Siri's story was typical. A broker, a woman herself from a northern village, approached the families in Siri's village with assurances of well paid work for their daughters. Siri's parents probably understood that the work would be as a prostitute, since they knew that other girls from their village had gone south to brothels. After some negotiation they were paid 50,000 baht (US$2,000) for Siri, a very significant sum for this family of rice farmers.[3] This exchange began the process of debt bondage that is used to enslave the girls. The contractual arrangement between the broker and the parents requires that this money be paid by the daughter's labor before she is free to leave or is allowed to send money home. Sometimes the money is treated as a loan to the parents, the girls being both the collateral and the means of repayment. In such cases the exorbitant interest charged on the loan means there is little chance that a girl's sexual slavery will ever repay the debt.

Siri's debt of 50,000 baht rapidly escalated. Taken south by the broker, Siri was sold for 100,000 baht to the brothel where she now works. After her rape and beating Siri was informed that the debt she must repay to the brothel equaled 200,000 baht. In addition, Siri learned of the other payments she would be required to make, including rent for her room, at 30,000 baht per month, as well as charges for food and drink, fees for medicine, and fines if she did not work hard enough or displeased a customer.

The total debt is virtually impossible to repay, even at Siri's higher rate of 400 baht. About 100 baht from each client is supposed to be credited to Siri to reduce her debt and pay her rent and other expenses; 200 goes to the pimp and the remaining 100 to the brothel. By this reckoning, Siri must have sex with three hundred men a month just to pay her rent, and what is left over after other expenses barely reduces her original debt. For girls who can charge only 100 to 200 baht per client, the debt grows even faster. This debt bondage keeps the girls under complete control as long as the brothel owner and the pimp believe they are worth having. Violence reinforces the control and any resistance earns a beating as well as an increase in the debt. Over time if the girl becomes a good and cooperative prostitute, the pimp may tell her she has paid off the debt and allow her to send small sums home. This "paying off" of the debt usually has nothing to do with an actual accounting of earnings but is declared at the discretion of the pimp, as a means to extend the brothel's profits by making the girl more pliable. Together with rare visits home, money sent back to the family operates to keep her at her job.

Most girls are purchased from their parents, as Siri was, but for others the enslavement is much more direct. Throughout Thailand agents travel to villages, offering work in factories or as domestics. Sometimes they bribe local officials to vouch for them, or they befriend the monks at the local temple to gain introductions. Lured by the promise of good jobs and the money that the daughters will send back to the village, the deceived families dispatch their girls with the agent, often paying for the privilege. Once they arrive in a city, the girls are sold to a brothel, where they are raped, beaten, and locked in. Still other girls are simply kidnapped. This is especially true of women and children who have come to visit relatives in Thailand from Burma or Laos. At bus and train stations, gangs watch for women and children who can be snatched or drugged for shipment to brothels.

Direct enslavement by trickery or kidnapping is not really in the economic interest of the brothel owners. The steadily growing market for prostitutes, the loss of girls to HIV infection, and the especially strong demand for younger and younger girls make it necessary for brokers and brothel owners to cultivate village families so that they can buy more daughters as they come of age. In Siri's case this means letting her maintain ties with her family and ensuring that after a year or so she send a monthly postal order for 10,000 baht to her parents. The monthly payment is a good investment, since it encourages Siri's parents to place their other daughters in the brothel as well. Moreover, the young girls themselves become willing to go when their older sisters and relatives returning for holidays bring stories of the rich life to be lived in the cities of the central plain. Village girls lead a sheltered life, and the appearance of women only a little older than themselves with money and nice clothes is tremendously appealing. They admire the results of this thing called prostitution with only the vaguest notion of what it is. Recent research found that young girls knew that their sisters and neighbors had become prostitutes, but when asked what it means to be a prostitute their most common answer was "wearing Western clothes in a restaurant."[4] Drawn by this glamorous life, they put up little opposition to being sent away with the brokers to swell an already booming sex industry.

By my own conservative estimate there are perhaps thirty-five thousand girls like Siri enslaved in Thailand. Remarkably, this is only a small proportion of the country's prostitutes. In the mid-1990s the government stated that there were 81,384 prostitutes in Thailand—but that official number is calculated from the number of registered (though still illegal) brothels, massage parlors, and sex establishments.

One Thai researcher estimated the total number of prostitutes in 1997 to be around 200,000.[5] Every brothel, bar, and massage parlor we visited in Thailand was unregistered, and no one working with prostitutes believes the government figures. At the other end of the spectrum are the estimates put forward by activist organizations such as the Center for the Protection of Children's Rights. These groups assert that there are more than 2 million prostitutes. I suspect that this number is too high in a national population of 60 million. My own reckoning, based on information gathered by AIDS workers in different cities, is that there are between half a million and 1 million prostitutes.

Of this number, only about one in twenty is enslaved. Most become prostitutes voluntarily, though some start out in debt bondage. Sex is sold everywhere in Thailand: barbershops, massage parlors, coffee shops and cafes, bars and restaurants, nightclubs and karaoke bars, brothels, hotels, and even temples traffic in sex. Prostitutes range from the high-earning "professional" women who work with some autonomy, through the women working by choice as call girls or in massage parlors, to the enslaved rural girls like Siri. Many women work semi-independently in bars, restaurants, and night clubs—paying a fee to the owner, working when they choose, and having the power to decide whom to take as a customer. Most bars and clubs cannot use an enslaved prostitute like Siri, as the women are often sent out on call and their clients expect a certain amount of cooperation and friendliness, Enslaved girls serve the lowest end of the market: the laborers, students, and workers who can afford only the 100 baht per half hour. It is low-cost sex in volume, and the demand is always there. For a Thai man, buying a woman is much like buying a round of drinks. But the reasons why such large numbers of Thai men use prostitutes are much more complicated and grow out of their culture, their history, and a rapidly changing economy.

■ ■ ■ "I DON'T WANT TO WASTE IT, SO I TAKE HER"

Until it was officially disbanded in 1910, the king of Thailand maintained a harem of hundreds of concubines, a few of whom might be elevated to the rank of "royal mother" or "minor wife." This form of polygamy was closely imitated by status-hungry nobles and emerging rich merchants of the nineteenth century. Virtually all men of any substance kept at least a mistress or a minor wife. For those with fewer resources, prostitution was a perfectly acceptable option, as renting took the place of out-and-out ownership.

Even today everyone in Thailand knows his or her place within a very elaborate and precise status system. Mistresses and minor wives continue to enhance any man's social standing, but the consumption of commercial sex has increased dramatically.[6] If an economic boom is a tide that raises all boats, then vast numbers of Thai men have now been raised to a financial position from which they can regularly buy sex. Nothing like the economic growth in Thailand was ever experienced in the West, but a few facts show its scale: in a country the size of Britain, one-tenth of the workforce moved from the land to industry in just the three years from 1993 to 1995; the number of factory workers doubled from less than 2 million to more than 4 million in the eight years from 1988 to 1995; and urban wages doubled from 1986 to 1996. Thailand is now the world's largest importer of motorcycles and the second-largest importer of pickup trucks, after the United States. Until the economic downturn of late 1997, money flooded Thailand, transforming poor rice farmers into wage laborers and fueling consumer demand.

With this newfound wealth, Thai men go to brothels in increasing numbers. Several recent studies show that between 80 and 87 percent of Thai men have had sex with a prostitute. Most report that their first sexual experience was with a prostitute. Somewhere between 10 and 40 percent of married men have paid for commercial sex within the past twelve months, as have up to 50 percent of single men. Though it is difficult to measure, these reports suggest something like 3 to 5 million regular customers for commercial sex. But it would be wrong to imagine millions of Thai men sneaking furtively on their own along dark streets lined with brothels; commercial sex is a social event, part of a good night out with friends. Ninety-five percent of men going to a brothel do so with their friends, usually at the end of a night spent drinking. Groups go out for recreation and entertainment, and especially to get drunk together. That is a strictly male pursuit, as Thai women usually abstain from alcohol. All-male groups out for a night on the town are considered normal in any Thai city, and whole neighborhoods are devoted to serving them. One man interviewed in a recent study explained, "When we arrive at the brothel; my friends take one and pay for me to take another. It costs them money; I don't want to waste it so I take her."[7] Having one's prostitute paid for also brings an informal obligation to repay in kind at a later date. Most Thais, men and women, feel that commercial sex is an acceptable part of an ordinary outing for single men, and about two-thirds of men and one-third of women feel the same about married men.[8]

For most married women, having their husbands go to prostitutes is preferable to other forms of extramarital sex. Most wives accept that men naturally want multiple partners, and prostitutes are seen as less threatening to the stability of the family.[9] Prostitutes require no long-term commitment or emotional involvement. When a husband uses a prostitute he is thought to be fulfilling a male role, but when he takes a minor wife or mistress, his wife is thought to have failed. Minor wives are usually bigamous second wives, often married by law in a district different than that of the men's first marriage (easily done, since no national records are kept). As wives, they require upkeep, housing, and regular support, and their offspring have a claim on inheritance: so they present a significant danger to the well-being of the major wife and her children. The potential disaster for the first wife is a minor wife who convinces the man to leave his first family, and this happens often enough to keep first wives worried and watchful.

For many Thai men, commercial sex is a legitimate form of entertainment and sexual release. It is not just acceptable: it is a clear statement of status and economic power. Such attitudes reinforce the treatment of women as mere markers in a male game of status and prestige. Combined with the new economy's relentless drive for profits, the result for women can be horrific. Thousands more must be found to feed men's status needs, thousands more must be locked into sexual slavery to feed the profits of investors. And what are the police, government, and local authorities doing about slavery? Every case of sex slavery involves many crimes—fraud, kidnap, assault, rape, sometimes murder. These crimes are not rare or random; they are systematic and repeated in brothels thousands of times each month. Yet those with the power to stop this tenor instead help it continue to grow and to line the pockets of the slaveholders.

■ ■ ■ MILLIONAIRE TIGER AND BILLIONAIRE GEESE

Who are these modern slaveholders? The answer is anyone and everyone—anyone, that is, with a little capital to invest. The people who appear to own the enslaved prostitutes—the pimps, madams, and brothel keepers—are usually just employees. As hired muscle, pimps and their helpers provide the brutality that controls women and makes possible their commercial exploitation. Although they are just employees, the pimps do rather well for themselves. Often living in the brothel, they receive a salary and add to that income by a number of scams; for example, food and drinks are sold to customers at inflated prices, and the pimps pocket the difference. Much more lucrative is their control of the price of sex. While each woman has a basic price, the pimps size up each customer and pitch the fee accordingly. In this way a client may pay two or three times more than the normal rate, and all of the surplus goes to the pimp. In league with the bookkeeper, the pimp systematically cheats the prostitutes of the little that is supposed to be credited against their debt. If they manage the sex slaves well and play all of the angles, pimps can easily make ten times their basic wage—a great income for an ex-peasant whose main skills are violence and intimidation, but nothing compared to the riches to be made by the brokers and the real slaveholders.

The brokers and agents who buy girls in the villages and sell them to brothels are only short-term slaveholders. Their business is part recruiting agency, part shipping company, part public relations, and part kidnapping gang. They aim to buy low and sell high while maintaining a good flow of girls from the villages. Brokers are equally likely to be men or women, and they usually come from the regions in which they recruit. Some are local people dealing in girls in addition to their jobs as police officers, government bureaucrats, or even schoolteachers. Positions of public trust are excellent starting points for buying young girls. In spite of the character of their work, they are well respected. Seen as job providers and sources of large cash payments to parents, they are well known in their communities. Many of the women brokers were once sold themselves; some spent years as prostitutes and now, in their middle age, make their living by supplying girls to the brothels. These women are walking advertisements for sexual slavery. Their lifestyle and income, their Western clothes and glamorous, sophisticated ways promise a rosy economic future for the girls they buy. That they have physically survived their years in the brothel may be the exception—many more young women come back to the village to die of AIDS—but the parents tend to be optimistic.

Whether these dealers are local people or traveling agents, they combine the business of procuring with other economic pursuits. A returned prostitute may live with her family, look after her parents, own a rice field or two, and buy and sell girls on the side. Like the pimps, they are in a good business, doubling their money on each girl within two or three weeks; but also like the pimps, their profits are small compared to those of the long-term slaveholders.

The real slaveholders tend to be middle-aged businessmen. They fit seamlessly into the community, and they suffer no social discrimination for what they do. If anything, they are admired as successful, diversified capitalists. Brothel ownership is normally only one of many business interests for the slaveholder. To be sure, a brothel owner may have some ties to organized crime, but in Thailand organized crime includes the police and much of the government. Indeed, the work of the modern slaveholder is best seen not as aberrant criminality but as a perfect example of disinterested capitalism. Owning the brothel that holds young girls in bondage is simply a business matter. The investors would say that they are creating jobs and wealth. There is no hypocrisy in their actions, for they obey an important social norm: earning a lot of money is good enough reason for anything.

The slaveholder may in fact be a partnership, company, or corporation. In the 1980s, Japanese investment poured into Thailand, in an enormous migration of capital that was called "Flying Geese."[10] The strong yen led to buying and building across the country, and while electronics firms built television factories, other investors found that there was much, much more to be made in the sex industry. Following the Japanese came investment from the so-called Four Tigers (South Korea, Hong Kong, Taiwan, and Singapore), which also found marvelous opportunities in commercial sex. (All five of these countries further proved to be strong import markets for enslaved Thai girls, as discussed below.) The Geese and the Tigers had the resources to buy the local criminals, police, administrators, and property needed to set up commercial sex businesses. Indigenous Thais also invested in brothels as the sex industry boomed; with less capital, they were more likely to open poorer, working-class outlets.

Whether they are individual Thais, partnerships, or foreign investors, the slaveholders share many characteristics. There is little or no racial or ethnic difference between them and the slaves they own (with the exception of the Japanese investors). They feel no need to rationalize their slaveholding on racial grounds. Nor are they linked in any sort of hereditary ownership of slaves or of the children of their slaves. They are not really interested in their slaves at all, just in the bottom line on their investment.

To understand the business of slavery today we have to know something about the economy in which it operates. Thailand's economic boom included a sharp increase in sex tourism tacitly backed by the government. International tourist arrivals jumped from 2 million in 1981 to 4 million in 1988 to over 7 million in 1996.[11] Two-thirds of tourists were unaccompanied men; in other words, nearly 5 million unaccompanied men visited Thailand in 1996. A significant proportion of these were sex tourists.

The recent downturn in both tourism and the economy may have slowed, but not dramatically altered, sex tourism. In 1997 the annual illegal income generated by sex workers in Thailand was roughly $10 billion, which is more than drug trafficking is estimated to generate.[12] According to ECPAT, an organization working against child prostitution, the economic crisis in Southeast Asia may have increased the exploitation of young people in sex tourism:

> According to Professor Lae Dilokvidhayarat from Chulalongkorn University, there has been a 10 percent decrease in the school enrollment at primary school level in Thailand since 1996. Due to increased unemployment, children cannot find work in the formal sector, but instead are forced to "disappear" into the informal sector. This makes them especially vulnerable to sexual exploitation. Also, a great number of children are known to travel to tourist areas and to big cities hoping to find work.
>
> We cannot overlook the impact of the economic crisis on sex tourism, either. Even though traveling costs to Asian countries are approximately the same as before mid 1997, when the crisis began, the rates for sexual services in many places are lower due to increased competition in the business. Furthermore, since there are more children trying to earn money, there may also be more so called situational child sex tourists, i.e. those who do not necessarily prefer children as sexual partners, but who may well choose a child if the situation occurs and the price is low."[13]

In spite of the economic boom, the average Thai's income is very low by Western standards. Within an industrializing country, millions still live in rural poverty. If a rural family owns its house and has a rice field, it might survive on as little as 500 baht ($20) per month. Such absolute poverty means a diet of rice supplemented with insects (crickets, grubs, and maggots are widely eaten), wild plants, and what fish the family can catch. If a family's standard of living drops below this level, which can be sustained only in the countryside, it faces hunger and the loss of its house or land. For most Thais, an income of 2,500 to 4,000 baht per month ($100 to $180) is normal. Government figures from December 1996 put two-thirds of the population at this level. There is no system of welfare or health care, and pinched budgets allow no space for saving. In these families, the 20,000 to 50,000 baht ($800 to $2,000) brought by selling a daughter provides a year's income. Such a vast sum is a powerful inducement that often blinds parents to the realities of sexual slavery.

■ ■ ■ DISPOSABLE BODIES

Girls are so cheap that there is little reason to take care of them over the long term. Expenditure on medical care or prevention is rare in the brothels, since the working life of girls in debt bondage is fairly short—two to five years. After that, most of the profit has been drained from the girl and it is more cost-effective to discard her and replace her with someone fresh. No brothel wants to take on the responsibility of a sick or dying girl.

Enslaved prostitutes in brothels face two major threats to their physical health and to their lives: violence and disease. Violence—their enslavement enforced through rape, beatings, or threats—is always present. It is a girl's typical introduction to her new status as a sex slave. Virtually every girl interviewed repeated the same story: after she was taken to the brothel or to her first client as a virgin, any resistance or refusal was met with beatings and rape. A few girls reported being drugged and then attacked;

others reported being forced to submit at gunpoint. The immediate and forceful application of terror is the first step in successful enslavement. Within hours of being brought to the brothel, the girls are in pain and shock. Like other victims of torture they often go numb, paralyzed in their minds if not in their bodies. For the youngest girls, who understand little of what is happening to them, the trauma is overwhelming. Shattered and betrayed, they often have few clear memories of what occurred.

After the first attack, the girl has little resistance left, but the violence never ends. In the brothel, violence and terror are the final arbiters of all questions. There is no argument; there is no appeal. An unhappy customer brings a beating, a sadistic client brings more pain; in order to intimidate and cheat them more easily, the pimp rains down terror randomly on the prostitutes. The girls must do anything the pimp wants if they are to avoid being beaten. Escape is impossible. One girl reported that when she was caught trying to escape, the pimp beat her and then took her into the viewing room; with two helpers he then beat her again in front of all the girls in the brothel. Afterward she was locked into a room for three days and nights with no food or water. When she was released she was immediately put to work. Two other girls who attempted escape told of being stripped naked and whipped with steel coat hangers by pimps. The police serve as slave catchers whenever a girl escapes; once captured, girls are often beaten or abused at the police station before being sent back to the brothel. For most girls it soon becomes clear that they can never escape, that their only hope for release is to please the pimp and to somehow pay off their debt.

In time, confusion and disbelief fade, leaving dread, resignation, and a break in the conscious link between mind and body. Now the girl does whatever it takes to reduce the pain, to adjust mentally to a life that means being used by fifteen men a day. The reaction to this abuse takes many forms: lethargy, aggression, self-loathing, suicide attempts, confusion, self-abuse, depression, full-blown psychoses, and hallucinations. Girls who have been freed and taken into shelters exhibit all of these disorders. Rehabilitation workers report that the girls suffer emotional instability; they are unable to trust or to form relationships, to readjust to the world outside the brothel, or to learn and develop normally. Unfortunately, psychological counseling is virtually unknown in Thailand, as there is a strong cultural pressure to keep mental problems hidden. As a result, little therapeutic work is done with girls freed from brothels. The long-term impact of their experience is unknown.

The prostitute faces physical dangers as well as emotional ones. There are many sexually transmitted diseases, and prostitutes contract most of them. Multiple infections weaken the immune system and make it easier for other infections to take hold. If the illness affects a girl's ability to have sex, it may be dealt with, but serious chronic illnesses are often left untreated. Contraception often harms the girls as well. Some slaveholders administer contraceptive pills themselves, continuing them without any break and withholding the monthly placebo pills so that the girls can work more nights of the month. These girls stop menstruating altogether.

Not surprisingly, HIV/AIDS is epidemic in enslaved prostitutes. Thailand now has one of the highest rates of HIV infection in the world. Officially, the government admits to 800,000 cases, but health workers insist there are at least twice that many. Mechai Veravaidya, a birth-control campaigner and expert who has been so successful that *mechai* is now the Thai word for condom, predicts there will be 4.3 million people infected with HIV by 2001.[14] In some rural villages from which girls are regularly trafficked, the infection rate is over 60 percent. Recent research suggests that the younger the girl, the more susceptible she is to HIV, because her protective vaginal mucous membrane has not fully developed. Although the government distributes condoms, some brothels do not require their use.

▪ ▪ ▪ BURMESE PROSTITUTES

The same economic boom that has increased the demand for prostitutes may, in time, bring an end to Thai sex slavery. Industrial growth has also led to an increase in jobs for women. Education and training are expanding rapidly across Thailand, and women and girls are very much taking part. The ignorance and deprivation on which the enslavement of girls depends are on the wane, and better-educated girls are much less likely to fall for the promises made by brokers. The traditional duties to family, including the debt of obligation to parents, are also becoming less compelling. As the front line of industrialization sweeps over northern Thailand, it is bringing fundamental changes. Programs on the television bought with the money from selling one daughter may carry warning messages to her younger sisters. As they learn more about new jobs, about HIV/AIDS, and about the fate of those sent to the brothels, northern Thai girls refuse to follow their sisters south. Slavery functions best when alternatives are few, and education and the media are opening the eyes of Thai girls to a world of choice.

For the slaveholders this presents a serious problem. They are faced with an increase in demand for prostitutes and a diminishing supply. Already the price of young Thai girls is spiraling upward. The slaveholders' only recourse is to look elsewhere, to areas where poverty and ignorance still hold sway. Nothing, in fact, could be easier: there remain large, oppressed, and isolated populations desperate enough to believe the promises of the brokers. From Burma to the west and Laos to the east come thousands of economic and political refugees searching for work; they are defenseless in a country where they are illegal aliens. The techniques that worked so well in bringing Thai girls to brothels are again deployed, but now across borders. Investigators from Human Rights Watch, which made a special study of this trafficking in 1993, explain:

> The trafficking of Burmese women and girls into Thailand is appalling in its efficiency and ruthlessness. Driven by the desire to maximize profit and the fear of HIV/AIDS, agents acting on behalf of brothel owners infiltrate ever more remote areas of Burma seeking unsuspecting recruits. Virgin girls are particularly sought after because they bring a higher price and pose less threat of exposure to sexually transmitted disease. The agents promise the women and girls jobs as waitresses or dishwashers, with good pay and new clothes. Family members or friends typically accompany the women and girls to the Thai border, where they receive a payment ranging from 10,000 to

20,000 baht from someone associated with the brothel. This payment becomes the debt, usually doubled with interest, that the women and girls must work to pay off, not by waitressing or dishwashing, but through sexual servitude.[15]

Once in the brothels they are in an even worse situation than the enslaved Thai girls: because they do not speak Thai their isolation is increased, and as illegal aliens they are open to even more abuse. The pimps tell them repeatedly that if they set foot outside the brothel, they will be arrested. And when they are arrested, Burmese and Lao girls and women are afforded no legal rights. They are often held for long periods at the mercy of the police, without charge or trial. A strong traditional antipathy between Thais and Burmese increases the chances that Burmese sex slaves will face discrimination and arbitrary treatment. Explaining why so many Burmese women were kept in brothels in Ranong, in southern Thailand, the regional police commander told a reporter for the *Nation:* "In my opinion it is disgraceful to let Burmese men [working in the local fishing industry] frequent Thai prostitutes. Therefore I have been flexible in allowing Burmese prostitutes to work here."[16]

A special horror awaits Burmese and Lao women once they reach the revolving door at the border. If they escape or are dumped by the brothel owners, they come quickly to the attention of the police, since they have no money for transport and cannot speak Thai. Once they are picked up, they are placed in detention, where they meet women who have been arrested in the periodic raids on brothels and taken into custody with only the clothes they are wearing. In local jails, the foreign women might be held without charge for as long as eight months while they suffer sexual and other abuse by the police. In time, they might be sent to the Immigrant Detention Center in Bangkok or to prison. In both places, abuse and extortion by the staff continue, and some girls are sold back to the brothels from there. No trial is necessary for deportation, but many women are tried and convicted of prostitution or illegal entry. The trials take place in Thai without interpreters, and fines are charged against those convicted. If they have no money to pay the fines, and most do not, they are sent to a factory-prison to earn it. There they make lightbulbs or plastic flowers for up to twelve hours a day; the prison officials decide when they have earned enough to pay their fine. After the factory-prison the women are sent back to police cells or the Immigrant Detention Center. Most are held until they can cover the cost of transportation (illegal aliens are required by law to pay for their own deportation); others are summarily deported.

The border between Thailand and Burma is especially chaotic and dangerous. Only part of it is controlled by the Burmese military dictatorship; other areas are in the hands of tribal militias or warlords. After arriving at the border, the deportees are held in cells by immigration police for another three to seven days. Over this time, the police extort money and physically and sexually abuse the inmates. The police also use this time to make arrangements with brothel owners and brokers, notifying them of the dates and places of deportation. On the day of deportation, the prisoners are driven in cattle trucks into the countryside along the border, far from any village, and then pushed out. Abandoned in the jungle, miles from any major road, they are given no food or water and have no idea where they are or how to proceed into Burma. As the immigration police drive away, the deportees are approached by agents and brokers who followed the trucks from town by arrangement with the police. The brokers offer work and transportation back into Thailand. Abandoned in the jungle, many women see the offer as their only choice. Some who don't are attacked and abducted. In either case, the cycle of debt bondage and prostitution begins again.

If they do make it into Burma, the women face imprisonment or worse. If apprehended by Burmese border patrols they are charged with "illegal departure" from Burma. If they cannot pay the fine, and most cannot, they serve six months' hard labor. Imprisonment applies to all those convicted—men, women, and children. If a girl or woman is suspected of having been a prostitute, she can face additional charges and long sentences. Women found to be HIV-positive have been imprisoned and executed. According to Human Rights Watch, there are consistent reports of "deportees being routinely arrested, detained, subjected to abuse and forced to porter for the military. Torture, rape and execution have been well documented by the United Nations bodies, international human rights organizations and governments."[17]

The situation on Thailand's eastern border with Laos is much more difficult to assess. The border is more open, and there is a great deal of movement back and forth. Lao police, government officials, and community leaders are involved in the trafficking, working as agents and making payments to local parents. They act with impunity, as it is very difficult for Lao girls to escape back to their villages; those who do find it dangerous to speak against police or officials. One informant told me that if a returning girl did talk, no one would believe her and she would be branded as a prostitute and shunned. There would be no way to expose the broker and no retribution; she would just have to resign herself to her fate. It is difficult to know how many Lao women and girls are brought into Thailand. In the northeast many Thais speak Lao, which makes it difficult to tell whether a prostitute is a local Thai or has actually come from Laos. Since they are illegal aliens, Lao girls will always claim to be local Thais and will often have false identity cards to prove it. In the brothels their lives are indistinguishable from those of Thai women.

■ ■ ■ ■ TO JAPAN, SWITZERLAND, GERMANY, THE UNITED STATES

Women and girls flow in both directions over Thailand's borders.[18] The export of enslaved prostitutes is a robust business, supplying brothels in Japan, Europe, and America. Thailand's Ministry of Foreign Affairs estimated in 1994 that as many as 50,000 Thai women were living illegally in Japan and working in prostitution. Their situation in these countries parallels that of Burmese women held in Thailand. The enticement of Thai women follows a familiar pattern. Promised work as cleaners, domestics, dishwashers, or cooks, Thai girls and women pay large fees to employment agents to secure jobs in rich, developed countries. When they arrive, they are brutalized and enslaved. Their debt bonds are significantly larger than those of enslaved prostitutes in Thailand, since they include airfares, bribes to immigration officials, the costs of false passports, and sometimes the fees paid to foreign men to marry them and ease their entry.

Variations on sex slavery occur in different countries. In Switzerland girls are brought in on "artist" visas as exotic dancers. There, in addition to being prostitutes, they must work as striptease dancers in order to meet the carefully checked terms of their employment. The brochures of the European companies that have leaped into the sex-tourism business leave the customer no doubt about what is being sold:

> Slim, sunburnt, and sweet, they love the white man in an erotic and devoted way. They are masters of the art of making love by nature, an art that we Europeans do not know. (Life Travel, Switzerland) [M]any girls from the sex world come from the poor north-eastern region of the country and from the slums of Bangkok. It has become a custom that one of the nice looking daughters goes into the business in order to earn money for the poor family . . . [Y]ou can get the feeling that taking a girl here is as easy as buying a package of cigarettes . . . little slaves who give real Thai warmth. (Kanita Kamha Travel, the Netherlands)[19]

In Germany they are usually bar girls, and they are sold to men by the bartender or bouncer. Some are simply placed in brothels or apartments controlled by pimps. After Japanese sex tours to Thailand began in the 1980s, Japan rapidly became the largest importer of Thai women. The fear of HIV in Japan has also increased the demand for virgins. Because of their large disposable incomes, Japanese men are able to pay considerable sums for young rural girls from Thailand. Japanese organized crime is involved throughout the importation process, sometimes shipping women via Malaysia or the Philippines. In the cities, the Japanese mob maintains bars and brothels that trade in Thai women. Bought and sold between brothels, these women are controlled with extreme violence. Resistance can bring murder. Because the girls are illegal aliens and often enter the country under false passports, Japanese gangs rarely hesitate to kill them if they have ceased to be profitable or if they have angered their slaveholders. Thai women deported from Japan also report that the gangs will addict girls to drugs in order to manage them more easily.

Criminal gangs, usually Chinese or Vietnamese, also control brothels in the United States that enslave Thai women. Police raids in New York, Seattle, San Diego, and Los Angeles have freed more than a hundred girls and women.[20] In New York, thirty Thai women were locked into the upper floors of a building used as a brothel. Iron bars sealed the windows and a series of buzzer-operated armored gates blocked exit to the street. During police raids, the women were herded into a secret basement room. At her trial, the brothel owner testified that she'd bought the women outright, paying between $6,000 and $15,000 for each. The women were charged $300 per week for room and board; they worked from 11:00 A.M. until 4:00 A.M. and were sold by the hour to clients. Chinese and Vietnamese gangsters were also involved in the brothel, collecting protection money and hunting down escaped prostitutes. The gangs owned chains of brothels and massage parlors through which they rotated the Thai women in order to defeat law enforcement efforts. After being freed from the New York brothel, some of the women disappeared—only to turn up weeks later in similar circumstances three thousand miles away, in Seattle. One of the rescued Thai women, who had been promised restaurant work and then enslaved, testified that the brothel owners "bought something and wanted to use it to the full extent and they didn't think those people were human beings."[21]

■ ■ ■ OFFICIAL INDIFFERENCE AND A GROWTH ECONOMY

In many ways, Thailand closely resembles another country, one that was going through rapid industrialization and economic boom one hundred years ago. Rapidly shifting its labor force off the farm, experiencing unprecedented economic growth, flooded with economic migrants, and run by corrupt politicians and a greedy and criminal police force, the United States then faced many of the problems confronting Thailand today. In the 1890s, political machines that brought together organized crime with politicians and police ran the prostitution and protection rackets, drug sales, and extortion in American cities. Opposing them were a weak and disorganized reform movement and a muckraking press. I make this comparison because it is important to explore why Thailand's government is so ineffective when faced with the enslavement of its own citizens, and also to remember that conditions can change over time. Discussions with Thais about the horrific nature of sex slavery often end with their assertion that "nothing will ever change this . . . the problem is just too big . . . and those with power will never allow change." Yet the social and economic underpinnings of slavery in Thailand are always changing, sometimes for the worse and sometimes for the better. No society can remain static, particularly one undergoing such upheavals as Thailand.

As the country takes on a new Western-style materialist morality, the ubiquitous sale of sex sends a clear message: women can be enslaved and exploited for profit. Sex tourism helped set the stage for the expansion of sexual slavery.

Sex tourism also generates some of the income that Thai men use to fund their own visits to brothels. No one knows how much money it pours into the Thai economy, but if we assume that just one-quarter of sex workers serve sex tourists and that their customers pay about the same as they would pay to use Siri, then 656 billion baht ($26.2 billion) a year would be about right. This is thirteen times more than the amount Thailand earns by building and exporting computers, one of the country's major industries, and it is money that floods into the country without any concomitant need to build factories or improve infrastructure. It is part of the boom raising the standard of living generally and allowing an even greater number of working-class men to purchase commercial sex.

Joining the world economy has done wonders for Thailand's income and terrible things to its society. According to Pasuk Phongpaichit and Chris Baker, economists who have analyzed Thailand's economic boom,

Government has let the businessmen ransack the nation's human and natural resources to achieve growth. It has not forced them to put much back. In many respects, the last generation of economic growth has been a disaster. The forests have been obliterated. The urban environment has deteriorated. Little has been done to combat the growth in industrial pollution and hazardous wastes. For many people whose labour has created the boom, the conditions of work, health, and safety are grim.

Neither law nor conscience has been very effective in limiting the social costs of growth. Business has reveled in the atmosphere of free-for-all. The machinery for social protection has proved very pliable. The legal framework is defective. The judiciary is suspect. The police are unreliable. The authorities have consistently tried to block popular organizations to defend popular rights.[22]

The situation in Thailand today is similar to that of the United States in the 1850s; with a significant part of the economy dependent on slavery, religious and cultural leaders are ready to explain why this is all for the best. But there is also an important difference: this is the new slavery, and the impermanence of modem slavery and the dedication of human-rights workers offer some hope.

NOTES

1. Siri is, of course, a pseudonym; the names of all respondents have been changed for their protection. I spoke with them in December 1996.

2. "Caught in Modern Slavery: Tourism and Child Prostitution in Thailand," Country Report Summary prepared by Sudarat Sereewat-Srisang for the Ecumenical Consultation held in Chiang Mai in May 1990.

3. Foreign exchange rates are in constant flux. Unless otherwise noted, dollar equivalences for all currencies reflect the rate at the time of the research.

4. From interviews done by Human Rights Watch with freed child prostitutes in shelters in Thailand, reported in Jasmine Caye, *Preliminary Survey on Regional Child Trafficking for Prostitution in Thailand* (Bangkok: Center for the Protection of Children's Rights, 1996), p. 25.

5. Kulachada Chaipipat, "New Law Targets Human Trafficking," *Bangkok Nation,* November 30, 1997.

6. Thais told me that it would be very surprising if a well-off man or a politician did not have at least one mistress. When I was last in Thailand there was much public mirth over the clash of wife and mistress outside the hospital room of a high government official who had suffered a heart attack, as each in turn barricaded the door.

7. Quoted in Mark Van Landingham, Chanpen Saengtienchai, John Knodel, and Anthony Pramualratana, *Friends, Wives, and Extramarital Sex in Thailand* (Bangkok: Institute of Population Studies, Chulalongkom University, 1995), p. 18.

8. Van Landingham et al., 1995, pp. 9–25.

9. Van Landingham et al., 1995, p. 53.

10. Pasuk Phongpaichit and Chris Baker, *Thailand's Boom* (Chiang Mai: Silkworm Books, 1996), pp. 51–54.

11. Center for the Protection of Children's Rights, *Case Study Report on Commercial Sexual Exploitation of Children in Thailand* (Bangkok, October 1996), p. 37.

12. David Kyle and John Dale, "Smuggling the State Back In: Agents of Human Smuggling Reconsidered," in *Global Human Smuggling: Comparative Perspectives,* ed. David Kyle and Rey Koslowski (Baltimore: Johns Hopkins University Press, 2001).

13. "Impact of the Asian Economic Crisis on Child Prostitution," *ECPAT International Newsletter* 27 (May 1, 1999), found at http://www.ecpat.net/eng/Ecpat_inter/IRC/articles.asp?articleID=143&NewsID=21.

14. Mechai Veravaidya, address to the International Conference on HIV/AIDS, Chiang Mai, September 1995. See also Gordon Fairclough, "Gathering Storm," *Far Eastern Review,* September 21, 1995, pp. 26–30.

15. Human Rights Watch, *A Modern Fornt of Slavery,* p. 3.

16. "Ranong Brothel Raids Net 148 Burmese Girls," *Nation* (July 16, 1993), p. 12.

17. Dorothy O. Thomas, ed., *A Modern Form of Slavery: Trafficking of Burmese Women and Girls into Brothels in Thailand* (New York: Human Rights Watch, 1993), p. 112.

18. *International Report on Trafficking in Women (Asia-Pacific Region)* (Bangkok: Global Alliance Against Traffic in Women, 1996); Sudarat Sereewat, *Prostitution: Thai-European Connection* (Geneva: Commission on the Churches' Participation in Development, World Council of Churches, n.d.). Women's rights and antitrafficking organizations in Thailand have also published a number of personal accounts of women enslaved as prostitutes and sold overseas. These pamphlets are disseminated widely in the hope of making young women more aware of the threat of enslavement. Good examples are Siriporn Skrobanek, *The Diary of Prang* (Bangkok: Foundation for Women, 1994); and White Ink (pseud.), *Our Lives, Our Stories* (Bangkok: Foundation for Women, 1995). They follow the lives of women "exported," the first to Germany and the second to Japan.

19. The brochures are quoted in Truong, *Sex, Money, and Morality: Prostitution and Tourism in Southeast Asia* (London: Zed Books, 1990), p. 178.

20. Carey Goldberg, "Sex Slavery, Thailand to New York," *New York Times* (September 11, 1995), p. 81.

21. Quoted in Goldberg.

22. Phongpaichit and Baker, 1996, p. 237.

My Secret Life as a Black Man

Anthony Walton

introduction

As you know, some of us are born poor, others rich, and most of us in between. Some of us are born to single mothers, others to married parents. Some of us are born to parents who have gone to graduate school, others to parents who have not finished high school. Some of us are born female, others male.

What is the point of such a recitation, to which we could add almost endless examples? It is that the circumstances we inherit at birth have significant consequences for what happens to us in life. They determine what sociologists call *life chances*—how the background factors that surround our birth affect our fate in life. They are part of our *social capital*, the capacities and opportunities—or their lack—that comes with our family circumstances. Sociologists regularly place these social factors under the sociological lens: social class, gender, race, religion, and historical period with its economic booms or busts, technological innovations, degree of political freedom, war or peace, and so on.

As significant as these external factors are in determining what happens to us in life and, ultimately, who we become, there also are internal matters. We all experience an "internal life"—self-conversations, the ways we "make sense" out of our experiences. Part of our internal life is self-control—that is, our evaluations of what we experience, the ways we want to react to situations and the ways we actually do. This rich "internal life" is essential both to our world view and to our interactions with others. Essential as it is for our being and our social life, however, our internal life is difficult to study. In this reading, a man who identifies himself as black shares some of his "internal life." I think that your understanding of racial relations will grow as you read this article.

Thinking Critically

As you read this selection, ask yourself:

1. What inner conflicts does the author reveal? What is the source of those conflicts?

2. What different "social worlds" does the author live in? How does he traverse (handle himself) in those different worlds?

3. Does the author have a "core" self? If so, what is it? Do you have one? If so, of what does it consist?

I have often thought of myself as having two lives: my life as a black man and my other, real life. Since grammar school I've felt a tension at play in my inner life, a pull between what was expected of me as a young black boy, adolescent, and man, and what I wanted as myself, Anthony. I've been at war, and the stakes of the battle are who I am and who I can become. When I was younger; I thought this struggle would end at some point. Now, at thirty-six, I realize it won't end; that its roots are as deep as the most fundamental problem of philosophy—the uneasy coexistence of body and soul. As William James writes in *The Principles of Psychology,* "Our bodies themselves, are they simply ours, or are they *us?*"

One night last November I walked along the pier at the southern tip of Miami Beach with an old friend from school, a white woman. The evening was unseasonably warm, and moonlit. We hadn't seen each other in eight or nine months, and we were chatting amiably, taking our time. My friend was excited about a book of poems by David Malouf and was exhorting me to read it.

About a third of the way out we passed a middle-aged black woman who remarked on my friend's considerable beauty and the color of her blond hair. I thought to myself, "How nice!," but when I entered the woman's frame of vision, she launched into a tirade. "Oh, I see," she hissed, "one of them who done married a white wife. Think you too good!" She followed us most of the way down the pier for what felt like an excruciating length of time, berating my friend for being with me, excoriating me for treason to the race—then she suddenly turned back and disappeared as abruptly as she had pounced.

I don't know if the woman was deranged or just angry, but the incident—this is what troubles me most—wasn't really anything new. That night in Miami was merely one more instance in which I'd offended another person, in this case a black person, by doing nothing more than living my own life.

I can remember conflicts years before with certain black kids in Aurora, Illinois, the town where I grew up, over my bookishness, my flagrant love of school and the library, and my tendency to make friends outside of the race and to join groups like Little League and Boy Scouts, activities considered insufficiently "black." One girl was so outraged by my failure to follow her tightly circumscribed ideas of how the black kids in our neighborhood should act that for two years she and the boys in her clique threw my books in the mud, picked fights with me after school, and threatened a white friend of mine in an attempt to stop us from sharing a locker. In the end, I withdrew from public school and enrolled in a Catholic school.

All along there were conflicts with white kids as well—over the appropriateness of my aspirations and the threat these aspirations posed to them. I wasn't in their group, and many seemed to think there was only so much achievement to go around. Along the way I also butted heads with black and white teachers, both groups declaring me too big for my britches, though for different reasons—some whites thinking I was uppity and arrogant, some blacks thinking I was more brazenly self-confident than was healthy for a young black.

Most troubling were the struggles with my parents, who for a long time disapproved of my "over-involvement" with the arts. I wanted to be Martin Scorsese

Originally appeared in *The Oxford American.* Reprinted by permission of Anthony Walton.

or Sting; in *their* scenario, I was to be a doctor or a pastor, the crown jewel of our family's long struggle up from slavery. At times my parents seemed heartbroken over our lack of common ground. To their thinking, I was courting disaster by turning my back on the way that black people had done things for ages.

Finally, there were the momentary, or ongoing, scrapes with white strangers—the wider world—those people too busy, fearful, or thoughtless to perceive others in any fashion other than as stereotypes. When these people gazed upon me, they saw only what their culture and society had constructed and coded as a "black man." And a six-foot, two-hundred-fifty pound one at that—a threat to doormen, security guards, and cabdrivers; someone suspicious, dangerous, but irrelevant.

Black strangers, like the woman in Miami, were often just as troubling, expecting me to conform completely to their ideological and cosmological positions, even though we knew nothing about each other.

The problem of defining the self, of authenticity is a problem for every human. But, for better and worse, it is more sharply and starkly dramatized for blacks. Walking down the street, I can't simply be lost in my thoughts, in my soul—in what I'll have for dinner, a movie I saw the night before, an essay I read about Flaubert—because I'm constantly jolted and reminded, by the looks in strangers' eyes, of *my body,* and of the assumptions and expectations that go along with it. What I think of as myself, my soul, is under crippling siege.

A black man . . . is still constantly being told—by society by the media, by white behavior and stricture, by other blacks—what he should think, what his soul's affinities should be, whom he should love and be in love with, what his ultimate loyalties are.

I have tried to imagine what the black woman in Miami thought she saw that evening and why she reacted the way she did. I can forgive her the rage, if not the bad manners. It was almost as if two different zones of reality and history—with their varied expectations of behavior and duty—had collided. To the woman, perhaps my white friend was the symbol of everything that had oppressed her and her people down through time. To me, she was someone I'd sat next to in class. I suppose the black woman and I each had to live up to, and live with, our respective interpretations of the scene, but as blacks we have historically been expected to agree with each other—which in this case was impossible.

The desires and intentions others have for me, however profound or superfluous, usually conflict with my own. And so of necessity I devised a way of navigating these treacherous shoals of expectation, a mode of being that allows me to maneuver through society black, white, rich, poor—and one that I suspect has cost me something. I learned, quite unconsciously, how to be a "black man," how to slide through the surface of any situation. I developed, in fact, a great many ways of being, a sense of the self as a shape-shifter, a kind of post-modern extrapolation of DuBois's "double-consciousness."

In Harlem, talk crap and slap palms; in Scarsdale, be the soul of probity; in Mississippi, agree with whoever is talking; with my parents, steer the conversation away from anything remotely "controversial." I became like Ralph Ellison's Rinehart, the chameleon of *Invisible Man*—all things to all people, whoever they wanted him to be.

A black man, if he chooses to enter mainstream society, must manipulate many contexts, must alter his appearance often and change his diction and demeanor as circumstances require. Classically, this was known as "bowing and scraping," but today, with a wider range of possibilities in a society that is itself fragmenting, the reality is far more complex.

A black man's "identity" in the boardroom of a bank is different from his "identity" as an anonymous black motorist stopped by the police, and both of those are different from his "identity" as a husband and father, or with his friends, be they black, white, or black and white. A day in Los Angeles that might start in South Central could finish in Orange County. How much skill and energy and psychic strength is required to "pass" in these wildly different places? These (and many more) fragments of identity are shifting and overlapping and contradicting one another daily.

Other questions of identity underlie and plague this fluid, protean self. Am I a human first? A male? A Christian? A black? A black male? Or am I a Southerner? A Midwesterner? A college graduate? A bourgeois? A writer?

I think it's safe to say that being black is not necessarily the irreducible fact of black people's lives. My parents, and millions of other blacks like them, think of themselves as African-Americans. They could be fairly described as militantly proud of that fact. But if you said to them, or many other blacks, that they had to choose between their Christianity or blackness, they would happily choose Christianity even if it meant they would be martyred.

My various modes of moving through and effacing a society, black and white, . . . were conceived as techniques for surviving the resulting fragmentation of self. I now see, as I get older, that the techniques *themselves* are something I must survive, as they pose a danger of leading me away from being true to myself (and thus true to others).

The problem, put simply, is one of authenticity—of preserving the capacity for being whole in a specific moment and honest with one's self, and with others.

I had been forced to consider if somehow I owed it to the woman on the pier to be strolling that night with a black woman. This brings me to the question, *Is there a me that is not defined by others, and not defined solely in opposition to them?*

The philosopher Charles Taylor has written, "Being true to myself means being true to my own originality, which is something that only I can articulate and discover. In articulating it, I am also defining myself."

Each of us is an original, and has an original way of existing as a human, though we may not ever fully realize it. Emerson emphasized that the soul was a unique and private thing, to be guarded from the world, to be mined, probed, and created in secret. But what does this notion of defining one's self mean to a black man?

Throughout my life what I've been hearing in various forms is, "Be true to your kind." But I wonder who, exactly, are my kind: the black kids who tried to stop me from going to the library or the old white lady librarian who, without my asking, set aside special books for me on subjects I liked? People who share my epidermal melanin content, and perhaps little else, or those who share my obsessive interests in Glenn Gould, Thelonious Monk, and string quartets? Am I my skin color, my gender, my family's social position? Or instead, am I my loyalties, my pleasures, those people and things I love? How do I choose who I am? How much is society choosing for me, and how much am I choosing for myself? Can I be, irreducibly, anything that I do not choose to be?

There are, classically, three constituents of identity—biology, culture, and belief—and the problem in our society is that we are always turning the categorical (abstractions humans invent in order to assign meaning and hierarchy) into the biological (descriptive facts that cannot be modified and that can have an irrevocable impact on one's fate). To describe someone as "black" or "Irish" or "Cuban" is to say something very different about that person than to describe him as male or as left-handed or as having heart disease, but we often invest the two kinds of description with equal authority. As Ellison wrote in *Invisible Man,* however, blackness is "not exactly a matter of a biochemical accident [of] my epidermis. . . . [it] occurs because of a peculiar disposition of the eyes of those with whom I come in contact." This "peculiar disposition," I might add, occurs in the eyes of blacks as well as whites.

It becomes tempting, taking into account the dangers of imprecise descriptors, to say that there is no such thing as a "black man," or any of the other socially constructed categories we have become used to declaiming. But we know that this is not quite true, or I wouldn't be writing this essay. . . .

When, late at night, I get on the elevator in the library of the college where I teach, the female student who reacts uncomfortably to my presence as we ride down alone is not necessarily interested in the fact that I'm carrying books by Emerson, Gordimer, and Rorty. On my good days, I shrug and say to myself, it's not me—not a black man—that she finds so alarming, but the general category of "male."

When I think of my lonely hours in the library, or in contemplation and in prayer, I don't see why my most personal affinities should be of interest, or meaning, to anyone but me and those few with whom I choose to open my self. Why must the people I love, the things and places I treasure, my lifetime's accumulation of an interior life, become subject to other people's politics, shallow rhetoric, and public scrutiny?

We live in a society that forces sincere and law-abiding people to break themselves into little pieces in order to survive it, to inhabit the margins of the culture rather than to embrace it whole. Democracy, in its pure, and even its corrupted form, should allow us to choose a self freely. Instead, in its modern-day American version, it leads, in the end, to a more fragmented self. The tragic legacy of our democracy as described by Ralph Ellison, is that as we are freed from sweeping social categories, from fixed, generational identities—and in order to flee the anguish of choice and responsibility, we simply create our own smaller categories and defend them viciously. We are "Asian," black," "gay," "suburban," "Latino," "white," "feminist," "conservative"—a legacy of soundbites, the commodified self, the "self" bought and sold for its utility.

It is almost structurally impossible for an American—and I stress that I'm speaking for more than black males here—simultaneously and openly to embrace and enjoy all of the aspects of the culture for which he or she might feel an affinity.

Are we becoming a nation of Rineharts, with different personas at work, at home, at play, at church? Is this the new human condition . . . Race, religion, gender, sexual preference, social class, economic power, age—definitions of some aspect of identity are always going to be at odds with others and preclude simple choices.

I am a black man, however, and I suspect that the question finally, is not "What does it mean to be a black man?" but rather, "What is living as a black man in this society doing to me, to my soul?" *Is* there a me aside from the black man? Am I finally, and only, my body, or are the soul and body of a black man two different things?

There is a Zen koan that says, "Show me your original face; show me the face you had before you were born." The question is, Can an American black man in the late twentieth century find that original face under the noise and expectations that surround and overwhelm him once he is in the world? Dare he show it? Can others see it?

"But This Is My Mother!" The Plight of Elders in Nursing Homes

Cynthia Loucks

introduction ■ ■ ■ ■

As discussed in the text, the globe is graying. Not only is the number of elderly increasing around the world, but also the elderly are becoming a larger proportion of the population of most countries. In the United States, a generation ago people age sixty-five and over made up 10 percent of the population. Today, about 13 percent of Americans are elderly. About the year 2050, the proportion of the elderly is expected to reach 20 percent.

By the middle of this century, then, on average every fifth person you see will be age sixty-five or older. (Of course, somewhere around this time you, too, will be elderly, so with your network of elderly friends almost everyone you see will be old.) But as you read in the text, age sixty-five is an arbitrary number, and there is no cross-cultural agreement about the age at which people become old. As you also read, neither is there a cross-cultural consensus on the meaning of "old."

There are global problems of old age, however, especially the dependency and frailty that sometimes accompany it. Around the world, the number of elderly has grown to such an extent that their medical care demands more and more of society's resources. In the United States, even though the average elderly American is independent and healthy, the costs of the medical treatment of the elderly have multiplied. No one has yet found a solution to this growing problem.

The frail elderly are especially problematic. What should be done when people grow old and can no longer take care of themselves? Every society has to find ways of taking care of their frail elderly, but, as with the Tiwi that you read about in the text, those solutions can be detrimental to the elderly. So it often is with our own particular solution—nursing homes, the topic of this selection by Cynthia Loucks.

Thinking Critically

As you read this selection, ask yourself:

1. What problems of nursing homes does the author describe? This is just the plight of one person in a single nursing home; why should we pay attention to it?

2. Inadequate care in nursing homes and the harm this does to the elderly have been documented for decades as a national problem. Why does this situation continue?

3. How are you going to assure that you will receive adequate health care when you grow old? How will you avoid being exploited?

*W*hether elders have bed sores is a good indicator of the quality of care that is being provided. Elders who can no longer move themselves must be repositioned regularly so that their body weight is not resting in any one place for too long. A head nurse on my mother's ward told me that nursing home regulations require that immobile residents be turned every two hours while in bed in order to shift their weight distribution and to vary the pressure on their body parts. If necessary, pillows can be used to position residents on their sides. But when there is a shortage of pillows, the efforts of conscientious aides who try to keep up with the necessary regimen are hampered.

In the course of a person's physical disintegration, bed sores become more difficult to prevent. When someone is very near death, subjecting them to the disturbance of repositioning can be unduly inconsiderate. However, until that point, nursing home staff need to follow the guidelines for preventing bed sores. The reality remains that in many facilities, including the one my mother was in, dependent elders are moved as little as once during an eight hour shift. Even then, most of the movements that occur are merely back and forth between bed and chair, which may not provide any relief if the weight of the body remains on the same spot. In addition, many nursing home residents are in effect lying down even when they are in their chairs, since the recliners are cranked back in order to use gravity to keep flaccid bodies from sliding onto the floor.

Other methods of preventing bed sores, such as gentle massage to stimulate circulation, are seldom employed by overworked staff in nursing homes. Although various devices can be used in chairs and beds to relieve sacral pressure—doughnut-shaped pillows, "egg crate" foam cushions and mattresses, gel-filled mattresses and pillows—these items are often in short supply in many nursing homes. A resident's personal cushion also can lie unnoticed in a closet where one staff person may have stored it and the next staff person does not rediscover it.

It distressed me a great deal to know that Mama couldn't turn herself over in bed or shift her weight in her chair without assistance. She easily could be left in an uncomfortable position for hours, unable to do anything about it. According to her last doctor, the one with geriatric training, part of the nature of Mama's condition was that she no longer felt the uncomfortable pressure or nerve stimuli that prompt the rest of us to shift our positions frequently. I hoped he was right and that Mama never felt too uncomfortable.

When immobile residents aren't being repositioned regularly, it often means they aren't being checked on frequently, either. As a result, nursing home residents have been found stuck in some very bizarre and even potentially life-threatening positions. Sometimes I would find Mama in an incredibly uncomfortable-looking posture. She would be so still, just staring, waiting, as though resigned to something she knew she was helpless to alter. On at least two occasions I know of, Mama somehow rolled to the side of her bed and wound up with her head stuck between the bed rails for who knows how long before someone found her. At the time, I was unaware of how terribly dangerous this phenomenon can actually be. I learned later that many nursing home residents have lost their lives from getting trapped in their bed rails and not being discovered in time to be rescued.

Mama also often slipped down in her chair, another typical side effect of paralysis and other conditions that impede the ability to resist gravity. It was part of the conundrum of having to be left fully upright after meals with no wherewithal to maintain the position herself. I feared that hours might go by before anyone noticed she had slumped. She could even slip all the way out of the chair and wind up injured on the floor before anyone might come to reposition her. I vividly remember one instance when I walked into Mama's room and found that she had slid so far out of her slippery vinyl recliner that only her sacrum and the back of her neck were in contact with the chair. Her chin was pressed to her chest and her legs were sticking out straight in front of her, well beyond the support of the chair's leg rest. She was staring straight ahead, her blank expression revealing little of the soul trapped in that poor old vessel.

I often wondered what Mama was thinking at those times, unsure whether she just checked out or maybe even went into some sort of trance induced by her extreme helplessness. I would notice a particularly blank expression on her face on such occasions, as well as sometimes when the aides were cleaning her, another undoubtedly unpleasant event. This common psychological response of distancing oneself in some way when under such circumstances is called dissociation. When something in life is too disagreeable, people employ defense mechanisms in order to handle the stress. What happens to the people who have to do this every day, several times a day, in order to deal with their circumstances? It is a question that needs to be addressed on behalf of all nursing home residents.

Another highly disconcerting and recurring event in Mama's life took place whenever she had to be transferred. In medical settings, to "transfer" someone is to move an immobilized person from one conveyance to another—from bed to geri-chair or wheelchair, from chair to toilet, etc., and back again. This particular aspect of caring for disabled elders is probably the most strenuous for all concerned. Those elders who cannot bear any weight on their feet are the most difficult to transfer. Even with a small person like Mama, who weighed less than one hundred pounds by the time she was admitted to the nursing home, the bulk and stiffness of the person render the process awkward.

Mama often screamed when she was being transferred, a habit that rattled many of her aides. I think she was frightened to be picked up, afraid she would be dropped or otherwise injured, which is not an unrealistic fear for someone in such impotent circumstances. To ease fears about being transferred and to limit the possibility of injury, there is an approved procedure for moving dependent residents. Two aides or nurses lift the resident along four points—the two armpits and the backs of the two knees—so that the person's weight is evenly distributed. In Mama's case, she was often transferred, whether by one aide or two, by lifting her up by her armpits only. Not only was that a very uncomfortable way to be lifted, but it also risked injury to her unsupported lower torso and limbs. Throughout Mama's stay in the nursing home I tried constantly to get the aides to use their other hand to support Mama beneath her knees. Trying to motivate them, I pointed out that Mama surely wouldn't cry out so much if they used this method. But with each subsequent visit I would see that the aides had reverted to their armpit-only transfer. Considering that Mama was probably transferred between bed and chair an average of 6 times per day, 365 days a year, it was quite an ordeal for her to endure.

There are other chronic physical care issues, albeit non-life-threatening, that are frequently left unattended to in nursing homes. For example, Mama's feet were often cold, so I bought her several pairs of socks and focused on trying to get the aides to remember to put them on her when she needed them. I shouldn't have been surprised when I realized they were putting socks on her all the time, even if her feet weren't cold. At times I would find Mama so hot that she was perspiring. It seemed like such a small thing to pay attention to—a person's skin temperature and then dressing her accordingly. Yet, such consideration was almost totally outside the bounds of the care that Mama received.

The paralysis that followed Mama's stroke and the subsequent lack of movement that ensued resulted in the contraction of her left arm and hand. During the first few months after Mama's arrival at the nursing home, a young woman came in from time to time to perform range-of-motion movements with Mama's limbs, a means for both reducing contraction and improving circulation. When the therapy was discontinued, for whatever reason I do not know, I didn't protest. The young woman had seemed so inexperienced, and Mama clearly didn't enjoy having her arms and legs tugged this way and that. I couldn't bring myself to insist on more.

Mama spent a lot of time either in bed or in her chair with her legs outstretched. Before long, her ankles became rotated such that her feet were always turned inward one another. Knowing she would never walk again, I didn't think it made a difference how her ankles were positioned so long as there were no indications of discomfort. The color and the condition of her skin looked all right. One of the nurses told me that people's ankles naturally rotated inward once they can no longer walk. I believed her and assumed that she had probably seen it happen many times before. But when I later learned how easily this condition could have been prevented by using pillows to hold her ankles in a neutral position, I felt remorse for having left it at that. I was not aware of the stress that this rotated position placed on all of Mama's connecting joints, and probably on the bones themselves, all the way up to her hips. (To see what this is like, lie down on your back when you are in bed tonight, with your legs outstretched, and slowly rotate your ankles inward as far as they will go. Notice the sensations that occur immediately, even as far up as the small of your back. Ouch!)

Mama's skin had gotten as thin as an old shirt that's been worn and washed so many times it has become transparent and easily torn. Yet, the aides would take a terry washcloth, coarse from heavy bleaching, and scrub her as though she had been digging ditches all day. Although stimulating the skin is beneficial, their methods looked excessive. When I suggested that Mama didn't need such vigorous bathing, they humored me and washed her more gently; but I had no doubt that as soon as I wasn't available to monitor them, they returned to doing it their way.

It wasn't long before Mama developed a skin rash. Considered a redhead (though her hair was more a deep auburn), Mama always had sensitive skin, so it was not surprising that it protested the treatment it received in the nursing home. The doctors and nurses discussed prescribing medication for her, both cortisone-based pills and lotions. As usual, the medical approach was to suppress the symptom without attempting to alleviate its cause.

Aides give bed baths by bringing a plastic tub of warm, soapy water to the bed of a resident, who then gets washed down with a washcloth. To my dismay, I discovered that after washing Mama, some of the aides simply dried her off without first rinsing her skin. Others would bring fresh water for rinsing her but would still use the same sudsy washcloth. The source of Mama's rash seemed obvious to me. When I pointed out the detrimental shortcuts, the aides countered that it was difficult to rinse her properly without getting the bed unduly wet. I suggested that they might try rinsing out the washcloth first with clean water and that if they used less soap when they filled up the plastic tub—it was usually frothing with suds—the rinsing might go more easily. They grudgingly agreed to try it, and Mama's rash soon subsided.

I also had to lobby to add moisturizing lotion to Mama's required skin-care regimen. I scrawled Mama's name in big black letters on her lotion dispenser in the hope that it would actually remain in her room. Since care supplies are seldom adequately stocked in nursing homes, staff freely "borrow" from one resident to give to another—the best solution they can find when needing something otherwise unavailable. Thanks partly to the ongoing vigilance of Aunt Margaret and the steady supply the family provided, lotion was always available. How often it was used on Mama, however, was less reliable. I bought facial moisturizer for Mama, too, but I could tell by how much remained in the jar that it was seldom applied by anyone else but me. I enjoyed rubbing the lotion onto her face. It was a chance to express the gentleness and tenderness that I felt for her, to nurture her in some small way.

It was also apparent that duties such as providing oral care were getting checked off on Mama's chart when they were not actually being performed. Her dentures had disappeared within a few weeks of her arrival at the nursing home. A nurse speculated that they were probably thrown out with her soiled laundry. Their loss, of course, did not preclude her need for oral care. One method of providing this care involves using a little sponge that is attached to the end of a stick. When dipped in water, the sponge emits a mouthwash-like substance. The sponge is then used to massage and freshen a person's mouth and gums without the need for rinsing. But like most medical supplies, these implements are ridiculously expensive and are invariably in short supply at nursing homes.

The physical care of nursing home residents is further complicated by the maladies that are endemic in today's long term care facilities, and Mama certainly wasn't immune to any of these problems. Urinary tract infections, diarrhea, congestion, dehydration, rashes, and bed sores—these ailments never seem to surprise the doctors, who attribute them to residents' advanced ages and poor physical conditions. While elders do tend to have diminished immune systems and increased susceptibility to sickness, especially when they are inactive, this knowledge should be a warning for increased preventive care rather than an excuse for the various skin, digestive, and bacterial problems that occur. These afflictions could be greatly reduced with good, consistent attention to residents' hygiene as well as to their prescribed care regimens. There should be no excuse for failing to avert the preventable.

When nursing home residents are no longer able to control the flow of their urine, they develop rashes from the prolonged exposure of their skin to the urine in their bedding and diapers. In typical fashion, nursing homes respond to the frequency of these rashes by inserting catheters into aged urethras. While reducing the need for frequent cleanup, catheters provide ideal conditions for the proliferation of infection-causing bacteria. Improperly used and monitored, as they often are in nursing homes, they can present other hazards as well. I once found that my mother had been placed in her bed lying on the tubing, which of course blocked the flow.

In addition, many elderly recipients of these contraptions, no longer constrained by subservience to authority, yank them out, causing subsequent irritation to tender tissue. After Mama suffered through several urinary tract infections, I decided that she, too, had had enough. I told the staff that I did not want any more foreign objects inserted anywhere into my mother and vetoed the further use of a catheter on her. While the doctors never seemed to question writing an order for a catheter and following it with the almost inevitable antibiotic prescription a week or two later, the nursing staff, who saw the human result of that cycle in increased bowel difficulties due to the loss of healthy intestinal flora, were more willing to break the cycle and acquiesce to my request, even though they had requested the catheter in the first place. One nurse admitted to me that she knew I was right, although overall, the staff was miffed that I expected them to keep Mama clean and dry enough to avoid further rashes.

Such medical aspects of Mama's care were never ending. I had to function as a conduit of information among the ever-changing nursing home staff, the doctor, and hospital staff whenever Mama was hospitalized for conditions such as internal bleeding episodes. It was especially important to provide the hospital staff with information because they never seemed to be notified of the particulars of Mama's health care. Once I was just in time to prevent a hospital nurse from attempting to feed Mama solid food, an act that would almost certainly have choked her.

I also had to keep trying to get Mama a diet that took into consideration her pre-existing condition of chronic colitis (inflammation of the colon). I needed to be on the lookout for cuts, sores, infections, and problems with her G-tube, so that these problems were attended to promptly, regularly, and effectively. I tried to be sure that she was not given treatments that would precipitate yet another condition requiring treatment. I checked that she was given sufficient fluids to avoid dehydration, which became a problem due to her inability to consume sufficient quantities at meal times and the unavailability of staff to provide the fluids she needed between meals.

It was very frustrating to review Mama's treatment and consider that she was in a reputable nursing home. At best, her care was tolerable, with rare instances of very good. Frequently, it was heedless, insensitive, rough, and even dangerous. Yet, I was determined to keep fighting for Mama, to keep taking yet another grievance to the head nurse, the doctor, the social worker, whomever I thought might be able to help us. There was never any question of giving up, even though overseeing Mama's care in that nursing home was truly the most demanding, frustrating, and disheartening job I have ever had.

It galled me again and again to witness the indifference with which so many of the nursing home staff treated my mother. They seemed unwilling to look at what they were doing and apparently regarded my efforts to intervene as just so much nagging. Even those who responded positively to my suggestions would either soon revert to their usual methods or not be taking care of my mother any more. Between staff rotations and people quitting, Mama never had the same caregivers for long, which deprived her of the comfort and reassurance that familiarity and continuity could have provided.

The unkindness that some of the aides displayed toward Mama—and that they would behave that way right in front of me—was not only distressing but downright baffling. Throughout her stay at the nursing home, when she wasn't too ill or too sleepy to respond, Mama always had an enthusiastically friendly greeting for one and all. To me it was a reflection of the wonderful graciousness that she managed to retain throughout so much of her ordeal.

One day a young male aide came into Mama's room to attend to her. True to form, Mama called out a cheery "Hi!" when the young man approached her bed. Silence. Seconds passed. Undaunted, Mama said "Hi!" again, with no less warmth or cheer. Her voice and what she said were clear and unmistakable. Still silence. Despite my pounding heart and the fury rising in my throat, I remained calm so as not to make a scene in front of Mama. I said to the young man, "She said 'hi' to you." As though coming out of a trance, he finally uttered a dull, flat "Hello." And without another word, he proceeded to perform his duties in an efficient but perfunctory manner. Mama fell silent.

When I later saw the aide in the corridor, I questioned him about his thoughtless behavior. Vaguely apologetic, he informed me that he had a lot on his mind. I was less than sympathetic and complained about the incident to the head nurse. She shared my dismay at the aide's behavior, agreeing that professional caregivers should leave their personal problems at the door when they come to work. It was good to have her agreement, but it didn't change anything.

I winced whenever I watched aides and nurses tend to Mama without speaking to her or speak to her without looking at her. I desperately wanted them to act in a manner that was kind, civil, and respectful. I knew what a difference it would make for Mama if they took a moment to explain what they were going to do and if they made an effort to listen to her, responding as much as possible to what she indicated.

All nursing home residents have psychological, emotional, and social needs regardless of their conditions. They need eye contact and whatever else seems appropriate to foster a feeling of connection and respect for their basic humanity. The lack of such behavior constitutes an assault on the human spirit and is, in many ways, the most painful offense for people to bear. It wounds more deeply than the discomfort and indignity of poor physical care.

PART
IV   Social Institutions

▪ ▪

In the previous parts of this book you have seen many of the social forces that influence your life, those that twist and turn you in one direction or another. You have read about culture and socialization, social control and deviance, and various forms of social stratification. In this part, we turn our focus onto *social institutions*—the standard ways that society sets up to meet its basic needs.

To exist, every society must solve certain basic problems. Babies must be nourished, children have to be socialized into adult roles, and the sex drive must be held within bounds. To help accomplish these things, every society has set up some form of marriage and family, the first social institution we meet on the stage of life. Social order—keeping people from robbing and killing one another—also has to be established. To accomplish this, each social group sets up some form of what we call politics. Goods and services also have to be produced and distributed. This leads to what is called the economy. The new generation also has to be taught how to view the world in the "correct" way, as well as to learn the skills to participate in the economy. For this, we have some form of education. Then there are views of the spiritual world, of God and morality, perhaps of an afterlife. For this, we have religion.

From birth we are immersed in social institutions, and we never escape from them. We are born into one (the family), we attend school in another (education), and we make our living in still another (economy). Even if we don't vote, the political institution surrounds us with the demands of its laws. Even if we don't worship at a church, synagogue, or mosque, we can't avoid religion, for religious principles are the foundation of law. Even closing most offices, schools, and factories on Sunday is based on religion. As life ends, social institutions continue to be significant—in the typical case a combination of family and the medical institution, followed by a final ceremony at a church or, as discussed in Reading 7, in a special room of a mortuary. There are even prescribed formalities as our body is lowered ceremoniously into the ground.

Social institutions, then, are another way that society nudges us to fit in. Like a curb or median is to an automobile, so social institutions are to our lives. They set boundaries around us, directing us to think and act along certain avenues, pushing us to turn one way instead of another.

Social institutions are so significant that sociologists specialize in them. Some sociologists focus on marriage and family, others study politics or the

153

economy, whereas still others do research on religion or education. After this introductory course, which is a survey of sociology, students usually can take courses on specific social institutions. Most departments of sociology teach a course on marriage and family. In large departments, there may be a course on each social institution, one on the sociology of religion, another on the sociology of education, and so on. In very large departments, the social institutions may be broken down into smaller components, and there may be several courses on the sociology of family, politics, education, and so on.

We open this fourth part of the book with a focus on the economic institution. As James Watson looks at the expansion of McDonald's into Hong Kong, he examines cultural consequences of the globalization of capitalism. The selection that follows has become a classic in sociology, C. Wright Mills' analysis of the ruling elite of the United States. What Mills calls the *power elite* is the group that makes the major decisions that affect our lives. Arlene and Jerome Skolnick, a husband and wife team of sociologists, then compare family life today with family life in "the idyllic past." In the selection on education, Peter and Patti Adler, another husband and wife team of sociologists, report on their study of college basketball players, analyzing why so few of them graduate from college. As you read this article, you will understand how the dynamics of organizations and subcultures defeat what should be the purpose of education. To examine religion, we turn to Marvin Harris' analysis of why letting cows wander about India's streets is functional for that society. We conclude this part with a look at the medical institution, a participant observation study by Daniel Chambliss, whose exploration behind the scenes of a hospital reveals a reality quite unlike that which is carefully cultivated and presented to us.

McDonald's in Hong Kong

James L. Watson

introduction

A key concept in sociology is *rationalization,* a term developed by Max Weber to refer to choosing the most efficient means to accomplish tasks. Weber, who noted that the traditional ways of doing things were passing, didn't know how far reaching and accurate his analysis would prove. In the Most Industrialized Nations, most traditional ways have passed into history and now are mere memories. From rationalization has come the dominance of the bottom line, calculating costs in order to produce the most gain. Rationality has become such a hallmark of contemporary social life that even cooking and serving meals—routine, everyday aspects of family life for millennia—are not immune to this process.

We all are familiar with McDonald's. Most of us have grown up with its hamburgers, fries, milk shakes, chicken nuggets, and other fast food. Some of us even celebrated our younger birthdays at McDonald's, with burgers, balloons, and cake, and playing with our friends at its party palaces—hardly able to stand it until we could return to that wonderland. Spreading over the land from its original single location in southern California, McDonald's has become part and parcel of U.S. culture. This process is so typical that the rationalization of society is sometimes called the *McDonaldization of society.* McDonald's matches our desire for having things done quickly, fitting in well with the microwave mentality that seems to characterize our lives.

But how does McDonald's translate? That is, when McDonald's is transplanted to a different culture, one where the customs and expectations differ markedly from ours, how does it fit in? Where is the adjustment—with McDonald's or with the culture, or with both? This is the focus of this reading, an analysis of the arrival and survival of McDonald's in Hong Kong.

Thinking Critically

As you read this selection, ask yourself:

1. What areas of your life are still marked by a traditional orientation? Are any of those areas giving way to rationality?

2. If rationality continues, little will be left of life that has not been rationalized. Can you identify areas of social life that cannot be rationalized?

3. What impact has McDonald's made on the culture of Hong Kong? In what ways do you see this as good or bad?

■ ■ ■ TRANSNATIONALISM AND THE FAST FOOD INDUSTRY

Does the roaring success of McDonald's and its rivals in the fast food industry mean that Hong Kong's local culture is under siege? Are food chains helping to create a homogenous, "global" culture better suited to the demands of a capitalist world order? Hong Kong would seem to be an excellent place to test the globalization hypothesis, given the central role that cuisine plays in the production and maintenance of a distinctive local identity. Man Tso-chuen's great-grandchildren are today avid consumers of Big Macs, pizza, and Coca-Cola; does this somehow make them less "Chinese" than their grandfather?

It is my contention that the cultural arena in places like Hong Kong is changing with such breathtaking speed that the fundamental assumptions underlining such questions are themselves questionable. Economic and social realities make it necessary to construct an entirely new approach to global issues, one that takes the consumers' own views into account. Analyses based on neomarxian and dependency (center/periphery) models that were popular in the 1960s and 1970s do not begin to capture the complexity of emerging transnational systems.

This [reading] represents a conscious attempt to bring the discussion of globalism down to earth, focusing on one local culture. The people of Hong Kong have embraced American-style fast foods, and by so doing they might appear to be in the vanguard of a worldwide culinary revolution. But they have not been stripped of their cultural traditions, nor have they become "Americanized" in any but the most superficial of ways. Hong Kong . . . constitutes one of the world's most heterogeneous cultural environments. Younger people, in particular, are fully conversant in transnational idioms, which include language, music, sports, clothing, satellite television, cybercommunications, global travel, and—of course—cuisine. It is no longer possible to distinguish what is local and what is not. In Hong Kong, as I hope to show in this chapter, the transnational *is* the local.

■ ■ ■ EATING OUT: A SOCIAL HISTORY OF CONSUMPTION

By the time McDonald's opened its first Hong Kong restaurant in 1975, the idea of fast food was already well established among local consumers. Office workers, shop assistants, teachers, and transport workers had enjoyed various forms of takeout cuisine for well over a century; an entire industry had emerged to deliver mid-day meals direct to workplaces. In the 1960s and 1970s thousands of street vendors produced snacks and simple meals on demand, day or night. Time has always been money in Hong Kong; hence, the dual keys to success in the catering trade were speed and convenience. Another essential characteristic was that the food, based primarily on rice or noodles, had to be hot. Even the most cosmopolitan of local consumers did not (and many still do not) consider cold foods, such as sandwiches and salads, to be acceptable meals. Older people in South China associate cold food with offerings to the dead and are understandably hesitant to eat it.

The fast food industry in Hong Kong had to deliver hot items that could compete with traditional purveyors of convenience foods (noodle shops, dumpling stalls, soup carts, portable grills). The first modern chain to enter the fray was Café de Coral, a local corporation that began operation in 1969 and is still a dominant player in the Hong Kong fast food market . . . .* Café de Coral's strategy was simple: It moved Hong Kong's street foods indoors, to a clean, well-lighted cafeteria that offered instant service and moderate prices; popular Cantonese items were then combined with (sinicized) "Western" foods that had been popular in Hong Kong for decades. Café de Coral's menu reads like the *locus classicus* of Pacific Rim cuisine: deep-fried chicken wings, curry on rice, hot dogs, roast pork in soup noodles, spaghetti with meat balls, barbecued ribs, red bean sundaes, Ovaltine, Chinese tea, and Coca-Cola (with lemon, hot or cold). The formula was so successful it spawned dozens of imitators, including three full-scale chains. . . .

McDonald's mid-1970s entry also corresponded to an economic boom associated with Hong Kong's conversion from a low-wage, light-industrial outpost to a regional center for financial services and high-technology industries. McDonald's takeoff thus paralleled the rise of a new class of highly educated, affluent consumers who thrive in Hong Kong's ever-changing urban environment—one of the most stressful in the world. These new consumers eat out more often than their parents and have created a huge demand for fast, convenient foods of all types. In order to compete in this market, McDonald's had to offer something different. That critical difference, at least during the company's first decade of operation, was American culture packaged as all-American, middle-class food. . . .

■ ■ ■ MENTAL CATEGORIES: SNACK VERSUS MEAL

As in other parts of East Asia, McDonald's faced a serious problem when it began operation in Hong Kong: Hamburgers, fries, and sandwiches were perceived as snacks (Cantonese *siu sihk,* literally "small eats"); in the local view these items did not constitute the elements of a proper meal. This perception is still prevalent among older, more conservative consumers who believe that hamburgers, hot dogs, and pizza can never be "filling." Many students stop at fast food outlets on their way home from school; they may share hamburgers and fries with their classmates and then eat a full meal with their families at home. This is not considered a problem by parents, who themselves are likely to have stopped for tea and snacks after work. Snacking with friends and colleagues provides a major opportunity for socializing (and transacting

---

*Seven of the world's ten busiest McDonald's restaurants are located in Hong Kong. When McDonald's first opened in 1975, few thought it would survive more than a few months. By January 1, 1997, Hong Kong had 125 outlets, which means that there was one McDonald's for every 51,200 residents, compared to one for every 30,000 people in the United States.

business) among southern Chinese. Teahouses, coffee shops, bakeries, and ice cream parlors are popular precisely because they provide a structured yet informal setting for social encounters. Furthermore, unlike Chinese restaurants and banquet halls, snack centers do not command a great deal of time or money from customers.

Contrary to corporate goals, therefore, McDonald's entered the Hong Kong market as a purveyor of snacks. Only since the late 1980s has its fare been treated as the foundation of "meals" by a generation of younger consumers who regularly eat non-Chinese food. Thanks largely to McDonald's, hamburgers and fries are now a recognized feature of Hong Kong's lunch scene. The evening hours remain, however, the weak link in McDonald's marketing plan; the real surprise was breakfast, which became a peak traffic period.

The mental universe of Hong Kong consumers is partially revealed in the everyday use of language. Hamburgers are referred to, in colloquial Cantonese, as *han bou bao*—*han* being a homophone for "ham" and *bao* the common term for stuffed buns or bread rolls. *Bao* are quintessential snacks, and however excellent or nutritious they might be, they do not constitute the basis of a satisfying (i.e., filling) meal. In South China that honor is reserved for culinary arrangements that rest, literally, on a bed of rice *(fan)*. Foods that accompany rice are referred to as *sung*, probably best translated as "toppings" (including meat, fish, and vegetables). It is significant that hamburgers are rarely categorized as meat *(yuk)*; Hong Kong consumers tend to perceive anything that is served between slices of bread (Big Macs, fish sandwiches, hot dogs) as *bao*. In American culture the hamburger is categorized first and foremost as a meat item (with all the attendant worries about fat and cholesterol content), whereas in Hong Kong the same item is thought of primarily as bread.

■ ■ ■ ■ FROM EXOTIC TO ORDINARY: McDONALD'S BECOMES LOCAL

Following precedents in other international markets, the Hong Kong franchise promoted McDonald's basic menu and did not introduce items that would be more recognizable to Chinese consumers (such as rice dishes, tropical fruit, soup noodles). Until recently the food has been indistinguishable from that served in Mobile, Alabama, or Moline, Illinois. There are, however, local preferences: the best-selling items in many outlets are fish sandwiches and plain hamburgers; Big Macs tend to be the favorites of children and teenagers. Hot tea and hot chocolate outsell coffee, but Coca-Cola remains the most popular drink.

McDonald's conservative approach also applied to the breakfast menu. When morning service was introduced in the 1980s, American-style items such as eggs, muffins, pancakes, and hash brown potatoes were not featured. Instead, the local outlets served the standard fare of hamburgers and fries for breakfast. McDonald's initial venture into the early morning food market was so successful that Mr. Ng hesitated to introduce American-style breakfast items, fearing that an abrupt shift in menu might alienate consumers who were beginning to accept hamburgers and fries as a regular feature of their diet. The transition to eggs, muffins, and hash browns was a gradual one, and today most Hong Kong customers order breakfasts that are similar to those offered in American outlets. But once established, dietary preferences change slowly: McDonald's continues to feature plain hamburgers (but not the Big Mac) on its breakfast menu in most Hong Kong outlets.

Management decisions of the type outlined above helped establish McDonald's as an icon of popular culture in Hong Kong. From 1975 to approximately 1985, McDonald's became the "in" place for young people wishing to associate themselves with the laid-back, nonhierarchical dynamism they perceived American society to embody. The first generation of consumers patronized McDonald's precisely because it was *not* Chinese and was *not* associated with Hong Kong's past as a backward-looking colonial outpost where (in their view) nothing of consequence ever happened. Hong Kong was changing and, as noted earlier, a new consumer culture was beginning to take shape. McDonald's caught the wave of this cultural movement and has been riding it ever since. . . .

Today, McDonald's restaurants in Hong Kong are packed—wall-to-wall—with people of all ages, few of whom are seeking an American cultural experience. Twenty years after Mr. Ng opened his first restaurant, eating at McDonald's has become an ordinary, everyday experience for hundreds of thousands of Hong Kong residents. The chain has become a local institution in the sense that it has blended into the urban landscape; McDonald's outlets now serve as rendezvous points for young and old alike. . . .

■ ■ ■ WHAT'S IN A SMILE? FRIENDLINESS AND PUBLIC SERVICE

American consumers expect to be served "with a smile" when they order fast food, but as noted in the Introduction, this is not true in all societies. In Hong Kong people are suspicious of anyone who displays what is perceived to be an excess of congeniality, solicitude, or familiarity. The human smile is not, therefore, a universal symbol of openness and honesty. "If you buy an apple from a hawker and he smiles at you," my Cantonese tutor once told me, "you know you're being cheated."

Given these cultural expectations, it was difficult for Hong Kong management to import a key element of the McDonald's formula—service with a smile—and make it work. Crew members were trained to treat customers in a manner that approximates the American notion of "friendliness." Prior to the 1970s, there was not even an indigenous Cantonese term to describe this form of behavior. The traditional notion of friendship is based on loyalty to close associates, which by definition cannot be extended to strangers. Today the concept of *public* friendliness is recognized—and verbalized—by younger people in Hong Kong, but the term many of them use to express this quality is "friendly," borrowed directly from English. McDonald's, through its television advertising, may be partly responsible for this innovation, but to date it has had little effect on workers in the catering industry.

During my interviews it became clear that the majority of Hong Kong consumers were uninterested in public displays of congeniality from service personnel. When shopping for fast food most people cited convenience, cleanliness, and table space as primary considerations; few even mentioned service except to note that the food should be delivered promptly. Counter staff in Hong Kong's fast food outlets (including McDonald's) rarely make great efforts to smile or to behave in a manner Americans would interpret as friendly. Instead, they project qualities that are admired in the local culture: competence, directness, and unflappability. In a North American setting the facial expression that Hong Kong employees use to convey these qualities would likely be interpreted as a deliberate attempt to be rude or indifferent. Workers who smile on the job are assumed to be enjoying themselves at the consumer's (and management's) expense: In the words of one diner I overheard while standing in a queue, "They must be playing around back there. What are they laughing about?"

■ ■ ■ CONSUMER DISCIPLINE?

[A] hallmark of the American fast food business is the displacement of labor costs from the corporation to the consumers. For the system to work, consumers must be educated—or "disciplined"—so that they voluntarily fulfill their side of an implicit bargain: We (the corporation) will provide cheap, fast service, if you (the customer) carry your own tray, seat yourself, and help clean up afterward. Time and space are also critical factors in the equation: Fast service is offered in exchange for speedy consumption and a prompt departure, thereby making room for others. This system has revolutionized the American food industry and has helped to shape consumer expectations in other sectors of the economy. How has it fared in Hong Kong? Are Chinese customers conforming to disciplinary models devised in Oak Brook, Illinois?

The answer is both yes and no. In general Hong Kong consumers have accepted the basic elements of the fast food formula, but with "localizing" adaptations. For instance, customers generally do not bus their own trays, nor do they depart immediately upon finishing. Clearing one's own table has never been an accepted pan of local culinary culture, owing in pan to the low esteem attaching to this type of labor. During McDonald's first decade in Hong Kong, the cost of hiring extra cleaners was offset by low wages. A pattern was thus established, and customers grew accustomed to leaving without attending to their own rubbish. Later, as wages escalated in the late 1980s and early 1990s, McDonald's tried to introduce self-busing by posting announcements in restaurants and featuring the practice in its television advertisements. As of February 1997, however, little had changed. Hong Kong consumers . . . have ignored this aspect of consumer discipline.

What about the critical issues of time and space? Local managers with whom I spoke estimated that the average eating time for most Hong Kong customers was between 20 and 25 minutes, compared to 11 minutes in the United States fast food industry. This estimate confirms my own observations of McDonald's consumers in Hong Kong's central business districts (Victoria and Tsimshatsui). A survey conducted in the New Territories city of Yuen Long—an old market town that has grown into a modern urban center—revealed that local McDonald's consumers took just under 26 minutes to eat.

Perhaps the most striking feature of the American-inspired model of consumer discipline is the queue. Researchers in many parts of the world have reported that customers refuse, despite "education" campaigns by the chains involved, to form neat lines in front of cashiers. Instead, customers pack themselves into disorderly scrums and jostle for a chance to place their orders. Scrums of this nature were common in Hong Kong when McDonald's opened in 1975. Local managers discouraged this practice by stationing queue monitors near the registers during busy hours and, by the 1980s, orderly lines were the norm at McDonald's. The disappearance of the scrum corresponds to a general change in Hong Kong's public culture as a new generation of residents, the children of refugees, began to treat the territory as their home. Courtesy toward strangers was largely unknown in the 1960s: Boarding a bus during rush hour could be a nightmare and transacting business at a bank teller's window required brute strength. Many people credit McDonald's with being the first public institution in Hong Kong to enforce queuing, and thereby helping to create a more "civilized" social order. McDonald's did not, in fact, introduce the queue to Hong Kong, but this belief is firmly lodged in the public imagination.

■ ■ ■ HOVERING AND THE NAPKIN WARS

Purchasing one's food is no longer a physical challenge in Hong Kong's McDonald's but finding a place to sit is quite another matter. The traditional practice of "hovering" is one solution: Choose a group of diners who appear to be on the verge of leaving and stake a claim to their table by hovering nearby, sometimes only inches away. Seated customers routinely ignore the intrusion; it would, in fact, entail a loss of face to notice. Hovering was the norm in Hong Kong's lower- to middle-range restaurants during the 1960s and 1970s, but the practice has disappeared in recent years. Restaurants now take names or hand out tickets at the entrance; warning signs, in Chinese and English, are posted: "Please wait to be seated." Customers are no longer allowed into the dining area until a table is ready.

Fast food outlets are the only dining establishments in Hong Kong where hovering is still tolerated, largely because it would be nearly impossible to regulate. Customer traffic in McDonald's is so heavy that the standard restaurant design has failed to reproduce American-style dining routines: Rather than ordering first and finding a place to sit afterward, Hong Kong consumers usually arrive in groups and delegate one or two people to claim a table while someone else joins the counter queues. Children make ideal hoverers and learn to scoot through packed restaurants, zeroing in on diners who are about to finish. It is one of the wonders of comparative ethnography to witness the speed with which Hong Kong children perform this reconnaissance duty. Foreign visitors are sometimes unnerved by hovering, but residents accept it as part of everyday life in one of the world's most densely populated cities. It is not surprising, therefore, that Hong Kong's fast food chains have made few efforts to curtail the practice.

Management is less tolerant of behavior that affects profit margins. In the United States fast food companies save money by allowing (or requiring) customers to collect their own napkins, straws, plastic flatware, and condiments. Self-provisioning is an essential feature of consumer discipline, but it only works if the system is not abused. In Hong Kong napkins are dispensed, one at a time, by McDonald's crew members who work behind the counter; customers who do not ask for napkins do not receive any. This is a deviation from the corporation's standard operating procedure and adds a few seconds to each transaction, which in turn slows down the queues. Why alter a well-tested routine? The reason is simple: napkins placed in public dispensers disappear faster than they can be replaced. . . .

Buffets, like fast food outlets, depend upon consumers to perform much of their own labor in return for reduced prices. Abuse of the system—wasting food or taking it home—is taken for granted and is factored into the price of buffet meals. Fast food chains, by contrast, operate at lower price thresholds where consumer abuse can seriously affect profits.

Many university students of my acquaintance reported that they bad frequently observed older people pocketing wads of paper napkins, three to four inches thick, in restaurants that permit self-provisioning. Management efforts to stop this behavior are referred to, in the Cantonese-English slang of Hong Kong youth, as the "Napkin Wars." Younger people were appalled by what they saw as the waste of natural resources by a handful of customers. As they talked about the issue, however, it became obvious that the Napkin Wars represented more—in their eyes—than a campaign to conserve paper. The sight of diners abusing public facilities reminded these young people of the bad old days of their parents and grandparents, when Hong Kong's social life was dominated by refugees who had little stake in the local community. During the 1960s and 1970s, economic insecurities were heightened by the very real prospect that Red Guards might take over the colony at any moment. The game plan was simple during those decades: Make money as quickly as possible and move on. In the 1980s a new generation of local-born youth began treating Hong Kong as home and proceeded to build a public culture better suited to their vision of life in a cosmopolitan city. In this new Hong Kong, consumers are expected to be sophisticated and financially secure, which means that it would be beneath their dignity to abuse public facilities. Still, McDonald's retains control of its napkins. . . .

▪ ▪ ▪ RONALD McDONALD AND THE INVENTION OF BIRTHDAY PARTIES

Until recently most people in Hong Kong did not even know, let alone celebrate, their birthdates in the Western calendrical sense; dates of birth according to the lunar calendar were recorded for divinatory purposes but were not noted in annual rites. By the late 1980s, however, birthday parties, complete with cakes and candles, were the rage in Hong Kong. Any child who was anyone had to have a party, and the most popular venue was a fast food restaurant, with McDonald's ranked above all competitors. The majority of Hong Kong people live in overcrowded flats, which means that parties are rarely held in private homes.

Except for the outlets in central business districts, McDonald's restaurants are packed every Saturday and Sunday with birthday parties, cycled through at the rate of one every hour. A party hostess, provided by the restaurant, leads the children in games while the parents sit on the sidelines, talking quietly among themselves. For a small fee celebrants receive printed invitation cards, photographs, a gift box containing toys and a discount coupon for future trips to McDonald's. Parties are held in a special enclosure, called the Ronald Room, which is equipped with low tables and tiny stools—suitable only for children. Television commercials portray Ronald McDonald leading birthday celebrants on exciting safaris and expeditions. The clown's Cantonese name, Mak Dong Lou Suk-Suk ("Uncle McDonald"), plays on the intimacy of kinship and has helped transform him into one of Hong Kong's most familiar cartoon figures. . . .

■ ■ ■ McDONALD'S AS A YOUTH CENTER

Weekends may be devoted to family dining and birthday parties for younger children, but on weekday afternoons, from 3:00 to 6:00 P.M., McDonald's restaurants are packed with teenagers stopping for a snack on their way home from school. In many outlets 80 percent of the late afternoon clientele appear in school uniforms, turning the restaurants into a sea of white frocks, light blue shirts, and dark trousers. The students, aged between 10 and 17, stake out tables and buy snacks that are shared in groups. The noise level at this time of day is deafening; students shout to friends and dart from table to table. Few adults, other than restaurant staff, are in evidence. It is obvious that McDonald's is treated as an informal youth center, a recreational extension of school where students can unwind after long hours of study. . . .

In contrast to their counterparts in the United States, where fast food chains have devised ways to discourage lingering, McDonald's in Hong Kong does not set a limit on table time. When I asked the managers of several Hong Kong outlets how they coped with so many young people chatting at tables that might otherwise be occupied by paying customers, they all replied that the students were "welcome." The obvious strategy is to turn a potential liability into an asset: "Students create a good atmosphere which is good for our business," said one manager as he watched an army of teenagers—dressed in identical school uniforms—surge into his restaurant. Large numbers of students also use McDonald's as a place to do homework and prepare for exams, often in groups. Study space of any kind, public or private, is hard to find in overcrowded Hong Kong. . . .

■ ■ ■ CONCLUSIONS: WHOSE CULTURE IS IT?

In concluding this [reading] I would like to return to the questions raised in my opening remarks: In what sense, if any, is McDonald's involved in these cultural transformations (the creation of a child-centered consumer culture, for instance)? Has the company helped to create these trends, or merely followed the market? Is this an example of American-inspired, transnational culture crowding out indigenous cultures? . . .

The deeper I dig into the lives of consumers themselves, in Hong Kong and elsewhere, the more complex the picture becomes. Having watched the processes of culture change unfold for nearly thirty years, it is apparent to me that the ordinary people of Hong Kong have most assuredly *not* been stripped of their cultural heritage, nor have they become the uncomprehending dupes of transnational corporations. Younger people—including many of the grandchildren of my former neighbors in the New Territories—are avid consumers of transnational culture in all of its most obvious manifestations: music, fashion, television, and cuisine. At the same time, however, Hong Kong has itself become a major center for the *production* of transnational culture, not just a sinkhole for its *consumption*. Witness, for example, the expansion of Hong Kong popular culture into China, Southeast Asia, and beyond: "Cantopop" music is heard on radio stations in North China, Vietnam, and Japan; the Hong Kong fashion industry influences clothing styles in Los Angeles, Bangkok, and Kuala Lumpur; and, perhaps most significant of all, Hong Kong is emerging as a center for the production and dissemination of satellite television programs throughout East, Southeast, and South Asia.

A lifestyle is emerging in Hong Kong that can best be described as postmodern, postnationalist, and flamboyantly transnational. The wholesale acceptance and appropriation of Big Macs, Ronald McDonald, and birthday parties are small, but significant aspects of this redefinition of Chinese cultural identity. In closing, therefore, it seems appropriate to pose an entirely new set of questions: Where does the transnational end and the local begin? Whose culture is it, anyway? In places like Hong Kong the postcolonial periphery is fast becoming the metropolitan center, where local people are consuming and simultaneously producing new cultural systems.

The Power Elite

C. Wright Mills

introduction ▪ ▪ ▪ ▪

A theme that has run through many of the preceding selections is how groups influence us—how they guide, direct, and even control our behavior. Our membership in some of these groups (as with gender in Reading 11) comes with birth and is involuntary. Other groups we join because we desire the membership. All groups—whether our membership is voluntary or involuntary—influence our thinking and behavior. The broad, overarching groups, which lay the general boundaries for our actions and even our attitudes and perceptions, are called *social institutions*. We are born and we die within social institutions. And between birth and death, we live within them—from family and school to politics and religion.

   A question central to much sociological research concerns power: Who has it, and how is it exercised? In this selection, C. Wright Mills says that power in U.S. society has become concentrated in our economic, political, and military institutions. Not only have these three social institutions grown larger and more centralized, but also they have become more interconnected. As a result, their power has outstripped that of our other social institutions. The interests of the top business, political, and military leaders have coalesced, says Mills, and using his term, these leaders form a *power elite*. This power elite makes the major decisions that so vitally affect our welfare and—with the dominance of the United States in global affairs—the welfare of the world.

Thinking Critically

As you read this selection, ask yourself:

1. If the members of the power elite don't meet with each other, how can they be considered the primary source of power in the United States today?

2. Not everyone agrees with Mills. Compare what Mills says in this selection with the pluralist view of power summarized in Chapter 15 of *Sociology*.

3. Mills identifies the top leaders of the top corporations as the pinnacle of U.S. power. Why doesn't he identify the top military or political leaders as this pinnacle?

The powers of ordinary men* are circumscribed by the everyday worlds in which they live, yet even in these rounds of job, family, and neighborhood they often seem driven by forces they can neither understand nor govern. "Great changes" are beyond their control, but affect their conduct and outlook nonetheless. The very framework of modern society confines them to projects not their own, but from every side, such changes now press upon the men and women of the mass society, who accordingly feel that they are without purpose in an epoch in which they are without power.

But not all men are in this sense ordinary. As the means of information and of power are centralized, some men come to occupy positions in American society from which they can look down upon, so to speak, and by their decisions mightily affect, the everyday worlds of ordinary men and women. They are not made by their jobs; they set up and break down jobs for thousands of others; they are not confined by simple family responsibilities; they can escape. They may live in many hotels and houses, but they are bound by no one community. They need not merely "meet the demands of the day and hour"; in some part, they create these demands, and cause others to meet them. Whether or not they profess their power, their technical and political experience of it far transcends that of the underlying population. What Jacob Burckhardt said of "great men," most Americans might well say of their elite: "They are all that we are not."

The power elite is composed of men whose positions enable them to transcend the ordinary environments of ordinary men and women; they are in positions to make decisions having major consequences. Whether they do or do not make such decisions is less important than the fact that they do occupy such pivotal positions: Their failure to act, their failure to make decisions, is itself an act that is often of greater consequence than the decisions they do make. For they are in command of the major hierarchies and organizations of modern society. They rule the big corporations. They run the machinery of the state and claim its prerogatives. They direct the military establishment. They occupy the strategic command posts of the social structure, in which are now centered the effective means of the power and the wealth and the celebrity which they enjoy.

The power elite are not solitary rulers. Advisers and consultants, spokesmen and opinion-makers are often the captains of their higher thought and decision. Immediately below the elite are the professional politicians of the middle levels of power, in the Congress and in the pressure groups, as well as among the new and old upper classes of town and city and region. Mingling with them, in curious ways which we shall explore, are those professional celebrities who live by being continually displayed but are never, so long as they remain celebrities, displayed enough. If such celebrities are not at the head of any dominating hierarchy, they do often have the

---

*As with the first article in this anthology, when Mills wrote, the literary custom was to use "men" to refer to both men and women and "his" to both hers and his. Although the writing style has changed, the sociological ideas are as significant as ever.

power to distract the attention of the public or afford sensations to the masses, or, more directly, to gain the ear of those who do occupy positions of direct power. More or less unattached, as critics of morality and technicians of power, as spokesmen of God and creators of mass sensibility, such celebrities and consultants are part of the immediate scene in which the drama of the elite is enacted. But that drama itself is centered in the command posts of the major institutional hierarchies.

The truth about the nature and the power of the elite is not some secret which men of affairs know but will not tell. Such men hold quite various theories about their own roles in the sequence of event and decision. Often they are uncertain about their roles, and even more often they allow their fears and their hopes to affect their assessment of their own power. No matter how great their actual power, they tend to be less acutely aware of it than of the resistances of others to its use. Moreover, most American men of affairs have learned well the rhetoric of public relations, in some cases even to the point of using it when they are alone, and thus coming to believe it. The personal awareness of the actors is only one of the several sources one must examine in order to understand the higher circles. Yet many who believe that there is no elite, or at any rate none of any consequence, rest their argument upon what men of affairs believe about themselves, or at least assert in public.

There is, however, another view: those who feel, even if vaguely, that a compact and powerful elite of great importance does now prevail in America often base that feeling upon the historical trend of our time. They have felt, for example, the domination of the military event, and from this they infer that generals and admirals, as well as other men of decision influenced by them, must be enormously powerful. They hear that the Congress has again abdicated to a handful of men decisions clearly related to the issue of war or peace. They know that the bomb was dropped over Japan in the name of the United States of America, although they were at no time consulted about the matter. They feel that they live in a time of big decisions; they know that they are not making any. Accordingly, as they consider the present as history, they infer that at its center, making decisions or failing to make them, there must be an elite of power.

On the one hand, those who share this feeling about big historical events assume that there is an elite and that its power is great. On the other hand, those who listen carefully to the reports of men apparently involved in the great decisions often do not believe that there is an elite whose powers are of decisive consequence.

Both views must be taken into account, but neither is adequate. The way to understand the power of the American elite lies neither solely in recognizing the historic scale of events nor in accepting the personal awareness reported by men of apparent decision. Behind such men and behind the events of history, linking the two, are the major institutions of modern society. *These hierarchies of state [politics] and corporation [business] and army [military] constitute the means of power* [italics added]; as such they are now of a consequence not before equaled in human history—and at their summits, there are now those command posts of modern society which offer us the sociological key to an understanding of the role of the higher circles in America.

Within American society, major national power now resides in the economic, the political, and the military domains. Other institutions seem off to the side of modern history, and, on occasion, duly subordinated to these. No family is as directly powerful in national affairs as any major corporation; no church is as directly powerful in the external biographies of young men in America today as the military establishment; no college is as powerful in the shaping of momentous events as the National Security Council. Religious, educational, and family institutions are not autonomous centers of national power; on the contrary, these decentralized areas are increasingly shaped by the big three, in which developments of decisive and immediate consequence now occur.

Families and churches and schools adapt to modern life; governments and armies and corporations shape it; and, as they do so, they turn these lesser institutions into means for their ends. Religious institutions provide chaplains to the armed forces where they are used as a means of increasing the effectiveness of its morale to kill. Schools select and train men for their jobs in corporations and their specialized tasks in the armed forces. The extended family has, of course, long been broken up by the industrial revolution, and now the son and the father are removed from the family, by compulsion if need be, whenever the army of the state sends out the call. And the symbols of all these lesser institutions are used to legitimate the power and the decisions of the big three.

The life-fate of the modern individual depends not only upon the family into which he was born or which he enters by marriage, but increasingly upon the corporation in which he spends the most alert hours of his best years; not only upon the school where he is educated as a child and adolescent, but also upon the state which touches him throughout his life; not only upon the church in which on occasion he hears the word of God, but also upon the army in which he is disciplined.

If the centralized state could not rely upon the inculcation of nationalist loyalties in public and private schools, its leaders would promptly seek to modify the decentralized educational system. If the bankruptcy rate among the top five hundred corporations were as high as the general divorce rate among the [57] million married couples, there would be economic catastrophe on an international scale. If members of armies gave to them no more of their lives than do believers to the churches to which they belong, there would be a military crisis.

Within each of the big three, the typical institutional unit has become enlarged, has become administrative, and, in the power of its decisions, has become centralized. Behind these developments there is a fabulous technology, for as institutions, they have incorporated this technology and guide it, even as it shapes and paces their developments.

The economy—once a great scatter of small productive units in autonomous balance—has become dominated by two or three hundred giant corporations, administratively and politically interrelated, which together hold the keys to economic decisions.

The political order, once a decentralized set of several dozen states with a weak spinal cord, has become a centralized, executive establishment which has taken up into itself many powers previously scattered, and now enters into each and every cranny of the social structure.

The military order, once a slim establishment in a context of distrust fed by state militia, has become the largest and most expensive feature of government, and, although well versed in smiling public relations, now has all the grim and clumsy efficiency of a sprawling bureaucratic domain.

In each of these institutional areas, the means of power at the disposal of decision makers have increased enormously; their central executive powers have been enhanced; within each of them modern administrative routines have been elaborated and tightened up.

As each of these domains becomes enlarged and centralized, the consequences of its activities become greater, and its traffic with the others increases. The decisions of a handful of corporations bear upon military and political as well as upon economic developments around the world. The decisions of the military establishment rest upon and grievously affect political life as well as the very level of economic activity. The decisions made within the political domain determine economic activities and military programs. There is no longer, on the one hand, an economy, and, on the other hand, a political order containing a military establishment unimportant to politics and to money-making. There is a political economy linked, in a thousand ways, with military institutions and decisions. On each side of the world-split running through central Europe and around the Asiatic rimlands, there is an ever-increasing inter-locking of economic, military, and political structures. If there is government intervention in the corporate economy, so is there corporate intervention in the governmental process. In the structural sense, this triangle of power is the source of the interlocking directorate that is most important for the historical structure of the present.

The fact of the interlocking is clearly revealed at each of the points of crisis of modern capitalist society—slump, war, and boom. In each, men of decision are led to an awareness of the interdependence of the major institutional orders. In the nineteenth century, when the scale of all institutions was smaller, their liberal integration was achieved in the automatic economy, by an autonomous play of market forces, and in the automatic political domain, by the bargain and the vote. It was then assumed that out of the imbalance and friction that followed the limited decisions then possible a new equilibrium would in due course emerge. That can no longer be assumed, and it is not assumed by the men at the top of each of the three dominant hierarchies.

For given the scope of their consequences, decisions—and indecisions—any one of these ramify into the others, and hence top decisions tend either to become coordinated or to lead to a commanding indecision. It has not always been like this. When numerous small entrepreneurs made up the economy, for example, many of them could fail and the consequences still remain local; political and military authorities did not intervene. But now, given political expectations and military commitments, can they afford to allow key units of the private corporate economy to break down in slump? Increasingly, they do intervene in economic affairs, and as they do so, the controlling decisions in each order are inspected by agents of the other two, and economic, military, and political structures are interlocked.

At the pinnacle of each of the three enlarged and centralized domains, there have arisen those higher circles which make up the economic, the political, and the military elites. At the top of the economy, among the corporate rich, there are the chief executives; at the top of the political order, the members of the political directorate; at the top of the military establishment, the elite of soldier-statesmen clustered in and around the Joint Chiefs of Staff and the upper echelon. As each of these domains has coincided with the others, as decisions tend to become total in their consequence, the leading men in each of the three domains of power—the warlords, the corporation chieftains, the political directorate—tend to come together, to form the power elite of America.

The higher circles in and around these command posts are often thought of in terms of what their members possess: They have a greater share than other people of the things and experiences that are most highly valued. From this point of view, the elite are simply those who have the most of what there is to have, which is generally held to include money, power, and prestige—as well as all the ways of life to which these lead. But the elite are not simply those who have the most, for they could not "have the most" were it not for their positions in the great institutions. For such institutions are the necessary bases of power, of wealth, and of prestige, and at the same time, the chief means of exercising power, of acquiring and retaining wealth, and of cashing in the higher claims for prestige.

By the powerful we mean, of course, those who are able to realize their will, even if others resist it. No one, accordingly, can be truly powerful unless he has access to the command of major institutions, for it is over these institutional means of power that the truly powerful are, in the first instance, powerful. Higher politicians and key officials of government command such institutional power; so do admirals and generals, and so do the major owners and executives of the larger corporations. Not all power, it is true, is anchored in and exercised by means of such institutions, but only within and through them can power be more or less continuous and important.

Wealth also is acquired and held in and through institutions. The pyramid of wealth cannot be understood merely in terms of the very rich; for the great inheriting families, as we shall see, are now supplemented by the corporate institutions of modern society: Every one of the very rich families has been and is closely connected—always legally and frequently managerially as well—with one of the multimillion-dollar corporations.

The modern corporation is the prime source of wealth, but, in latter-day capitalism, the political apparatus also opens and closes many avenues to wealth. The amount as well as the source of income, the power over consumers' goods as well as over productive capital, are determined by position within the political economy. If our interest in the very rich goes beyond their lavish or their miserly consumption, we must examine their relations to modern forms of corporate property as well as to the state; for such relations now determine the chances of men to secure big property and to receive high income.

Great prestige increasingly follows the major institutional units of the social structure. It is obvious that prestige depends, often quite decisively, upon access to the publicity machines that are now a central and normal feature of all the big institutions of modern America. Moreover, one feature of these hierarchies of corporation, state, and military establishment is that their top positions are increasingly interchangeable. One result of this is the accumulative nature of prestige. Claims for prestige, for example, may be initially based on military roles, then expressed in and augmented by an educational institution run by corporate executives; and cashed in, finally, in the political order, where, for [top military leaders who become president, such as] General Eisenhower and those [they represent], power and prestige finally meet at the very peak. Like wealth and power, prestige tends to be cumulative: The more of it you have, the more you can get. These values also tend to be translatable into one another: The wealthy find it easier than the poor to gain power; those with status find it easier than those without it to control opportunities for wealth.

If we took the one hundred most powerful men in America, the one hundred wealthiest, and the one hundred most celebrated away from the institutional positions they now occupy, away from their resources of men and women and money, away from the media of mass communication that are now focused upon them— then they would be powerless and poor and uncelebrated. For power is not of a man. Wealth does not center in the person of the wealthy. Celebrity is not inherent in any personality. To be celebrated, to be wealthy, to have power requires access to major institutions, for the institutional positions men occupy determine in large part their chances to have and to hold these valued experiences.

The people of the higher circles may also be conceived as members of a top social stratum, as a set of groups whose members know one another, see one another socially and at business, and so, in making decisions, take one another into account. The elite, according to this conception, feel themselves to be, and are felt by others to be, the inner circle of "the upper social classes." They form a more or less compact social and psychological entity; they have become self-conscious members of a social class. People are either accepted into this class or they are not, and there is a qualitative split, rather than merely a numerical scale, separating them from those who are not elite. They are more or less aware of themselves as a social class and they behave toward one another differently from the way they do toward members of other classes. They accept one another, understand one another, marry one another, tend to work and to think if not together at least alike.

Now, we do not want by our definition to prejudge whether the elite of the command posts are conscious members of such a socially recognized class, or whether considerable proportions of the elite derive from such a clear and distinct class. These are matters to be investigated. Yet in order to be able to recognize what we intend to investigate, we must note something that all biographies and memoirs of the wealthy and the powerful and the eminent make clear: No matter what else they may be, the people of these higher circles are involved in a set of overlapping "crowds" and intricately connected "cliques." There is a kind of mutual attraction among those who "sit on the same terrace"—although this often becomes clear to them, as well as to others, only at the point at which they feel the need to draw the line; only when, in their common defense, they come to understand what they have in common, and so close their ranks against outsiders.

The idea of such ruling stratum implies that most of its members have similar social origins, that throughout their lives they maintain a network of internal connections, and that to some degree there is an interchangeability of position between the various hierarchies of money and power and celebrity. We must, of course, note at once that if such an elite stratum does exist, its social visibility and its form, for very solid historical reasons, are quite different from those of the noble cousinhoods that once ruled various European nations.

That American society has never passed through a feudal epoch is of decisive importance to the nature of the American elite, as well as to American society as a historic whole. For it means that no nobility or aristocracy, established before the capitalist era, has stood in tense opposition to the higher bourgeoisie. It means that this bourgeoisie has monopolized not only wealth but prestige and power as well. It means that no set of noble families has commanded the top positions and monopolized the values that are generally held in high esteem; and certainly that no set has done so explicitly by inherited right. It means that no high church dignitaries or court nobilities, no entrenched landlords with honorific accouterments, no monopolists of high army posts have opposed the enriched bourgeoisie and in the name of birth and prerogative successfully resisted its self-making.

But this does *not* mean that there are no upper strata in the United States. That they emerged from a "middle class" that had no recognized aristocratic superiors does not mean they remained middle class when enormous increases in wealth made their own superiority possible. Their origins and their newness may have made the upper strata less visible in America than elsewhere. But in America today there are in fact tiers and ranges of wealth and power of which people in the middle and lower ranks know very little and may not even dream. There are families who, in their well-being, are quite insulated from the economic jolts and lurches felt by the merely prosperous and those farther down the scale. There are also men of power who in quite small groups make decisions of enormous consequence for the underlying population. . . .

16

Family in Transition

Arlene S. Skolnick and Jerome H. Skolnick

introduction

The social institution that introduces us to society is the family. Because it is within the family that we learn our basic orientations to social life, the family is considered to be the basic building block of society. Within this great socializer, we learn our language and the basic norms that guide our behavior. It is here that we are introduced to ways of eating and dressing, to ideas of punctuality and neatness, and to highly refined norms that are difficult to put into words, such as how loudly we should laugh at people's jokes or how much self-centeredness we are allowed to display as we interact with others. Our family also teaches us its views of gender, race–ethnicity, social class, religion, politics, work, school, people with disabilities, people on welfare, children, and the elderly. From our family, we even learn attitudes about our own intelligence, attractiveness, and our body. This early socialization becomes part of our basic outlook on life—the ways we evaluate others and ourselves.

Like our other social institutions, U.S. families are changing. They have become smaller, they have accumulated a lot of debt, parental authority has decreased, people are marrying later, more children are born to single mothers, and divorce has made families fragile. (Some sociologists point out that because parents used to die much younger, today's children have about the same chance of living through childhood with both their biological parents as did children of two hundred years ago. Either way, marriage *is* fragile.) Sometimes, we look at the past with nostalgia. If only we could have family life like it used to be in those *Leave It to Beaver* years! The comparisons of present and past family life in this reading should hold a few surprises.

Thinking Critically

As you read this selection, ask yourself:

1. Do you think you would prefer the family life of the 1950s or 1960s to that of today? Why?

2. What do the Skolnicks mean when they say that "ambivalence sets close relationships apart from less intimate ones"?

3. What are the major differences between family life of the past and that of today?

Everybody agrees that families have changed dramatically over the past several decades, but there is no consensus on what the changes mean. The majority of women, including mothers of young children, are now working outside the home. Divorce rates have risen sharply. (But they have leveled off since 1979.) Twenty-eight percent of children are living in single parent families. Cohabitation—once called "shacking up" or "living in sin"—is a widespread practice. The sexual double standard—the norm that demanded virginity for the bride, but not the groom—has largely disappeared from mainstream American culture. There are mother-only families, father-only families, grandparents raising grandchildren, and gay and lesbian families.

Indeed, the growing public acceptance of homosexuals is one of the most striking trends of recent time, despite persisting stigma and the threat of violence. Local governments and some leading corporations have granted gays increasing recognition as domestic partners entitled to spousal benefits. In June 2003, the Supreme Court struck down the last state laws that made gay sex a crime. The following November 18, the Massachusetts Supreme Judicial Court ruled that gays have the right to marry. These rulings have set off a national debate and a demand by conservatives to sponsor a Constitutional amendment forbidding same-sex marriage.

Does all of this mean the family is "in decline"? In crisis? Are we witnessing a moral meltdown? Why is there so much anxiety about the family? Why do so many families feel so much stress and strain? We can't answer these questions if we assume that family life takes place in a social vacuum. Social and economic circumstances have always had a profound impact on families, and when the world outside changes in important ways, families must also reshape themselves.

All these shifts in family life are part of an ongoing global revolution. All industrialized nations, and many of the emerging ones, have experienced similar changes. In no other Western country, however, has family change been so traumatic and divisive as in the United States. For example, the two-earner family is the most common family pattern in the United States; 75 percent of mothers of children under 18 and more than 60 percent of those with young children work outside the home. Yet the question of whether mothers "should" work is still a fiercely debated issue—except if the mother is on welfare.

Thus, the typical pattern for public discussion of family issues is a polarized, emotional argument. Lurching from one hot topic to another, every issue is presented as an either-or choice: Which is better for children—two parents or one? Is divorce bad or good for children? Should mothers of young children work or not?

This kind of argument makes it difficult to discuss the issues and problems facing the family in a realistic way. It doesn't describe the range of views among family scholars, and it doesn't fit the research evidence. For example, the right question to ask about divorce is "Under what circumstances is divorce harmful or beneficial to children?" (Amato, 1994). In most public debates about divorce, however, that question is never asked, and the public never hears the useful information they should.

Still another problem with popular discourse about the family is that it exaggerates the amount of change that has actually occurred. For example, consider . . . that only 7 percent of American households fit the model of the traditional family. This number, or something like it, is often cited by conservatives as proof that the institution is in danger of disappearing unless the government steps in to restore marriage and the two-parent family. At the opposite end of the political spectrum are those who celebrate the alleged decline of the traditional family and welcome the new family forms that have supposedly replaced it.

But is it true that only 7 percent of American households are traditional families? It all depends, as the saying goes, on how you define "traditional." The statement is true if you count only families with children under 18 in which only the husband works outside the home. But if the wife works too, as most married women now do, the family doesn't count as "traditional" by that definition. Neither does the recently married couple who do not have children yet. The couple whose youngest child turns 18 is no longer counted as a "traditional" family either.

Despite the current high divorce rates (actually down from 1979), Americans have not abandoned the institution of marriage. The United States has the highest marriage rate in the industrial world. About 90 percent of Americans marry at some point in their lives, and virtually all who do either have, or want children. Further, surveys repeatedly show that family is central to the lives of most Americans. Family ties are their deepest source of satisfaction and meaning, as well as the source of their greatest worries (Mellman, Lazarus, and Rivlin, 1990). In sum, family life in the United States is a complex mixture of both continuity and change.

While the transformations of the past three decades do not mean the end of family life, they have brought a number of new difficulties. For example, although most families now depend on the earnings of wives and mothers, the rest of society has not caught up to the new realities. For example, most schools are out of step with parents' working hours—they let out at 3:00, and still maintain the long summer vacations that once allowed children to work on the family farm. Most jobs, especially well-paying ones, are based on the male model; that is, a worker who can work full-time or longer without interruptions. An earnings gap persists between men and women in both blue-collar and white-collar jobs. Employed wives and mothers still bear most of the workload in the home.

■ ■ ■ ■ UNDERSTANDING THE CHANGING FAMILY

During the same years in which the family was becoming the object of public anxiety and political debate, a torrent of new research on the family was pouring forth. The study of the family had come to excite the interest of scholars in a range of disciplines—history, demography, economics, law, and psychology. As a result of this research, we now have much more information available about families of the past, as well as current families, than we have ever had before.

The main outcome of this research has been to debunk myths about family life, both past and present. Nevertheless, the myths persist and help to fuel the cultural wars over family change.

The Myth of Universality

To say that families are the same everywhere is in some sense true. Yet families also vary in many ways—in who is included as a family member, emotional environments, living arrangements, ideologies, social and kinship networks, and economic and other functions. Although anthropologists have tried to come up with a single definition of family that would hold across time and place, they generally have concluded that doing so is not useful (Geertz, 1965; Stephens, 1963).

For example, although marriage is virtually universal across cultures, the definition of marriage is not the same. Although many cultures have weddings and notions of monogamy and permanence, some lack one or more of these attributes. In some cultures, the majority of people mate and have children without legal marriage and often without living together. In other societies, husbands, wives, and children do not live together under the same roof.

In our own society, the assumption of universality has usually defined what is normal and natural both for research and therapy and has subtly influenced our thinking to regard deviations from the nuclear family as sick, perverse, or immoral. As Suzanne Keller (1971) once observed, "The fallacy of universality has done students of behavior a great disservice by leading us to seek and hence to find a single pattern that has blinded us to historical precedents for multiple legitimate family arrangements."

The Myth of Family Harmony

"Happy families are all alike; each unhappy family is unhappy in its own way." This well-known quotation from Leo Tolstoy is a good example of the widespread tendency to divide families into two opposite types—happy or unhappy, good or bad, "normal" or "dysfunctional." The sitcom families of the 1950s—*Ozzie and Harriet, Leave It to Beaver,* and the rest—still serve as "ideal" models for how families should be.

But few families, then or now, fit neatly into either category. Even the most loving relationships inevitably involve negative feelings as well as positive ones. It is this ambivalence that sets close relationships apart from less intimate ones. Indeed, from what we have learned about the Nelson family over the years, the real Ozzie and Harriet did not have an Ozzie and Harriet family.

Only in fairly recent times has the darker side of family life come to public attention. For example, child abuse was only "discovered" as a social problem in the 1960s. In recent years, family scholars have been studying family violence such as child or spousal abuse to better understand the normal strains of family life. More police officers are killed and injured dealing with family fights than in dealing with any other kind of situation; of all the relationships between murderers and their victims, the family relationship is most common. Studies of family violence reveal that it is much more widespread than had been assumed, cannot easily be attributed to mental illness, and is not confined to the lower classes. Family violence seems to be a product of psychological tensions and external stresses that can affect all families at all social levels.

The study of family interaction has also undermined the traditional image of the happy, harmonious family. About three decades ago, researchers and therapists began to bring mental patients and their families together to watch how they behaved with one another. Oddly, researchers had not studied whole family groups before.

At first the family interactions were interpreted as pathogenic: a parent expressing affection in words but showing nonverbal hostility; alliances being made between different family members; families having secrets; or one family member being singled out as a scapegoat to be blamed for the family's troubles. As more and more families were studied, however, such patterns were found in many families, not just in those families with a schizophrenic child. Although this line of research did not uncover the cause of schizophrenia, it revealed that normal, ordinary families can often seem dysfunctional, or, in the words of one study, they may be "difficult environments for interaction."

The Myth of Parental Determinism

The kind of family a child grows up in leaves a profound, lifelong impact. But a growing body of studies shows that early family experience is not the all-powerful, irreversible influence it has sometimes been thought to be. An unfortunate childhood does not doom a person to an unhappy adulthood. Nor does a happy childhood guarantee a similarly blessed future (Emde and Harmon, 1984; Macfarlane, 1964; Rubin, 1996).

Any parent knows that child rearing is not like molding clay or writing on a blank slate. Rather, it's a two-way process in which both parent and child influence each other. Children come into this world with their own temperaments and other characteristics. Moreover, from a very early age, children are active perceivers and thinkers. Finally, parents and children do not live in a social vacuum; children are also influenced by the world around them and the people in it—relatives, family friends, their neighborhoods, other children, their schools, as well as the media.

The traditional view of parental determinism has been challenged by the extreme opposite view. Psychologist Judith Rich Harris asserts that parents have very little impact on their children's development. In her book, *The Nurture Assumption: Why Children Turn Out the Way They Do* (1998), Harris argues that genetics and peer groups, not parents, determine how a child will develop. As in so many debates about the family, both extremes oversimplify complex realities.

The Myth of a Stable Past

Laments about the current state of decay of the family imply some earlier era when the family was more stable and harmonious. Historians have not, in fact, located a golden age of the family. Nor have they found any time or place when families did not vary in many ways from whatever the standard model was. Indeed, they have found that premarital sexuality, illegitimacy, and generational conflict can best be studied as a part of family life itself rather than as separate categories of deviation.

The most shocking finding of recent years is the prevalence of child abandonment and infanticide throughout European history. It now appears that infanticide provided a major means of population control in all societies lacking reliable contraception, Europe included, and that it was practiced by families on legitimate children (Hrdy, 1999).

Rather than being a simple instinctive trait, having profound love for a newborn child seems to require two: the infant must have a decent chance of surviving, and the parents must feel that the infant is not competing with them and their older children in a struggle for survival. Throughout many centuries of European history, both of these conditions were lacking.

Another myth about the family is that it has been a static, unchanging form until recently, when it began to come apart. In reality, families have always been in flux; when the world around them changes, families have to change in response. At periods when a whole society undergoes some major transformation, family change may be especially rapid and dislocating.

In many ways, the era we are living through today resembles two earlier periods of family crisis and transformation in U.S. history (see Skolnick, 1991). The first occurred in the early nineteenth century, when the industrial era moved work out of the home (Ryan, 1981). In the older pattern, most people lived on farms. A father was not just the head of the household, but also boss of the family enterprise. Mother and children and hired hands worked under his supervision.

But when work moved out, so did the father and the older sons and daughters, leaving behind the mother and the younger children. These dislocations unleashed an era of personal stress and cultural confusion. Eventually, a new model of family emerged that not only reflected the new separation of work and family, but also glorified it.

The household now became idealized as "home sweet home," an emotional and spiritual shelter from the heartless world outside. Many of our culture's most basic ideas about the family and gender were formed at this time. The mother-at-home, father-out-at-work model that most people think of as "traditional" was in fact the first version of the modern family.

Historians label this nineteenth century model of the family "Victorian" because it became influential in England and Western Europe, as well as in the United States, during the reign of Queen Victoria. It reflected, in idealized form, the nineteenth-century middle-class family. The Victorian model became the prevailing cultural definition of family, but few families could live up to the ideal in all its particulars. Working-class, black, and ethnic families, for example, could not get by without the economic contributions of wives, mothers, and daughters. Even for middle-class families, the Victorian ideal prescribed a standard of perfection that was virtually impossible to fulfill (Demos, 1986).

Eventually, social change overtook the Victorian model. Beginning around the 1880s, another period of rapid economic, social, and cultural change unsettled Victorian family patterns, especially their gender arrangements. Several generations of so-called new women challenged Victorian notions of femininity.

They became educated, pursued careers, became involved in political causes—including their own—and created the first wave of feminism. This ferment culminated in the victory of the women's suffrage movement. It was followed by the 1920s' jazz-age era of flappers and flaming youth—the first, and probably the major, sexual revolution of the twentieth century.

Another cultural crisis ensued, until a new cultural blueprint emerged—the companionate model of marriage and the family. The new model was a modern, more relaxed version of the Victorian family; companionship and sexual intimacy were now defined as central to marriage.

This highly abbreviated history of family and cultural change forms the necessary backdrop for understanding the family upheavals of the late twentieth and early twenty-first centuries. As in earlier times, major changes in the economy and society have destabilized an existing model of family life and the everyday patterns and practices that have sustained it.

We have experienced a triple revolution: first, the move toward a postindustrial service and information economy; second, a life course revolution brought about by reductions in mortality and fertility; and third, a psychological transformation rooted mainly in rising educational levels. Although these shifts have profound implications for everyone, women have been the pacesetters of change. Most women's lives and expectations over the past three decades, inside and outside the family, have departed drastically from those of their own mothers. Men's lives today also are different from their fathers' generation, but to a much lesser extent.

■ ■ ■ THE TRIPLE REVOLUTION

The Postindustrial Family

A service and information economy produces large numbers of jobs that, unlike factory work, seem suitable for women. Yet as Jessie Bernard (1982) once observed, the transformation of a housewife into a paid worker outside the home sends tremors through every family relationship. It blurs the sharp contrast between men's and women's roles that mark the breadwinner/housewife pattern. It also reduces women's economic dependence on men, thereby making it easier for women to leave unhappy marriages.

Beyond drawing women out of the home, shifts in the nature of work and a rapidly changing globalized economy have unsettled the lives of individuals and families at all class levels. The well-paying industrial jobs that once enabled a blue-collar worker to own a home and support a family are no longer available. The once secure jobs that sustained the "organization men" and their families in the 1950s and 1960s have been made shaky by downsizing, an unstable economy, corporate takeovers, and a rapid pace of technological change.

The new economic uncertainty has also made the transition to adulthood increasingly problematic. In the postwar years, particularly in the United States, young people entered adulthood in one giant step. They found jobs, often out of high school, married young, left home, and had children quickly. Today, few young adults can afford to marry and have children in their late teens or early twenties. In an economy where a college degree is necessary to earn a living wage, early marriage impedes education for both men and women.

Those who do not go on to college have little access to jobs that can sustain a family. Particularly in the inner cities of the United States, growing numbers of young people have come to see no future for themselves in the ordinary world of work. In middle-class families, a narrowing opportunity structure has increased anxieties about downward mobility for offspring and parents as well. The "incompletely launched young adult syndrome" has become common: Many young adults fail to launch careers and become successfully independent adults, and many even come home to crowd their parents' empty nest (Schnaiberg and Goldenberg, 1989).

The Life Course Revolution

We cannot hope to understand current predicaments of family life without understanding how drastically the basic realities of life and death changed over the twentieth century. In 1900, average life expectancy was 47 years. Infants had the highest mortality rates, but young and middle-aged adults were often struck down by infectious diseases. Before the turn of the twentieth century, only 40 percent of women lived through all the stages of a normal life course: growing up, marrying, having children, and surviving with a spouse to the age of 50 (Uhlenberg, 1980).

Declining mortality rates have had a profound effect on women's lives. Women today are living longer and having fewer children. When infant and child mortality rates fall, women no longer have five, seven, or nine children to ensure that two or three will survive to adulthood. After rearing children, the average woman can look forward to three or four decades without maternal responsibilities.

One of the most important changes in contemporary marriage is the potential length of marriage and the number of years spent without children in the home. Our current high divorce rates may be a by-product of this shift. By the 1970s, the statistically average couple spent only 18 percent of their married lives raising young children, compared with 54 percent a century ago (Bane, 1976). As a result, marriage is becoming defined less as a union between parents raising a brood of children and more as a personal relationship between two individuals.

A Psychological Revolution

The third major transformation is a set of psychocultural changes that might be described as "psychological gentrification" (Skolnick, 1991). That is, cultural advantages once enjoyed only by the upper classes—in particular, education—have been extended to those lower down on the socioeconomic scale. Psychological gentrification also involves greater leisure time, travel, and exposure to information, as well as a general rise in the standard of living. Despite the persistence of poverty, unemployment, and economic insecurity in the industrialized world, far less of the population than in the historical past is living at the level of sheer subsistence.

Throughout Western society, rising levels of education and related changes have been linked to a complex set of shifts in personal and political attitudes. One of these is a more psychological approach to life—greater introspectiveness and a yearning for warmth and intimacy in family and other relationships (Veroff, Douvan, and Kulka, 1981). There is also evidence of an increasing preference on the part of both men and women for a more companionate ideal of marriage and a more democratic family. More broadly, these changes in attitude have been described as a shift to "postmaterialist values," emphasizing self-expression, tolerance, equality, and a concern for the quality of life (Inglehart, 1990).

The multiple social transformations of our era have brought both costs and benefits: Family relations have become both more fragile and more emotionally rich; longevity has brought us a host of problems as well as the gift of extended life. Although change has brought greater opportunities for women, persisting gender inequality means women have borne a large share of the costs of these gains. But we cannot turn the clock back to the family models of the past.

Despite the upheavals of recent decades, the emotional and cultural significance of the family persists. Family remains the center of most people's lives and, as numerous surveys show, is a cherished value. Although marriage has become more fragile, the parent-child relationship—especially the mother-child relationship—remains a core attachment across the life course (Rossi and Rossi, 1990). The family, however, can be both "here to stay" and beset with difficulties.

Most European countries have recognized for some time that governments must play a role in supplying an array of supports to families' health care, children's allowances, housing subsidies, support for working parents and children (such as child care, parental leave, and shorter work days for parents), as well as an array of services for the elderly. Each country's response to these changes, as we noted earlier, has been shaped by its own political and cultural traditions. The United States remains embroiled in a cultural war over the family; many social commentators and political leaders have promised to reverse the recent trends and restore the "traditional" family. In contrast, other Western nations, including Canada and other English-speaking countries, have responded to family change by trying to remedy the problems brought about by economic and social transformations. As a result of these policies, these countries have been spared much of the poverty and other social ills that have plagued the United States in recent decades.

Looking Ahead

The world at the beginning of the twenty-first century is vastly different from what it was at the beginning, or even the middle, of the twentieth century. Families are struggling to adapt to new realities. The countries that have been at the leading edge of family change still find themselves caught between yesterday's norms, today's new realities, and an uncertain future. As we have seen, changes in women's lives have been a pivotal factor in recent family trends. In many countries there is a considerable difference between men's and women's attitudes and expectations of one another. Even where both partners accept a more equal division of labor in the home, there is often a gap between beliefs and behavior. In no country have employers, the government, or men fully caught up to the changes in women's lives.

Families have always struggled with outside circumstances and inner conflict. Our current troubles inside and outside the family are genuine, but we should never forget that many of the most vexing issues confronting us derive from benefits of modernization few of us would be willing to give up—for example, longer, healthier lives, and the ability to choose how many children to have and when to have them.

When most people died before they reached age 50, there was no problem of a large elderly population to care for. Nor was adolescence a difficult stage of life when children worked; education was a privilege of the rich, and a person's place in society was determined by heredity rather than choice.

In short, family life is bound up with the social, economic, and cultural circumstances of particular times and places. We are no longer peasants, Puritans, pioneers, or even suburbanites circa 1955. We face a world earlier generations could hardly imagine, and we must find new ways to cope with it.

REFERENCES

Amato, P. R. 1994. Life span adjustment of children to their parents' divorce. *The Future of Children* 4, no. 1 (Spring).

Bane, M. J. 1976. *Here to Stay.* New York: Basic Books.

Bernard, J. 1982. *The Future of Marriage.* New York: Bantam.

Demos, J. 1986. *Past, Present, and Personal.* New York: Oxford University Press.

Emde, R. N., and R. J. Harmon, eds. 1984. *Continuities and Discontinuities in Development.* New York: Plenum Press.

Geertz, G. 1965. The impact of the concept of culture on the concept of man. In *New Views of the Nature of Man,* edited by J. R. Platt. Chicago: University of Chicago Press.

Harris, J. R. 1998. *The Nurture Assumption: Why Children Turn Out the Way They Do.* New York: Free Press.

Hrdy, S. B. 1999. *Mother Nature.* New York: Pantheon Books.

Inglehart, R. 1990. *Culture Shift.* N.J.: Princeton University Press.

Keller, S. 1971. Does the family have a future? *Journal of Comparative Studies,* Spring.

Macfarlane, J. W. 1964. Perspectives on personality consistency and change from the guidance study. *Vita Humana* 7: 115–126.

Mellman, A., E. Lazarus, and A. Rivlin. 1990. Family time, family values. In *Rebuilding the Nest,* edited by D. Blankenhorn, S. Bayme, and J. Elshtain. Milwaukee, WI: Family Service America.

Rossi, A. S., and P. H. Rossi. 1990. *Of Human Bonding: Parent-Child Relations across the Life Course.* Hawthorne, NY: Aldine de Gruyter.

Rubin, L. 1996. *The Transcendent Child.* New York: Basic Books.

Ryan, M. 1981. *The Cradle of the Middle Class.* New York: Cambridge University Press.

Schnaiberg, A., and S. Goldenberg. 1989. From empty nest to crowded nest: The dynamics of incompletely launched young adults. *Social Problems* 36, no. 3 (June): 251–269.

Skolnick, A. 1991. *Embattled Paradise: The American Family in an Age of Uncertainty.* New York: Basic Books.

Stephens, W. N. 1963. *The Family in Cross-Cultural Perspective.* New York: World.

Veroff, J., E. Douvan, and R. A. Kulka. 1981. *The Inner American: A Self-Portrait from 1957 to 1976.* New York: Basic Books.

College Athletes and Role Conflict

Peter Adler and Patricia A. Adler

introduction

In earlier societies, there was no separate social institution called education. There were no special buildings called schools, and no people who earned their living as teachers. Instead, as an integral part of growing up, children learned what was necessary to get along in life. If hunting or cooking were the essential skills required for survival and taking on adult roles in their group, then people who already possessed those skills taught them to children. Socialization into adult roles by family and friends was education.

With an informal system of passing on knowledge and skills no longer adequate, a formal social institution known as education has become highly significant in industrial and postindustrial societies. With each generation, the amount of education that young people are expected to attain has increased. A hundred years ago, graduating from the eighth grade was considered to be sufficient education for almost everyone. Only a few young people went on to *higher* education in a place called *high* school. Today, in contrast, most youth are asked, "Where are you going to college?" This question is also asked of every top high school athlete, who everyone presumes will be awarded a scholarship to college. Many of the athletes who do get scholarships fail to graduate from college. Why should this be, since they have such a tremendous opportunity that, in many instances, can fundamentally change their lives? The Adlers' analysis should give you good insights into the reasons.

Thinking Critically

As you read this selection, ask yourself:

1. Why is it common for athletes who receive college scholarships to fail to graduate from college? What part does the athlete subculture play in this?

2. What role conflicts do college athletes experience? Why?

3. If you were the president of a "Top 10" college and you wanted to dramatically increase the college graduation rate of your athletes, based on the findings in this selection, what would you do?

Athletes attend colleges and universities for the ostensible purpose of getting an education while they exercise and refine their athletic skills, but recent studies note that this ideal has become increasingly corrupted. Reports by journalists, former athletes, and social scientists note the commercialization of big-time college athletics, where the money and prestige available to universities have turned their athletic programs into business enterprises that emphasize winning at all costs, often neglecting the education goals of their institutions. The equality of the exchange between college athletes and their educational institutions has therefore been sharply questioned, with many critics leveling charges that universities have exploited their athletes by making excessive demands of them and failing to fulfill their educational promises to them. Several studies have suggested that these factors . . . result in [athletes] having lower grades and less chance of graduating than other students. . . . Drawing on four years of intensive participant observation with a major college basketball team, this article examines college athletes' academic experiences. . . .

■ ■ ■ METHODS AND SETTING

For four years the authors studied a major college basketball program via participant-observation. . . . The research was conducted at a medium-size private university with a predominantly white, suburban, and middle-class student body. The university's academic standards were demanding as it was striving to enhance its academic reputation. The athletic department, as a whole, had a recent history of success. Players were generally recruited from the region, were 70% black, and ranged from the lower to the middle classes. The basketball program fit what Coakley and Frey termed *big-time college athletics.* Although it could not compare to the really large universities, its recent success had compensated for its size and lack of historical tradition. The national ranking and past success of the basketball team and other teams in sending graduating members into the professional leagues imbued the entire athletic milieu with a sense of seriousness and purpose.

The basketball players' circle of significant others was largely predetermined by athletic environment. The role-set members fell into three main categories: athletic, academic, and social. Within the athletic realm, in addition to their teammates, athletes related primarily to the coaching staff, trainers, team managers, secretaries, and athletic administrators. Secondary role-set members included boosters, fans, and the news media. Within the academic realm, athletes' role-set members consisted of professors, tutors, classmates, and, to a lesser extent, academic counselors and administrators. Within the social realm, athletes related to girlfriends, local friends, and students (non-athletes), but most especially to their college athlete peers: the teammates and dormmates who were members of their subculture.

▪ ▪ ▪ ROLE EXPECTATIONS

Most incoming college athletes observed approached their academic role with initial feelings of idealism. They were surrounded by family and cultural messages
that college would enhance their upward mobility and benefit their lives in many
ways. They never doubted this assertion. Because of their academic experiences in
high school, few athletes questioned their ability to succeed in college ("I graduated high school, didn't I?"). Athletes' idealism about their impending academic
experience was further strengthened by the positive tone coaches had taken toward
academics during the recruiting process. Entering freshmen commonly held the following set of prior expectations about their academic role: (1) they would go to
classes and do the work (phrased as "putting the time in"); (2) they would graduate
and get a degree, and (3) there would be no problems.

Approximately 47% ($N = 18$) of the entering athletes observed showed their
initially high academic aspirations and expectations by requesting to be placed in a
preprofessional major in the colleges of business, engineering, or arts and sciences.
Despite warnings from coaches and older teammates about how difficult it would
be to complete this coursework and play ball, they felt they could easily handle the
demands. These individuals planned to use college athletics as a stepping-stone to
career opportunities. As one freshman stated:

> I goin' to use basketball to get an education. Sure I'd like to make the NBA someday,
> but right now I've got to have something to fall back on if I don't.

Another group of freshmen, who had already accorded academics a less salient
role (45%, $N = 17$), were enrolled by coaches in more "manageable" majors, such
as physical education or recreation. Most of these individuals, though, believed that
they too would get a degree. They had few prior expectations about academics, but
assumed that they would make it through satisfactorily. Someone had taken care of
these matters in high school, and they felt that college would be no different. Only
a few individuals from the sample (8%, $N = 3$) entered college expecting to turn
professional shortly thereafter. From the beginning these individuals disdained the
academic role.

Much of this initial idealism was based on an inaccurate picture of college.
Athletes did not anticipate the focus on analytical thinking and writing they would
encounter, expecting that college courses would be an extension of their high school
experiences. One sophomore reflected back on his expectations:

> I didn't think about it much, but when I did, I thought it'd be more or less the same
> here as it be back in high school, no big change. I be passin' all my courses there, but
> I still be goin' out every night.

In their first weeks on campus during their summer program, this early idealism was once again bolstered. Repeatedly the head coach stressed the importance of
earning a degree. He cared about his players as people and wanted them to build a

future out of their college experience. In fact, one of the main reasons athletes' parents encouraged their sons to attend this university was because of the head coach's integrity and good values. Once the school year began, athletes attended required nightly study halls, were told that tutors were available, and were constantly reminded by the coach to go to class. One freshman, interviewed during the preseason period, showed his idealism through his expectations and impressions:

> I'm here for two reasons: to get my degree and play basketball. I don't think it's goin' to be no problem to get my degree. I want to graduate in four years and I think I will. I think that's really important to Coach, too, because in practice he always mentions how important the degree is and everything.

Contrary to popular sentiment, most of the athletes observed began their college careers with a positive attitude toward academics. While their athletic role was unquestionably the most salient and their social role secondary, the academic role was still a critical dimension of their self-identity. Their behavior in the academic realm reflected this; they missed few classes, and turned in assignments regularly. For most this period lasted anywhere from one semester to two years.

■ ■ ■ ROLE CONFLICT

After two semesters in school and a full basketball season, athletes began to realize that their academic expectations had not been entirely accurate. Their early naive idealism gave way to disappointment and cynicism. . . . A major change athletes encountered in shifting from high school to college basketball lay in their athletic role. In large part this was due to the professionalization process they underwent. As one junior remarked:

> In high school, basketball was fun and games, but now it's a job. We get to the gym, we gotta work. You gotta put your all into it no matter how you feelin' that day. 'Cause this is big business. There's a lotta money ridin' on us.

Compounding the professionalization was a dramatic increase in pressure. The basketball players were all public figures in the local area who received intense news coverage. They clearly knew how important winning was to the coaches, boosters, and fans.

The players' athletic role often encroached on their academic role. They soon discovered that handling both roles was not always possible. A primary reason was the time conflict: some courses they wanted or needed for their majors were only offered in the afternoons during practice time; road trips caused them to miss key lectures, examinations, or review sessions, and banquets and other booster functions (which occurred at least once a week) cut into their studying time. At some point during this freshman year, most athletes realized that they did not have the time to perform as well as they had originally hoped in the academic role. . . .

Athletes' perceptions of their athletic–academic role conflict was also influenced by the role model of their coaches. While the coaches sincerely cared about their players' academic responsibilities and achievements, they had their own priorities. Once the season began, they were too busy with their athletic work to pay much attention to academics. The pressures of recruiting, funding, and winning absorbed their energy. Despite their best preseason intentions, once practice officially began in October, the coaches became predominantly concerned with their players as athletes and ended up passing on the pressures of their organizational demands and constraints. Like their players, they were faced with a complex situation to which they often reacted, rather than acted. While they verbally stressed the importance of academics, they accorded athletic and team functions higher salience than school obligations: players' athletic time was strictly regulated, but their academic time was not. Players' behavior in practice, at games, at booster events, and on road trips was carefully monitored, yet their performance in class was not. Despite the coaches' concern about academics, the predominant message that athletes received was that, in contrast to academics, athletics had to be strictly adhered to because a powerful role-set member was always present.

ACADEMIC ROLE

During the school year, players began to notice other characteristics of their academic role that undercut their coaches' verbal emphasis on scholarship. One of the first was their lack of autonomy over their course (and sometimes major) selection. An assistant coach picked out classes and registered the athletes without consulting them. Assistant coaches bought their books, added and dropped courses for them, and contacted their professors if they had to be absent or were doing poorly in their work. By taking care of these academic matters for them, the coaches served as intermediaries between players and the academic realm. Consequently, most athletes failed to develop the knowledge, initiative, or the interest to handle these academic matters themselves, or to develop significant relationships with their professors or other academic role-set members. Thus, when the coaches were too busy to attend to these details, the players were unable to manage for themselves. As one senior remarked:

> Most of those guys don't even know how to fill out an add-drop card, so when they want to switch classes they just do it, and they tell the coaches to switch them. They figure it's not their job. But a lot of guys get Fs because the coaches never got around to it. The only reason I got through is that my girlfriend did it for me. I don't even know how to read a schedule of classes or where to get one.

Despite their occasional lapses, the fact that coaches managed these administrative matters gave athletes a false sense of security, a feeling that someone was always looking out for them academically and would make sure that they were given another chance. The athletes believed that they could fail to perform academically and not have to pay the consequences. They developed the perception that . . . they would be taken care of academically, and that they need not overly involve themselves in this arena. . . .

Concomitant with this lack of autonomy came a new freedom. Unlike high school, their attendance at classes was not compulsory. Being able to skip classes placed a greater responsibility for self-motivation on them. When their motivation waned, athletes developed a pattern of slipping behind in their attendance and classwork until their problems compounded. When athletes did attend class, they often encountered another set of difficulties or disillusionments. In the classroom athletes thought that many professors labeled them as jocks. This image was fostered by the fact that they were surrounded in their classes by other athletes (also placed there by assistant coaches), and that they were identified early in the semester to their professor as athletes (because assistant coaches called or sent out reports to monitor their academic progress). They therefore encountered different expectations and treatment than the general student body. Whether they were given greater tolerance (extra tutoring sessions, relaxed deadlines, relaxed academic standards) or less tolerance ("Those guys think they're entitled to special treatment because they're athletes, and I'm going to show them they're wrong"), they were treated as less than full adults. This special treatment reinforced the differentiation between these two roles and their perceptions of themselves as athletes more than students. When they returned to the dormitory rooms at night, exhausted and sore from practicing, it became easier for them to rationalize, procrastinate, and fritter away their time instead of studying.

Athletes also became disinterested in their academic role because of the content of their classes. The level of disinterest varied between the athletes enrolled in arts and sciences, business, or engineering courses, and those taking physical education or recreation courses. Many of those in the latter category had wanted and expected to take courses in college that were either entertaining, vocational, or in some way relevant to their everyday lives. This was not what they found. Instead, they were enrolled in courses that they considered comical and demeaning. One sophomore articulated the commonly held view:

> How could I get into this stuff? They got me taking nutrition, mental retardation, square dancing, and camp counseling. I thought I was goin' to learn something here. It's a bunch o' BS.

Players enrolled in more rigorous academic courses were often unequipped for the demanding calibre of the work. Many did not have the knowledge, interests, skills, or study habits to compete with other students. With their inadequate training, tight schedules, and waning motivation, athletes became frustrated, bored, and disinterested. Players often stopped going to classes they did not like, yet never officially withdrew from them. When they did poorly on the first test, they gave up on the course, figuring "to hell with it, I'm not gonna try." The positive feedback from their academic role that the athletes anticipated often was replaced by a series of disappointments. As a result they often spent their days lying around the dormitory rooms, watching television, and convincing each other not to go to class. Athletes' academic failures then brought them feelings of inadequacy and uncertainty, as one player described:

> When I first came here I thought I'd be goin' to class all the time and I'd study and that'd be it. But I sure didn't think it meant studyin' all the time. Back in high school you just be memorizin' things, but that's not what they want here. Back in high school I thought I be a pretty good student, but now I don't know.

Players' experiences in the classroom were very different from their preconceptions. The work was harder and they were not taken care of to the extent they had imagined. The intense competition of the athletic arena led them to be obsessed with success. Their frequent academic failures (or at best mediocre grades) led athletes to distance themselves from self-involvement in the academic role. It was better not to try than to try and fail. And they derived plenty of support for this tack within the peer subculture.

■ ■ ■ SOCIAL ROLE

Athletes' social experiences at the university were predominantly with other athletes. Initially they had expected to derive both friendship and status recognition from other students as they had in high school. Instead they found themselves socially isolated. Geographically they were isolated by being housed in an athletic dormitory on a remote side of the campus. Temporally they were cut off by the demands of their practices, games, study halls, and booster functions. Culturally they were racially, socially, and economically different from the rest of the student body. Physically, they were different from other students in size and build, and many students, especially women, found them imposing or occasionally intimidating.

These factors left other athletes as their primary outlets for social relations. Housed together in a dormitory reserved almost exclusively for male athletes (primarily football and basketball players), they bonded together into a reference group and peer subculture. Relations within this group were made especially cohesive by the intensity of their living, playing, and traveling together. A junior described this living situation:

> Living in the jock dorm the privacy is limited. Everybody knows everythin' 'bout what you doin' and who you seein'. You got to live with these same faces twelve months out of the year, they like your brothers, and we all one big family, like it or not. You just got to fit in.

Within the dormitory, athletes briefed each other about what to expect from and think about various individuals, and how to handle certain situations. They formed generalized attitudes and beliefs about what things were important and what things were not. The peer subculture provided them with a set of norms that guided their interpretations of and actions within their various roles.

One of the peer subculture's strongest influences lay in its anti-intellectual and anti-academic character. Typically, dormitory conversation centered on athletic and social dimensions of their lives with little reference to academic, cultural, or intellectual pursuits. In fact, individuals who displayed too much interest, effort, or success in academics were often ridiculed, as one player described:

> When most of the other guys are making Ds or Fs, if I work hard and I get a B on a test, if I go back to the dorm and they all see I got a B, then they goin' "snap on" [make fun of] me. So most of the guys, they don't try. They all act like it's a big joke.

The athletes' peer subculture conflicted with their academic role in five ways: (1) by discouraging them from exerting effort in academics; (2) by providing them with distractions that made it harder for them to study; (3) by providing them with role models who appeared to be getting through college while according their academic role negligible identity salience; (4) by discouraging them from seeking out and associating with other students who could have provided greater academic role modeling; and (5) by providing excuses and justifications that legitimated their academic failures.

The conflict between their athletic, academic, and social roles pulled the athletes in too many directions. One junior expressed his continuing distress over this role conflict:

> When I think about it I get tense and frustrated, you just can't be everything they expect you to be and what you want to be. Something's gotta give. It's either cut off my social life, or flunk out of school, or not do the things I have to do to be able to make pro.

■ ■ ■ ROLE CONFLICT RESOLUTIONS

Athletes' expectations for their academic role were gradually replaced by feelings of anomie as they came to perceive the disparity between the recruiting and cultural rhetoric they had encountered and the reality of college life. In order to successfully negotiate their college experience they had to find some way to resolve this role conflict, which they did by realigning the expectations, priorities, and identity salience [the significance of a role, or how much one identifies with it] of their roles.

The biggest change in their core identity salience lay in the growth of their athletic role. While athletics had always been the first priority for most, it now engulfed them. This shift was brought about by the demands and expectations of their athletic role set and by their own desire to cling to their dreams of making it in the NBA. First, the head coach overwhelmed athletes by the intensity of his power and role demands. He expected them to place basketball before everything else. He influenced their view of their present and future life chances by framing these for them based on athletic priorities. He heard about everything they did and reprimanded them for violations of his behavior code. Yet it was the intensity of the athletic experience itself that ensured their self-immersion in this role. The glamour and excitement of playing for a big-time athletic program offered even the most marginal players their most fulfilling gratification and rewards. One player described the impossibility of maintaining any balance between his athletic and other roles:

> When I go to sleep at night what do you think I be thinking? History? Sociology? No way. I hear coach yelling in my ear, "Run, run, get on the ball, play defense, Robinson. Damn, Robinson, can you move your feet, son?" During the season I sleep, eat, and breathe basketball.

In addition, the athletic role pervaded and dominated the identity of their other roles in social and academic situations. On campus they were recognized as athletes first and students second. Off campus and even out of uniform, they were constantly responsible for "representing the program." Their appearance and demeanor reflected on their teammates, their coaches, their basketball program, and the entire university. They therefore had to relinquish a great deal of privacy and freedom.

The growth of the athletic role's identity salience was further endorsed by their peer subculture. Most of the athletes in their dormitory had reprioritized their roles and become engulfed by athletics. These significant others offered them a model of role conflict resolution that adopted the coach's perspective on the predominance of athletics, maintained the secondary importance of having a social life, and reshuffled academics to an even lower identity salience. All of the athletes realigned the identity salience of these roles in this manner, progressively detaching themselves from academics.

These changes in athletes' identities led to a series of pragmatic adjustments in their academic goals. Of the individuals who began with preprofessional majors, only one-fourth of them stayed with these all the way through college and graduated. They did so primarily without the academic care and concern they had originally anticipated. They ceased attending classes regularly, diminished their efforts to get to know professors, did not bother to get class notes or reading assignments until just before tests, and exerted the minimum amount of effort necessary to get by. More commonly, these individuals reassessed their academic goals and found that some adjustment was necessary. A second group (the remaining three-fourths of this original group) adjusted by both shifting their behavior and by changing from their preprofessional program to a more manageable major. While this shift meant that they had abandoned both their academic idealism and their earlier career goals, they still held to the goal of graduating. The predominant attitude changed to getting a diploma regardless of the major. As one player commented, "When you apply for a job all that matters is if you have that piece of paper. They don't care what you majored in." Many of the athletes in this group managed to graduate or keep on a steady course toward graduation. Much like Merton's innovators, they retained the socially approved goal but replaced their earlier means with a creative alternative.

Athletes who began their college careers with lower initial academic aspirations and who majored in physical education or recreation from the start made corresponding adjustments. Approximately one-fifth of these in this group originally held on to their initial goal and managed to graduate in one of these fields. Like the preprofessional majors, they did so with less concern than they had displayed on entering. The other four-fifths came to the realization, usually relatively late, that their chances for graduating from college were unrealistic. They therefore shifted their orientation toward maintaining their athletic eligibility. A junior's remarks illustrated how this shift to maintaining eligibility affected his attitude toward his academic role:

> I used to done thought I was goin' to school, but now I know it's not for real. . . . I don't have no academic goals. A player a coach is counting on, that's all he think about is ball. That's what he signed to do. So what you gotta do is show up, show your smilin' face. Try as hard as you can. Don't just lay over in the room. That's all the coach can ask. Or else you may not find yourself playing the next year. Or even that year.

By their senior year, when they had met their final eligibility requirements, many members of this last group abandoned the academic role entirely. They either anticipated going to one of the professional leagues, or they knew that their scholarships would soon expire and they would have to look for a job. In either case, wasting their time in class no longer seemed necessary.

■ ■ ■ DISCUSSION

. . . In their academic role, many college athletes received poor or marginal grades and had to relinquish or readjust the academic goals they held on entering college. This perception awakened them to the conflict between their expectations that college would be much like high school and their realizations that the academic demands at the university were greater than they could achieve. Their emphasis on competition and winning, derived from their athletic role, made the failure especially difficult to accept.

When faced with extreme role conflict, individuals doing very poorly in their classes engaged in role distance, diminishing the importance of this role to their self-identity. Individuals from stronger academic backgrounds fared slightly better, however, and did not as greatly diminish their [identity with the] academic role. . . . As individuals assessed their relative strengths and weaknesses within given roles, they accorded higher salience to those in which they were evaluated positively and lower salience to those in which they were negatively evaluated. . . .

Most athletes' initial commitment to the academic role was induced by cultural expectations and by the encouragement of others, but that commitment was not firmly embedded in their self-conceptions. Once they got to college, their commitment to work hard academically was easily dislodged by their first few adverse experiences and by the peer culture's devaluation of academics. In contrast, their commitment to the athletic role was entrenched, because this was their dream since childhood. No matter how little playing time they received or how much the coach criticized them, they clung to the primary self-identification as athletes. . . .

As college athletes learned the nature of their new status they learned that they were seen as basketball players by nearly everyone they encountered. Their athletic identity pervaded and dominated the identity of their other roles in almost all other situations. This designation was true in their academic and social lives both on campus and off, and it grew more pervasive as they progressed through their playing careers and advanced to more visible team positions. . . . When people are constantly identified by one role to the near total exclusion of their others, they become increasingly committed to that role and it is likely to take precedence in influencing their self-conceptions. . . .

Athletes' position at the university was characterized by "institutional powerlessness," as their coaches had the ability to control all aspects of their lives. By influencing their personal time, academic schedules, and playing role on the team, coaches could dominate not only their athletic role, but their social and academic roles as well. Regardless of the players' own goals, expectations, or desires, they had to take into consideration the wishes and demands of the coach. Players also believed . . . that the coach could . . . keep them eligible to play if he wanted, even if they got into academic difficulty. The omnipotence of their athletic over their academic role influenced them to shift greater identity salience to the role where the apparent power lay. . . .

India's Sacred Cow

Marvin Harris

introduction

A generation ago, some "experts" predicted that with the rise of science and rationality U.S. culture would become so secularized that religion would quietly fade into the background. Only in a few superstitious, backward corners of society would a remnant of religion remain. Events proved otherwise, of course, and today religion is as vital for Americans as it was in the past. Tens of millions of Americans seek guidance and solace in religion. They look to religion to answer many of the perplexing questions they face in life, ones for which science offers no answers.

Like the other social institutions, religion is interconnected with the other parts of society. When it comes to our own religion, it often is difficult to perceive these interconnections. What affects us directly, such as what occurs in our own congregation, synagogue, or mosque, gets our attention, not abstract connections. When we look at unfamiliar religions, in contrast, we are seeing customs that are not part of our taken-for-granted assumptions. The unfamiliarity or "strangeness" of these religious practices prompts us to ask questions. For example, we might wonder why cows are allowed to wander India's city streets and country roads. For Indians, however, this is part of their background assumptions of life, and for them the sight of cows even in a city's heavy street traffic does not prompt questions. Similarly, we may wonder why deprived and hungry Indians don't eat these cattle. As Harris considers such matters, he makes the essential interconnections between religion and other aspects of culture more evident.

Thinking Critically

As you read this selection, ask yourself:

1. What interconnections are there between your religion (assuming you have one) and other aspects of your culture? Another way of asking this is: How do your religion and culture reinforce or influence one another?

2. If you are a religious person, what questions does your religion answer that science does not?

3. Why are cows allowed to wander freely about India? How is this functional for Indian society? How is it dysfunctional?

News photographers that came out of India during the famine of the late 1960s showed starving people stretching out bony hands to beg for food while sacred cattle strolled behind undisturbed. The Hindu, it seems, would rather starve to death than eat his cow or even deprive it of food. The cattle appear to browse unhindered through urban markets eating an orange here, a mango there, competing with people for meager supplies of food.

By Western standards, spiritual values seem more important to Indians than life itself. Specialists in food habits around the world like Fred Simons at the University of California at Davis consider Hinduism an irrational ideology that compels people to overlook abundant, nutritious foods for scarcer, less healthful foods.

What seems to be an absurd devotion to the mother cow pervades Indian life. Indian wall calendars portray beautiful young women with bodies of fat white cows, often with milk jetting from their teats into sacred shrines.

Cow worship even carries over into politics. In 1966 a crowd of 120,000 people, led by holy men, demonstrated in front of the Indian House of Parliament in support of the All-Party Cow Protection Campaign Committee. In Nepal, the only contemporary Hindu kingdom, cow slaughter is severely punished. As one story goes, the car driven by an official of a United States agency struck and killed a cow. In order to avoid the international incident that would have occurred when the official was arrested for murder, the Nepalese magistrate concluded that the cow had committed suicide.

Many Indians agree with Western assessments of the Hindu reverence for their cattle, the zebu, or *Bos indicus,* a large-humped species prevalent in Asia and Africa. M. N. Srinivas, an Indian anthropologist, states: "Orthodox Hindu opinion regards the killing of cattle with abhorrence, even though the refusal to kill vast numbers of useless cattle which exist in India today is detrimental to the nation." Even the Indian Ministry of Information formerly maintained that "the large animal population is more a liability than an asset in view of our land resources." Accounts from many different sources point to the same conclusion: India, one of the world's great civilizations, is being strangled by its love for the cow.

The easy explanation for India's devotion to the cow, the one most Westerners and Indians would offer, is that cow worship is an integral part of Hinduism. Religion is somehow good for the soul, even it if sometimes fails the body. Religion orders the cosmos and explains our place in the universe. Religious beliefs, many would claim, have existed for thousands of years and have a life of their own. They are not understandable in scientific terms.

But all this ignores history. There is more to be said for cow worship than is immediately apparent. The earliest Vedas, the Hindu sacred texts from the second millennium B.C., do not prohibit the slaughter of cattle. Instead, they ordain it as part of sacrificial rites. The early Hindus did not avoid the flesh of cows and bulls; they ate it at ceremonial feasts presided over by Brahman priests. Cow worship is

From Human Nature Magazine/Harris. *Human Nature Magazine: India's Sacred Cow.* © 1978 Wadsworth, a part of Cengage Learning, Inc. Reproduced by permission. www.cengage.com/permissions

a relatively recent development in India; it evolved as the Hindu religion developed and changed.

This evolution is recorded in royal edicts and religious texts written during the last 3,000 years of Indian history. The Vedas from the first millennium B.C. contain contradictory passages, some referring to ritual slaughter and others to a strict taboo on beef consumption. A. N. Bose, in *Social and Rural Economy of Northern India, 600 B.C.–200 A.D.,* concludes that many of the sacred-cow passages were incorporated into the texts by priests of a later period.

By 200 A.D. the status of Indian cattle had undergone a spiritual transformation. The Brahman priesthood exhorted the population to venerate the cow and forbade them to abuse it or to feed on it. Religious feasts involving the ritual slaughter and consumption of livestock were eliminated and meat eating was restricted to the nobility.

By 1000 A.D., all Hindus were forbidden to eat beef. Ahimsa, the Hindu belief in the unity of all life, was the spiritual justification for this restriction. But it is difficult to ascertain exactly when this change occurred. An important event that helped to shape the modern complex was the Islamic invasion, which took place in the eighth century A.D. Hindus may have found it politically expedient to set themselves off from the invaders, who were beefeaters, by emphasizing the need to prevent the slaughter of their sacred animals. Thereafter, the cow taboo assumed its modern form and began to function much as it does today.

The place of the cow in modern India is every place—on posters, in the movies, in brass figures, in stone and wood carvings, on the streets, in the fields. The cow is a symbol of health and abundance. It provides the milk that Indians consume in the form of yogurt and ghee (clarified butter), which contribute subtle flavors to much spicy Indian food.

This, perhaps, is the practical role of the cow, but cows provide less than half the milk produced in India. Most cows in India are not dairy breeds. In most regions, when an Indian farmer wants a steady, high-quality source of milk he usually invests in a female water buffalo. In India the water buffalo is the specialized dairy breed because its milk has a higher butterfat content than zebu milk. Although the farmer milks his zebu cows, the milk is merely a by-product.

More vital than zebu milk to South Asian farmers are zebu calves. Male calves are especially valued because from bulls come oxen, which are the mainstay of the Indian agricultural system.

Small, fast oxen drag wooden plows through late-spring fields when monsoons have dampened the dry, cracked earth. After harvest, the oxen break the grain from the stalk by stomping through mounds of cut wheat and rice. For rice cultivation in irrigated fields, the male water buffalo is preferred (it pulls better in deep mud), but for most other crops, including rainfall rice, wheat, sorghum, and millet, and for transporting goods and people to and from town, a team of oxen is preferred. The ox is the Indian peasant's tractor, thresher, and family car combined; the cow is the factory that produces the ox.

If draft animals instead of cows are counted, India appears to have too few domesticated ruminants, not too many. Since each of the 70 million farms in India require a draft team, it follows that Indian peasants should use 140 million animals in the fields. But there are only 83 million oxen and male water buffalo on the sub-continent, a shortage of 30 million draft teams.

In other regions of the world, joint ownership of draft animals might overcome a shortage, but Indian agriculture is closely tied to the monsoon rains of late spring and summer. Field preparation and planting must coincide with the rain, and a farmer must have his animals ready to plow when the weather is right. When the farmer without a draft team needs bullocks most, his neighbors are all using theirs. Any delay in turning the soil drastically lowers production.

Because of this dependence on draft animals, loss of the family oxen is devastating. If a beast dies, the farmer must borrow money to buy or rent an ox at interest rates so high that he ultimately loses his land. Every year foreclosures force thousands of poverty-stricken peasants to abandon the countryside for the overcrowded cities.

If a family is fortunate enough to own a fertile cow, it will be able to rear replacements for a lost team and thus survive until life returns to normal. If, as sometimes happens, famine leads a family to sell its cow and ox team, all ties to agriculture are cut. Even if the family survives, it has no way to farm the land, no oxen to work the land, and no cows to produce oxen.

The prohibition against eating meat applies to the flesh of cows, bulls, and oxen, but the cow is the most sacred because it can produce the other two. The peasant whose cow dies is not only crying over a spiritual loss but over the loss of his farm as well.

Religious laws that forbid the slaughter of cattle promote the recovery of the agricultural system from the dry Indian winter and from periods of drought. The monsoon, on which all agriculture depends, is erratic. Sometimes, it arrives early, sometimes late, sometimes not at all. Drought has struck large portions of India time and again in this century, and Indian farmers and the zebus are accustomed to these natural disasters. Zebus can pass weeks on end with little or no food and water. Like camels, they store both in their humps and recuperate quickly with only a little nourishment.

During drought the cows often stop lactating and become barren. In some cases the condition is permanent but often it is only temporary. If barren animals were summarily eliminated, as Western experts in animal husbandry have suggested, cows capable of recovery would be lost along with those entirely debilitated. By keeping alive the cows that can later produce oxen, religious laws against cow slaughter assure the recovery of the agricultural system from the greatest challenge it faces—the failure of the monsoon.

The local Indian governments aid the process of recovery by maintaining homes for barren cows. Farmers reclaim any animal that calves or begins to lactate. One police station in Madras collects strays and pastures them in a field adjacent to the station. After a small fine is paid, a cow is returned to its rightful owner when the owner thinks the cow shows signs of being able to reproduce.

During the hot, dry spring months most of India is like a desert. Indian farmers often complain they cannot feed their livestock during this period. They maintain the cattle by letting them scavenge on the sparse grass along the roads. In the cities the cattle are encouraged to scavenge near food stalls to supplement their scant diet. These are the wandering cattle tourists report seeing throughout India.

Westerners expect shopkeepers to respond to these intrusions with the deference due a sacred animal; instead, their response is a string of curses and the crack of a long bamboo pole across the beast's back or a poke at its genitals. Mahatma Gandhi was well aware of the treatment sacred cows (and bulls and oxen) received in India. "How we bleed her to take the last drop of milk from her. How we starve her to emaciation, how we ill-treat the calves, how we deprive them of their portion of milk, how cruelly we treat the oxen, how we castrate them, how we beat them, how we overload them" (Gandhi, 1954).

Oxen generally receive better treatment than cows. When food is in short supply, thrifty Indian peasants feed their working bullocks and ignore their cows, but rarely do they abandon the cows to die. When cows are sick, farmers worry over them as they would over members of the family and nurse them as if they were children. When the rains return and when the fields are harvested, the farmers again feed their cows regularly and reclaim their abandoned animals. The prohibition against beef consumption is a form of disaster insurance for all India.

Western agronomists and economists are quick to protest that all the functions of the zebu cattle can be improved with organized breeding programs, cultivated pastures, and silage. Because stronger oxen would pull the plow faster, they could work multiple plots of land, allowing farmers to share their animals. Fewer healthy, well-fed cows could provide Indians with more milk. But pastures and silage require arable land, land needed to produce wheat and rice.

A look at Western cattle farming makes plain the cost of adopting advanced technology in Indian agriculture. In a study of livestock production in the United States, David Pimentel of the College of Agriculture and Life Sciences at Cornell University, found that 91 percent of the cereal, legume, and vegetable protein suitable for human consumption is consumed by livestock. Approximately three quarters of the arable land in the United States is devoted to growing food for livestock. In the production of meat and milk, American ranchers use enough fossil fuel to equal more than 82 million barrels of oil annually.

Indian cattle do not drain the system in the same way. In a 1971 study of livestock in West Bengal, Stewart Odend'hal (1972) of the University of Missouri found that Bengalese cattle ate only the inedible remains of subsistence crops—rice straw, rice hulls, the tops of sugar cane, and mustard-oil cake. Cattle graze in the fields after harvest and eat the remains of crops left on the ground; they forage for grass and weeds on the roadsides. The food for zebu cattle costs the human population virtually nothing. "Basically," Odend'hal says, "the cattle convert the items of little direct human value into products of immediate utility."

In addition to plowing the fields and producing milk, the zebus produce dung, which fires the hearths and fertilizes the fields of India. Much of the estimated 800 million tons of manure produced annually is collected by the farmers' children as they follow the family cows and bullocks from place to place. And when the children see the droppings of another farmer's cattle along the road, they pick those up also. Odend'hal reports that the system operates with such high efficiency that the children of West Bengal recover nearly 100 percent of the dung produced by their livestock.

From 40 to 70 percent of all manure produced by Indian cattle is used as fuel for cooking; the rest is returned to the fields as fertilizer. Dried dung burns slowly, cleanly, and with low heat—characteristics that satisfy the household needs of Indian women. Staples like curry and rice can simmer for hours. While the meal slowly cooks over an unattended fire, the women of the household can do other chores. Cow chips, unlike firewood, do not scorch as they burn.

It is estimated that the dung used for cooking fuel provides the energy-equivalent of 43 million tons of coal. At current prices, it would cost India an extra 1.5 billion dollars in foreign exchange to replace the dung with coal. And if the 350 million tons of manure that are being used as fertilizer were replaced with commercial fertilizers, the expense would be even greater. Roger Revelle of the University of California at San Diego has calculated that 89 percent of the energy used in Indian agriculture (the equivalent of about 140 million tons of coal) is provided by local sources. Even if foreign loans were to provide the money, the capital outlay necessary to replace the Indian cow with tractors and fertilizers for the fields, coal for the fires, and transportation for the family would probably warp international financial institutions for years.

Instead of asking the Indians to learn from the American model of industrial agriculture, American farmers might learn energy conservation from the Indians. Every step in an energy cycle results in a loss of energy to the system. Like a pendulum that slows a bit with each swing, each transfer of energy from sun to plants, plants to animals, and animals to human beings involves energy losses. Some systems are more efficient than others; they provide a higher percentage of the energy inputs in a final, useful form. Seventeen percent of all energy zebus consume is returned in the form of milk, traction, and dung. American cattle raised on Western rangeland return only 4 percent of the energy they consume.

But the American system is improving. Based on techniques pioneered by Indian scientists, at least one commercial firm in the United States is reported to be building plants that will turn manure from cattle feedlots into combustible gas. When organic matter is broken down by anaerobic bacteria, methane gas and carbon dioxide are produced. After the methane is cleansed of the carbon dioxide, it is available for the same purposes as natural gas—cooking, heating, electric generation. The company constructing the biogasification plant plans to sell its product to a gas-supply company, to be piped through the existing distribution system. Schemes similar to this one could make cattle ranches almost independent of utility and gasoline companies; for methane can be used to run trucks, tractors, and cars as well as to supply heat and electricity. The relative energy self-sufficiency that the Indian peasant has achieved is a goal American farmers and industry are now striving for.

Studies of Odend'hal's understate the efficiency of the Indian cow, because dead cows are used for purposes that Hindus prefer not to acknowledge. When a cow dies, an Untouchable, a member of one of the lowest ranking castes in India, is summoned to haul away the carcass. Higher castes consider the body of the dead cow polluting; if they handle it, they must go through a rite of purification.

Untouchables first skin the dead animal and either tan the skin themselves or sell it to a leather factory. In the privacy of their homes, contrary to the teachings of Hinduism, untouchable castes cook the meat and eat it. Indians of all castes rarely acknowledge the existence of these practices to non-Hindus, but most are aware that beefeating takes place. The prohibition against beefeating restricts consumption by the higher castes and helps distribute animal protein to the poorest sectors of the population that otherwise would have no source of these vital nutrients.

Untouchables are not the only Indians who consume beef. Indian Muslims and Christians are under no restriction that forbids them beef, and its consumption is legal in many places. The Indian ban on cow slaughter is state, not national, law and not all states restrict it. In many cities, such as New Delhi, Calcutta, and Bombay, legal slaughterhouses sell beef to retail customers and to restaurants that serve steak.

If the caloric value of beef and the energy costs involved in the manufacture of synthetic leather were included in the estimate of energy, the calculated efficiency of Indian livestock would rise considerably. As well as the system works, experts often claim that its efficiency can be further improved. Alan Heston (et al., 1971), an economist at the University of Pennsylvania, believes that Indians suffer from an overabundance of cows simply because they refuse to slaughter the excess cattle. India could produce at least the same number of oxen and the same quantities of milk and manure with 30 million fewer cows. Heston calculates that only 40 cows are necessary to maintain a population of 100 bulls and oxen. Since India averages 70 cows for every 100 bullocks, the difference, 30 million cows, is expendable.

What Heston fails to note is that sex ratios among cattle in different regions of India vary tremendously, indicating that adjustments in the cow population do take place. Along the Ganges River, one of the holiest shrines of Hinduism, the ratio drops to 47 cows for every 100 male animals. This ratio reflects the preference for dairy buffalo in the irrigated sectors of the Gangetic Plains. In nearby Pakistan, in contrast, where cow slaughter is permitted, the sex ratio is 60 cows to 100 oxen.

Since the sex ratios among cattle differ greatly from region to region and do not even approximate the balance that would be expected if no females were killed, we can assume that some culling of herds does take place; Indians do adjust their religious restrictions to accommodate ecological realities.

They cannot kill a cow but they can tether an old or unhealthy animal until it has starved to death. They cannot slaughter a calf but they can yoke it with a large wooden triangle so that when it nurses it irritates the mother's udder and gets kicked to death. They cannot ship their animals to the slaughterhouse but they can sell them to Muslims, closing their eyes to the fact that the Muslims will take the cattle to the slaughterhouse.

These violations of the prohibition against cattle slaughter strengthen the premise that cow worship is a vital part of Indian culture. The practice arose to prevent the population from consuming the animal on which Indian agriculture depends. During the first millennium B.C., the Ganges Valley became one of the most densely populated regions of the world.

Where previously there had been only scattered villages, many towns and cities arose and peasants farmed every available acre of land. Kingsley Davis, a population expert at the University of California at Berkeley, estimates that by 300 B.C. between 50 million and 100 million people were living in India. The forested Ganges Valley became a windswept semidesert and signs of ecological collapse appeared; droughts and floods became commonplace, erosion took away the rich topsoil, farms shrank as population increased, and domesticated animals became harder and harder to maintain.

It is probable that the elimination of meat eating came about in a slow, practical manner. The farmers who decided not to eat their cows, who saved them for procreation to produce oxen, were the ones who survived the natural disasters. Those who ate beef lost the tools with which to farm. Over a period of centuries, more and more farmers probably avoided beef until an unwritten taboo came into existence.

Only later was the practice codified by the priesthood. While Indian peasants were probably aware of the role of cattle in their society, strong sanctions were necessary to protect zebus from a population faced with starvation. To remove temptation, the flesh of cattle became taboo and the cow became sacred.

The sacredness of the cow is not just an ignorant belief that stands in the way of progress. Like all concepts of the sacred and the profane, this one affects the physical world; it defines the relationships that are important for the maintenance of Indian society.

Indians have the sacred cow, we have the "sacred" car and the "sacred" dog. It would not occur to us to propose the elimination of automobiles and dogs from our society without carefully considering the consequences, and we should not propose the elimination of zebu cattle without first understanding their place in the social order of India.

Human society is neither random nor capricious. The regularities of thought and behavior called culture are the principal mechanisms by which we human beings adapt to the world around us. Practices and beliefs can be rational or irrational, but a society that fails to adapt to its environment is doomed to extinction. Only those societies that draw the necessities of life from their surroundings without destroying those surroundings inherit the earth. The West has much to learn from the great antiquity of Indian civilization, and the sacred cow is an important part of that lesson.

REFERENCES

Gandhi, Mohandas K. 1954. *How to Serve the Cow.* Bombay: Navajivan Publishing House.

Heston, Alan, et al. 1971. "An Approach to the Sacred Cow of India." *Current Anthropology* 12, 191–209.

Odend'hal, Stewart. 1972. "Gross Energetic Efficiency of Indian Cattle in Their Environment." *Journal of Human Ecology* 1, 1–27.

Just Another Routine Emergency

Daniel F. Chambliss

introduction

In social life, appearances may not be everything, but they certainly are essential for getting along. Just as buildings have façades—attractive front exteriors that are designed to give a good impression of what might be inside—so social groups and organizations have façades. Some organizations even hire public relations firms to put out favorable messages to the public. To cultivate images of caring, others contribute to charitable causes. Oil companies that exploit the environment publish expensive, glossy ads and brochures to convince the public that they care more about the environment than *Greenpeace* or *The Sea Shepherds* do.

As mentioned in the introduction to Part II, some say that the first wisdom of sociology is that nothing is as it appears. If so, the first task of sociology is to look behind the scenes. Beneath the social façade put out for public consumption lies a different reality. As in the case of some oil companies, the reality may conflict greatly with their carefully cultivated public image. But in the typical case, the hidden reality has more to do with mundane matters: dissension within the group that leaders want to keep from the public or less dedication to the public welfare than the organization wants to reveal. At times, the façade may be designed to give an appearance of competence and order, while the hidden reality is a looming incompetence and disorder. As Chambliss takes us behind the social façade of the hospital, he reveals a reality unfamiliar to most of us.

Thinking Critically

As you read this selection, ask yourself:

1. What lies behind the scenes of hospitals?

2. How do hospital workers keep outsiders from seeing past their social façade?

3. From information in this reading, prove or disprove this statement: From their inappropriate humor, we can see that doctors and nurses don't really care about their patients.

Every unit in the hospital . . . has its own normality, its own typical patients, number of deaths, and crises to be faced. But just as predictably, every unit has its emergencies that threaten the routine and challenge the staff's ability to maintain workaday attitudes and practices. Emergencies threaten the staff's ability to carry on as usual, to maintain their own distance from the patient's suffering, and to hold at bay their awe at the enormity of events. Occasionally breakdowns occur in unit discipline or the ability to do the required work.

Staff follow several strategies when trying to manage the threat of breakdowns: they will keep outsiders outside, follow routinization rituals, or use humor to distance themselves. Finally, even when all efforts fail, they will keep going, no matter what. Consider in turn each of these implicit maxims:

1. KEEP OUTSIDERS OUTSIDE

Every hospital has policies about visiting hours, designed not only to "let patients rest" but also to protect staff from outsiders' interference in their work. Visitors are limited to certain hours, perhaps two to a patient room for fifteen-minute visits; they may have to be announced before entering the unit or may be kept waiting in a room down the hall. No doubt many such policies are good for the patient. No doubt, too, they keep visitors out of the nurse's way, prevent too many obtrusive questions or requests for small services, and prevent curious laypersons from seeing the messier, less presentable sides of nursing care.

When visitors cannot be physically excluded, they can still be cognitively controlled, that is, prevented from knowing that something untoward is happening. Typically, the staff behave in such episodes as if everything were OK, even when it is not. This is similar to what Erving Goffman observed in conversations: when the shared flow of interaction is threatened by an accidental insult or a body failure such as a sneeze or flatulence, people simply try to ignore the break in reality and carry on as if nothing has happened. Such "reality maintenance" is often well-orchestrated, requiring cooperation on the part of several parties. For Goffman, normal people in normal interactions accept at face value each other's presentation of who they are:

> A state where everyone temporarily accepts everyone else's line is established. This kind of mutual acceptance seems to be a basic structural feature of interaction, especially the interaction of face-to-face talk. It is typically a "working" acceptance, not a "real" one.[1]

And when this routine breaks down, the immediate strategy is simple denial:

> When a person fails to prevent an incident, he can still attempt to maintain the fiction that no threat to face has occurred. The most blatant example of this is found

where the person acts as if an event that contains a threatening expression has not occurred at all.[2]

In the hospital, the unexpected entrance of outsiders into a delicate situation can disrupt the staff's routine activities and create unmanageable chaos. To avoid this, the staff may pretend to outsiders that nothing special is happening; this pretense itself can be part of the routine. During a code (resuscitation) effort I witnessed, there were three such potential disruptions by outsiders: another patient calling for help, a new incoming patient being wheeled in, and the new patient's family members entering the unit. All three challenges were handled by the staff diverting the outsiders from the code with a show, as if nothing were happening:

> Code in CCU [Cardiac Care Unit] . . . woman patient, asystole [abnormal ventricle contractions]. Doc (res[ident]) pumping chest—*deep* pumps, I'm struck by how far down they push. Serious stuff. Matter of factness of process is striking. This was a surprise code, not expected. Patient was in Vtak [ventricular fibrillation], pulse started slowing, then asystole. N[urse]s pumping for a while, RT [Respiratory Therapist] ambu-bagging [pumping air into lungs]. Maybe 7–8 people in patient's room working. Calm, but busy. Occasionally a laugh.
>
> Pt in next room (no more than 10 feet away) called for nurse—a doc went in, real loose and casual, strolled in, pt said something; doc said, "There's something going on next door that's taking people's time; we'll get to you"—real easy, like nothing at all happening. Then strolls back to code room. Very calm. . . .
>
> Two N[urse]s came into unit wheeling a new patient. One said, "Uh, oh, bad time," very quietly as she realized, going in the door, that a code was on. Somebody said, "Close the door"—the outside door to the unit, which the Ns with the new pt were holding open. . . .
>
> When the new pt was brought in and rolled into his room, the family with him was stopped at unit door, told to stay in waiting room and "we'll call you" with a casual wave of hand, as if this is routine. [No one said a code was on. Patient lying on gurney was wheeled in, went right by the code room and never knew a thing.] [Field Notes]

This is a simple example of protecting the routine from the chaos of a panicking patient or a horrified family; the outsiders never knew that a resuscitation was occurring fifteen feet away. The staff's work was, in their own eyes, routine; their challenge was protecting that routine from outside disruption.

▪ ▪ ▪ 2. FOLLOW ROUTINIZATION RITUALS

The staff's sense of routine is maintained by the protective rituals of hospital life. Under stress, one may use them more and more compulsively, falling back on the old forms to reconvince oneself that order is still present. Frantic prayers in the foxhole are the prototype cases.

Most prominent of such rituals in hospitals are "rounds," the standard ritual for the routine handling of patient disasters in the hospital. "Rounds" is the generic term for almost any organized staff group discussion of patients' conditions. "Walking rounds" refers to a physician walking through the hospital, usually trailed by various residents and interns, going from patient to patient and reviewing their condition. "Grand rounds" are large meetings of the medical staff featuring the presentation of an interesting case, with elaborate discussion and questions, for the purpose of education and review of standard practices. Nursing rounds usually consist of a meeting between the staff for one (outgoing) shift reporting to the staff of the next (incoming) shift on the condition of all patients on the floor. Here the staff collectively explains what has happened and why, bringing every case into the staff's framework of thinking, and systematically enforcing the system's capability for handling medical problems without falling to pieces. In rounds, the staff confirm to each other that things are under control. Once a week, for instance, the Burn Unit at one hospital holds rounds in their conference room with a group of residents, one or two attending, several nurses, the social workers, dieticians, and physical therapists. The patients here are in terrible shape; one can sometimes hear moans in the hallway outside as patients are taken for walks by the nurses. But rounds continue:

> Macho style of the docs very evident. . . . Resident will present a case, then the attendings take rapid-fire shots at what he [the resident] had done: wrong dressing, wrong feeding schedule, failure to note some abnormality in the lab results. Much of the talk was a flurry of physiological jargon, many numbers and abbreviations. The intensity of the presentation, the mercilessness of the grilling, is surprising. . . . Focus is on no errors made in situation of extreme pressure—i.e., both in patient treatment and then here in rounds presenting the case. Goal here is to be predictable, *controlled,* nothing left out. [Field Notes]

■ ■ ■ 3. USE HUMOR TO DISTANCE YOURSELF

Keeping outsiders away and following the standard rituals for maintaining normality can help, but sometimes the pathos of hospital life becomes psychologically threatening to staff members. One response is to break down, cry, and run out, but this is what they are trying to avoid; the more common reaction is the sort of black humor that notoriously characterizes hospitals and armies everywhere. Humor provides an outlet; when physical space is not available, humor is a way to separate oneself psychologically from what is happening. It says both that I am not involved and that this really isn't so important. (In brain surgery, when parts of that organ are, essentially, vacuumed away, one may hear comments like "There goes 2d grade, there go the piano lessons," etc.) With laughter, things seem less consequential, less of a burden. What has been ghastly can perhaps be made funny:

> Today they got a 600-gram baby in the Newborn Unit. When Ns heard [the baby] was in Delivery, they were praying, "Please God let it be under 500 grams"—because that's the definite cutoff under which they won't try to save it—but the doc said admit it anyway. Ns unhappy.

> I came in the unit tonight; N came up to me and said brightly, with a big smile, "Have you seen our fetus?" Ns on the Newborn Unit have nicknames for some. There's "Fetus," the 600-gram one; "Munchkin"; and "Thrasher," in the corner, the one with constant seizures. Grim humor, but common. ["Fetus" was born at 24 weeks, "Munchkin" at 28.] [Field Notes]

The functions of such humor for medical workers have been described in a number of classic works of medical sociology. Renée Fox, writing in her book *Experiment Perilous* about physicians on a metabolic research unit, says, "The members of the group were especially inclined to make jokes about events that disturbed them a good deal," and she summarizes that

> by freeing them from some of the tension to which they were subject, enabling them to achieve greater detachment and equipoise, and strengthening their resolve to do something about the problems with which they were faced, the grim medical humor of the Metabolic Group helped them to come to terms with their situation in a useful and professionally acceptable way.[3]

Fox and other students of hospital culture (notably Rose Coser)[4] have emphasized that humor fills a functional purpose of "tension release," allowing medical workers to get on with the job in the face of trauma; their analyses usually focus on jokes explicitly told in medical settings. This analysis is correct as far as it goes, but in a sense I think it almost "explains away" hospital humor—as if to say that "these people are under a lot of strain, so it's understandable that they tell these gruesome jokes." It suggests, in a functionalist fallacy, that jokes are made because of the strain and that things somehow aren't "really" funny.

But they are. An appreciation of hospital life must recognize that funny things—genuinely funny, even if sometimes simultaneously horrible—do happen. Hospitals are scenes of irony, where good and bad are inseparably blended, where funny things happen, where to analytically excuse laughter as a defense mechanism is simultaneously to deny the human reality, the experience, that even to a non-stressed outsider *this is funny*.[5] The humor isn't found only in contrived jokes but in the scenes one witnesses; laughter can be spontaneous, and it's not always nervous. True, one must usually have a fairly normalized sense of the hospital to laugh here, but laugh one does.

Certainly, the staff make jokes:

> In the OR [operating room]:
> "This is his [pt's] 6th time [for a hernia repair]."
> "After two, I hear you're officially disabled."
> "Oh good, does that mean he gets a special parking place?"
> [Field Notes]
> In the ICU [Intensive Care Unit], two Ns—one male, one female—working on pt.
> Nurse 1 (male): "This guy has bowel sounds in his scrotum."
> Nurse 2 (female): "In his scrotum?"

> Nurse 1: "Yeah, didn't you pick that up?"
> Nurse 2: "I didn't put my stethoscope there!" (Big laughs.) [Field Notes]

Sometimes jokes are more elaborate and are obviously derived from the tragedy of the situation:

> In another ICU, staff member taped a stick to the door of the unit, symbolizing (for them) "The Stake," a sign of some form of euthanasia [perhaps the expression sometimes used, "to stake" a patient, derives from the myth that vampires can only be killed by driving a stake through the heart]. Periodically word went around that a resident had just won the "Green Stake Award," meaning that he or she had, for the first time, allowed or helped a patient to die. [Field Notes]
>
> Some colorful balloons with "Get Well Soon" were delivered to a patient's room. The patient died the following night. Someone on the staff moved the balloons to the door of another patient's room; that patient died! Now the staff has put the balloons at the door of the patient they believe is "most likely to die next." [Field Notes]

But jokes have to be contrived; they are deliberate efforts at humor and so make a good example of efforts to distance oneself, or to make the tragic funny. But the inherent irony of the hospital is better seen in situations that spontaneously provoke laughter. These things are funny in themselves; even an outsider can laugh at them:

> Nurse preparing to wheel a patient into the OR tells him, "Take out your false teeth, take off your glasses . . . ," and continuing, trying to make a joke, "Take off your leg, take out your eyes." The patient said, "Oh, I almost forgot—" and pulled out his [false] eye! [Interview]

Or:

> Lady patient [Geriatric floor] is upset because she called home, there's no answer; she's afraid her husband has died. Sylvia [a nurse] told her he probably just went somewhere for lunch, but patient said he would have called. She's afraid.
>
> [Later] Sylvia went back in lady's room—she's crying. Husband called! Sylvia happy, smiling, "You should be happy!" "But," says the old lady, "he called to say he was out burying the dog!"
>
> Sylvia had to leave the room because she was starting to laugh; she and Janie laughing at this at the N's station, saying it's really sad but funny at the same time. [Field Notes]

Or:

> In looking at X-rays of a patient's colon, the resident explains to the team a shadow on the film: "Radiology says it could be a tumor, or it might just be stool." Jokes all around about how "helpful" Rays [Radiology] is. [Field Notes]

One needn't be under pressure to find such things funny. People do laugh to ease pressure or to distance oneself. But sometimes the distance comes first: laughter is made possible by the routinization that has gone before.

■ ■ ■ ■ **4. WHEN THINGS FALL APART, KEEP GOING**

Sometimes routinization fails: outsiders come into the room and, seeing their dead mother, break down, screaming and wailing; or a longtime, cared-for patient begins irretrievably to "decompensate" and lose blood pressure, sliding quickly to death; or emergency surgery goes bad, the trauma shakes the staff, and there are other patients coming in from the ambulances. Any of these can destroy the staff's sense of "work as usual." In such cases, the typical practice seems to be, remarkably: just keep going. Trauma teams specialize in the psychological strength (or cold-bloodedness, perhaps) to continue working when the world seems to be falling apart. Finally, nurses and physicians are notable for continuing to work even, in the final case, after the patient is for almost all purposes dead, or will be soon.

> A resident said to the attending [physician] on one floor, discussing a terminal patient: "If we transfuse him, he might get hepatitis."
> Another resident: "By the time he gets hepatitis he'll be dead."
> Attending: "OK, so let's transfuse." [Field Notes]

Perseverance is a habit; it's also a moral imperative, a way of managing disaster as if it were routine.

In every unit there are nurses known for being good under pressure. These are people who, whatever their other skills (and, typically, their other skills are quite good), are able to maintain their presence of mind in any crisis. Whereas "being organized" is a key quality for nurses in routine situations, staying calm is crucial in emergency situations. Compare two nurses known for remaining calm (Mavis and Anna) to two others who are prone to alarm (Linda and Julie):

> Mavis [in Neonatal ICU] is cited as a good nurse (great starting IVs, e.g.) who doesn't get shook, even in a code, even if her pt is dying, she still keeps doing what you're supposed to do. Linda, by contrast, is real smart, very good technically, but can freak out, start yelling, etc., if things are going badly. [Field Notes]
> Julie [in Medical ICU], hurrying around, looks just one step ahead of disaster, can't keep up, etc. Doc says something about the patient in room 1. Julie says, walking past, "He's not mine," keeps going. But Anna, calm, walks in pt's room—pt with oxygen mask, wants something. Anna goes out, calmly, comes back in a minute w/cup of crushed ice, gives pt a spoonful to ease thirst. She *always* seems to be doing that little thing that others "don't have time for"—never flustered and yet seems to get more done than anyone else. [Field Notes, Interview]

But to "keep going" depends not so much on the individual fortitude of nurses such [as] Mavis and Anna, but on the professional and institutional habits of the nursing staff and the hospital. The continuance of care even in the face of obvious failure of efforts is itself a norm. Whatever one's personal disposition, one keeps working; the staff keep working, often when the patient is all but dead, or "dead" but not officially recognized as such:

> Dr. K., walking rounds with four residents, discussing a 30-year-old male patient, HIV-positive, gone totally septic [has bloodstream infection, a deadly problem], no hope at all of recovery—Dr. K. says this is a "100 percent mortality" case; so they decide how to proceed with minimal treatment, at the end of which Dr. K. says brightly, "And if he codes—code him!" [Field Notes]

Coding such a patient is an exercise in technique; there is no hope entailed, no optimism, no idea that he might be saved. There is only the institutional habit which substitutes for hope, which in many cases obviates the staff's pessimism or lack of interest. When standard procedure is followed, courage is unnecessary. It is one thing to be routinely busy, caring for vegetative patients; it happens every day. It is quite another to handle emergency surgery with no time and a life at stake. Sometimes such a case will challenge all the staff's resources—their personal fortitude, their habitualization of procedures, the self-protection offered by an indefatigable sense of humor. To maintain one's composure while under tremendous pressures of time and fatefulness requires all the courage a staff can muster.

One such case was that of emergency surgery on a thirty-five-year-old woman who came to Southwestern Regional hospital in severe abdominal pain; she was diagnosed with a ruptured ectopic [tubal] pregnancy estimated at sixteen weeks. The case provides us with a dramatic example of the pressure placed on the staff to retain their composure in the face of disaster.

The long description which follows is graphic. The scene was more than bloody; it was grotesque. More than one staff member—including one member of the surgical team itself—left the room during the operation, sickened. Other nurses, even very experienced ones, told me they have never witnessed such a scene and hope never to witness one. I include it here, in some detail, to exemplify both what health professionals face in their work and how, incredibly, some of them can carry on. The description is reconstructed from Field Notes (some written at the time on the inside of a surgical mask, some on sheets of paper carried in a pocket), and from interviews afterward with participants:

> Saturday night OR suite; hasn't been busy. Only one case so far, a guy who got beat up with a tire iron (drug deal), finished about 8:30 P.M. It's about 10:00. 2 Ns—the Saturday night staff—sitting around in the conference room, just chatting and waiting for anything that happens.
>
> Call comes over intercom: ruptured tubal (pregnancy) just came in OR, bringing to the crash room. 35-year-old black woman, very heavy—250 pounds maybe—apparently pregnant for 16 weeks, which means she's been in pain for 10 weeks or more without coming in. Friends brought her to ER screaming in pain. Blood pressure is at "60 over palpable," i.e., the diastolic doesn't even register on the manometer. She's obviously bleeding bad internally, will die fast if not opened up. Ns run to OR

and set up fast. I've never seen people work so quickly here, no wasted motion at all. This is full speed *emergency*.

When patient is rolled in, fully conscious, there are more than a dozen staff people in the room, including three gynecological surgery residents, who will operate; all three are women. The surgeons are scrubbed and gowned and stand in a line, back from the table, watching without moving, the one in charge periodically giving orders to the nurses who are setting up. At one point there are twelve separate people working on the patient—IVs going into both arms, anesthesiologist putting mask on pt to gas, nurse inserting a Foley [bladder] catheter, others tying pt's arms to the straightout arms of the table, others scrubbing the huge belly, an incredible scene. The patient is shaking terribly, in pain and fear. Her eyes are bugging out, looking around terribly fast. She's whimpering, groaning as needles go in, crying out softly. No one has time even to speak to her; one nurse briefly leans over and speaks into her ear something like "try not to worry, we're going to take care of you," but there is no time for this. I've never seen anyone so afraid, sweating and crying and the violent shaking.

As soon as they have prepped her—the belly cleansed and covered with Opsite, in a matter of minutes, very, very fast, the anesthesiologist says, "All set?" And someone says "yes," and they gas her. I'm standing right by her head, looking to the head side of the drape which separates her head from her body; the instant that her eyes close, I look to the other side—and the surgeon has already slit her belly open. No hesitation at all, maybe before the patient was out.

What happened next, more extraordinary than the very fast prep, was the opening. Usually in surgery the scalpel makes the skin cut, then slowly scissors are used, snipping piece by piece at muscle, the Bovie cauterizing each blood vessel on the way, very methodical and painstaking. This was nothing like that. It was an entirely different style. They cut fast and deep, sliced her open deep, just chopped through everything, in a—not a panic, but something like a "blitzkrieg," maybe—to get down into the Fallopian tube that had burst and was shooting blood into the abdomen.

When they first got into the abdominal cavity, usually there would be some oozing blood; here as they opened blood splattered out all over the draping on the belly. It was a godawful mess, blood everywhere. They had one surgeon mopping up with gauze sponges, another using a suction pump, a little plastic hose, trying to clean the way. Unbelievable. They got down to the tubes, reaching down and digging around with their hands. And then they found it—suddenly out of this bloody mess down in the abdomen, with the surgeons groping around trying to feel where things were, out of this popped up, right out of the patient and, literally, onto the sheet covering her, the 16-week fetus itself. Immediately one surgeon said mock-cheerfully, "It's a boy!" "God, don't do that," said the scrub tech, turning her head away.

The scrub tech then began to lose it, tears running down her cheeks. Two other people on the team—there were maybe six around the table—said about the same time, nearly together, "Damien!" and "Alien!" recalling recent horror movies, "children of the devil" themes. The fetus lay on the sheet just below the open abdomen for a few moments. The head surgery resident, working, just kept working. The scrub tech should have put the fetus into a specimen tray, but she was falling to pieces fast, crying, and starting to have trouble handing the proper tools to the surgeon, who said something like, "What are you doing?" At this point the circulating nurse, a man, said, "If nobody else will do it," picked up the fetus and put it in a specimen tray, which he then covered with a towel and put aside. He then told another nurse to help him into a gown—he wasn't scrubbed. This violates sterile technique badly, for him to start handling tools, but the scrub tech was becoming a problem. The circulating nurse then quickly gowned and gloved, gently pulled the scrub tech aside and said, "I'll do it." The scrub tech ran out of the room in tears. And the circulating nurse began passing tools to the surgeons himself. It is the circulating nurse's responsibility to handle problems this way, and he did. Another nurse had gone out to scrub properly, and when she came back, maybe ten minutes later, she gowned and gloved and relieved him; so he (the circulating nurse) went back to his regular job of charting the procedure, answering the phone, etc.

By this time, things were under control; the bleeding was stopped, the tube tied off. The other tube was OK and left alone so the pt can get pregnant again. The blood in the abdomen was cleaned up—over 1500 cc's were lost, that's just under a half-gallon of blood. The pt would have died fast if they hadn't gotten in there.

Within two hours after the patient had first rolled in, the room was quiet, only three staff members left, two surgeons and the scrub nurse closing up and talking quietly. Most of the mess—the bloody sponges, the used tools, and all—was gone, cleared away, and all the other staff people, including the chief surgeon, had left. Very calm. The patient, who two hours ago was on the end of a fast terrible death, will be out of the hospital in two days with no permanent damage beyond the loss of one Fallopian tube. [Field Notes, Interviews]

In this situation, we can see two somewhat distinct problems in maintaining the routine order of things: first, the challenge simply in getting the work done; and second, the challenge of upholding the moral order of the hospital.[6] The first issue was resolved by replacing the scrub tech so the operation could continue. The second issue is trickier. The scrub tech's response appeared to be set off not by the horror of what she saw—the bloody fetus—but by the reaction of the assisting surgeon—"It's a boy!" I can only guess that the joke was too much for her. In continuing to work without her, and continuing without noticeable change of demeanor, the surgical team was asserting not only the imperative to protect the operational routine but also, I think, to protect the moral order of emergency surgery as well. That order includes:

1. The job comes first, before personal reactions of fear or disgust.
2. Cynicism is an acceptable form of expression if it helps to maintain composure and distance.
3. The medical team is rightfully in charge and above what may be happening in the OR [operating room].
4. Preserving life is the central value; others (such as niceties of language or etiquette) fall far behind.

There is clearly a morality here. Just as clearly, it is not the morality of everyday life.

NOTES

1. Erving Goffman, "On Face-Work," in *Interaction Ritual: Essays on Face-to-Face Behavior* (New York: Pantheon Books, 1967), p. 11.

2. Ibid., pp. 17–18.

3. Renée C. Fox, *Experiment Perilous* (New York: Free Press, 1959; reprint ed., Philadelphia: University of Pennsylvania Press, 1974), pp. 80–82.

4. Rose Laub Coser, "Some Social Functions of Laughter," in Lewis Coser, *The Pleasures of Sociology*, edited and with an introduction and notes by Lewis Coser (New York: New American Library, 1980), pp. 81–97.

5. The genius of Shem's *House of God* is that it accepts this fact and presents it honestly.

6. I am indebted to Robert Zussman, who suggested these in his review of the manuscript.

Like it or not, we are destined to live in the midst of rapid social change. Social change is so extensive that little remains the same from one generation to the next. Social change is so swift that it even threatens to leave us stumbling around in a previous era. We have to learn new skills—and relearn old ones. When U.S. physicians complete medical school, for example, they have received a top-notch education and are familiar with the latest developments in their profession. If they fail to continue taking courses in their specialties, however, in a short time they fall woefully behind.

Some of the many changes in which we are immersed are small and of little consequence for our lives. A fast food outlet opens where a gas station used to be. The new models of cars sprout new lines—ever so slightly. Computers appear in new colors and slightly modified designs. Our college adds a course and drops another. A band, singer, or actor becomes an overnight sensation, then drops quickly from sight.

Other changes are broader, and have greater impact on us. Cities grow so large that they expand into one another, and no longer can you tell where one ends and the other leaves off. Increasingly, these megacities influence U.S. culture, changing the ways we view life. Politicians pass new laws that force us to change our behavior. Upset about some social condition, people band together in social movements, their protests echoing throughout the society.

In their consequences, some changes are huge. As the globalization of capitalism sweeps millions of jobs away from us, transplanting them into parts of the world where labor is cheaper, our own economic future may become uncertain. Markets heat up as credit is overexpanded, and as the stock market drops and banks refuse to lend, the aftershocks affect us all. The mass media grow more powerful, increasingly shaping public opinion and placing the affairs of the nation in fewer hands. Computers change the way we work, are educated, have our illnesses diagnosed, and how we fight wars. They even change the way we think, although this fundamental impact is so recent—and so subtle—that we currently have little understanding of it.

To conclude this book, then, we shall consider social change. Farai Chideya opens this final part by giving us a background for understanding some of the changes that Latino migration is bringing. Social movements are also in the forefront of change, and in the following selection James Jasper and Dorothy Nelkin analyze the animal rights movement. Reinforcing the analysis of Reading 9 ("Job on the Line") and Reading 14 ("McDonald's in Hong Kong"), we then turn our focus on what is perhaps the most far sweeping social change the world is experiencing—the globalization of capitalism. William Wishard examines the major trends that are enveloping the world's nations, uprooting the ways that we "do social life," challenging our orientations, and sometimes creating resentments that lead to violent opposition.

20................

Border Blues: The Dilemma of Illegal Immigration

Farai Chideya

introduction ▪ ▪ ▪ ▪

Changes in urbanization and population ordinarily seem remote, something occurring at a distance that has little relevance for our own lives. These changes, however, are two of the most significant events that the world is experiencing. They are so significant that it is difficult to exaggerate their impact not only on society but also on our own future. As our society has urbanized—as increasing numbers of people have moved from village and farm to the city, the city has expanded its influence. Today, U.S. culture so revolves around urban life that even rural life has been urbanized. To say *U.S. culture* is to say *urban* culture. Similarly significant are changes in population, which sociologists call *demographic shifts*. On a global level, population growth and population shrinkage affect the welfare of nations. They set up conditions for vast migrations, bringing ethnic changes that transform nations—and conflicts that reverberate around the world.

A demographic shift that is having a major impact on the United States is migration from Mexico and South America. This migration has been so extensive in the past decade that Latinos have replaced African Americans as the largest ethnic group in the country. It is too early to tell what changes this demographic shift will bring to U.S. social institutions and to popular culture, but we can be certain that they will be extensive. In this selection, Farai Chideya provides a background for understanding this fundamental shift in our population, as well as an insider's perspective into some of the experiences of illegal immigrants.

Thinking Critically

As you read this selection, ask yourself:

1. Why is this vast migration occurring? Look for both social and personal factors.

2. What changes to U.S. social institutions and culture is this demographic shift likely to bring?

3. What solutions would you propose to solve the problem of illegal immigration? What problems would your solutions solve? What problems would they create? In formulating your answer, be sure to take the main points of this article into consideration.

The land around El Paso, Texas, is an imposing desert scene painted in tones of ochre and red clay—stark mountains, vast sky, arid plains. It's so far west that it's the only major Texas city in the mountain, rather than the central, time zone. Atop a nearby mountain is the massive Christo Rey—an imposing figure of Jesus hewn out of tons of stone. It seems like a peaceful vista, but this land is the staging ground for a colossal clash of cultures—the meeting of Mexico and the United States at the border. The biggest clash is not between Mexico and the United States per se, but between many competing visions of what Mexican immigration means to the United States. Mexican immigration has been decried as an "illegal alien invasion," an erosion of America's job base, even the beginnings of a plot to return the Southwest to Mexican hands. And sometimes Mexican Americans themselves are perceived with suspicion, in the belief their allegiance is pledged to Mexico, not the United States.

What's the reality behind these perceptions? And what's life on the border like?. . . I've spent virtually my whole life living on the East Coast, where the Latino communities are dominated by Puerto Ricans, Dominicans, Cubans. I groove to Latin hip-hop and Afro-Cuban sounds, but I hadn't heard much Mexican-American music like ranchero and Tejano. I know a good plate of *pernil* when I eat one, but I couldn't tell you from *tortas*. And I've heard more opinions over whether Puerto Rico should become independent than I've heard firsthand accounts of life on the border. In other words, when I came to El Paso I was starting at ground zero. Why did I choose El Paso? Well, first, this border city has been the site of a well-publicized crackdown on illegal immigration. Second, it's been deeply impacted by government policies like NAFTA. But third, and most important to me, El Paso is not majority Anglo but 70 percent Latino and Mexican American, a place where there are bound to be differences of opinion between members of the Latino community. . . .

[W]hile trade with Mexico has been good for Texas in general, the NAFTA free trade treaty has hit El Paso's economy hard. The city already has an unemployment rate double the national average. Now plants that used to pay workers five dollars an hour in El Paso can pay them five dollars a day just across the border in Juarez—and not pay duty on the goods shipped back to the United States. Among the issues I want to explore here in El Paso are not just questions of Mexican-American identity—how they see themselves—but also how they see their (real or distant) cousins across the border. Do the residents of El Paso look upon the Mexicans as brothers, economic competitors—or a bit of both?

One of the first people I meet in El Paso gives me a hint of the differences in opinion about border issues. Nora is chic, almost out of place in the grungy alternative bar we're both sitting in, with high cheekbones, light skin, and curly black hair cut in a bob. "I hate to say it, but I agree with him," she says. "They need to learn English." The "him" Nora is talking about is a black city councilman who chewed out a citizen who addressed a town hall meeting in Spanish. The "they"—an implicit "they"—are recent Mexican immigrants. Nora, who used to model in New York and now works in the local clothing industry, takes the councilman's side. But some local cartoonists lampooned the politician's outrage, and many residents wrote letters of protest to the newspaper.

Many El Paso residents are from first- or second-generation immigrant families, people who remember life in Mexico and have direct family ties across the border. But it's a mistake to think that they encompass all of El Paso's Latinos. A large proportion of El Paso families, like Nora's, are *Tejano,* a term which means that her forebears have lived in Texas for generations—i.e., even before it was part of the United States. (As many Tejanos like to say, "We didn't cross the border. The border crossed us.") The unique Tex-Mex culture of the Tejanos gave rise to one of the biggest Latina singing sensations, Selena, whose premature death in 1995 woke America up to the size of the Latino community. And one lesson America has yet to learn about the Latino community is how many different cultural and political perspectives there are—even within a single group, like Mexican Americans.

Those different perspectives come into direct conflict when it comes to an issue as controversial as the border. I focused on two groups of people familiar with El Paso: the enforcers who try to keep people out, and the border crossers desperate to stay in America.

THE ENFORCERS

Melissa Lucio gets the radio call at noon on a scorching summer day. An electric sensor just inside the U.S. border's been tripped; agents are looking around but they haven't found anyone yet. She heads for the sensor's coordinates and pulls up alongside a couple of agents. They're beating the bushes around a splotch of water halfway between a pond and a puddle. After a minute, a guy about thirty-five years old steps out of a thicket with a resigned look on his face and a satchel slung over his shoulder. A Mexican worker who's crossed illegally into the States, he also happens to be wearing an OFFICIAL U.S. TAXPAYER baseball cap. When I laughingly point this out to Melissa, she goes me one better. "We had a guy who walked in with a Border Patrol hat the other day. We asked him where he got it and he said he found it on the bank of the river. The officer's name was still written on the inside—he'd lost it over a year ago."

Melissa's just one of the thousands of U.S. Border Patrol agents charged with the thankless (and some would say impossible) task of keeping illegal immigrants out of America and catching them once they come in. A Mexican-American El Paso native, she's also the wife of another Mexican-American Border Patrol agent. Just thirty years old, she's also the mother of five sons. With her thick black hair pulled back in a neat French braid, her brown uniform replete with two-way radio and gun, Melissa rides the Texas–Mexico–New Mexico border tracking and detaining border crossers. Sometimes she gets help from the electronic signals of hidden sensors, but much of the time she relies on her own eyes, scanning the horizon and bending toward the earth to interpret "signs"—the scant marks and footprints in the dry earth which she reads for vital clues of time and direction. The day is hot and clear. Recent rains have made it easier to track signs—and have also put desert flowers into bloom. Melissa's comments as she navigates the covered-cab truck around bumps and gullies are punctuated with interjections about the wildlife—"Beautiful bird!" "Really cool lizard!" "Check out that jackrabbit!" But her ear is always tuned to the radio, and she's tough when she has to be. If her truck gets stuck, she breaks off branches and digs it out; if a suspect in a vehicle takes off into a residential area, she pursues and radios the local police. As we traverse highways, dirt roads, and long stretches of pristine desert, we don't run into any other female agents out in the field.

The man Melissa has just picked up doesn't protest when she puts him in the covered back area of the truck. In fact, he reaches into his satchel, pulls out a newspaper, and starts to read. At my request, she asks him where he was going and what he was going to do.

"*¿Para dónde vas?*" she asks.

"*Para Coronado,*" he answers.

Coronado is an affluent area, replete with a country club, where he was headed to cut yards. "He was actually closer to the east side of Juarez," Melissa translates, "and I asked him why he didn't cross over there. And he said there's a lot of *cholos* [bandits] stealing and robbing in that area. He says it's easier to cross over here. He says he doesn't come often, but every once in a while when he needs money."

One stereotype of illegal immigrants is that they're a bunch of welfare cheats. But this crosser, and most of the ones that Melissa picks up, are coming in strictly to work—sometimes to stay for the day and go back that night. The economics are clear cut. The starting wage in the *maquiladoras*, or twin plants—so named because they're owned by U.S. corporations who maintain both Mexican factories and their "twins" across the border—is about five dollars a day. The wages for yard work are far, far higher. "If they have their own tools, they could make sixty bucks a day," Melissa says. "If not, it could be thirty or forty." In other words, one day per week of work in the United States earns more than an entire week's labor in Mexico. Of course, there'd be no point crossing the border if U.S. employers weren't willing, even eager, to give undocumented workers jobs. If a border crosser makes it in every day, the payoff is good even relative to U.S. workers. "If you think about minimum wage, four sixty per hour with taxes taken out, [the border crossers] are going to make more," she says. "Even the Mexican police officers, some of them make four hundred dollars per month if they're lucky."

I ask Melissa if the people she picks up ever give her flack for being Mexican American and picking up Mexicans. "I've only had one person say, 'Don't you think you're being mean?'" she says. "And I say, if you had a job, you would do it to the best of your ability, right? They say 'Yeah.'"—she draws the word out to give it a dubious inflection. "And I say that's just what I'm doing. I've got five children. I want to maintain my household. And they understand."

"Like this education issue," she continues. "Let's say you educate them, and then what? They're illegal in the United States so they can't obtain work. Or let's say they become legal, then they're going to be competing against my children or me for a job that could have very well been mine." She's no fan of NAFTA, which she believes has knocked the wind out of an already weakened local economy. "Not a month goes by that you don't hear about a local company that's up and relocating to Mexico," she says. "It may be a good law, but not for the people who live paycheck to paycheck."

We drop our passenger off at the Paso Del Norte processing station, a short-term holding area that seems appropriately located in the middle of nowhere. Inside the plain building is a bullpen of officers at their desks, surrounded by large cells where individuals are sorted by gender, age, and area of origin. Locals—people from Juarez and nearby border areas—are the easiest to process and return. People from the interior of Mexico, farther south, are interviewed by Mexican officials and given bus fare home. And last of all are detainees from Central America, some of whom have traveled hundreds upon hundreds of miles from Honduras and points south, only to be caught on the final leg of their journey. There are men and women, old and young—really young. One of the kids in the pen, who flashes me an impish grin when I check him out, looks about twelve.

"Oh, we get kids who are eight, nine, ten. I ask them, 'Your Mom, doesn't she worry about you?' And some of their parents do, but they really run wild. If they know a lady at a bakery [in the United States] will give them sweet-breads, stuff like that, they'll come. Some of them have friends they come to goof off with. This is what they do. This is recreation."

By the time they're sixteen—which is the age of the next border crosser we pick up—they're usually crossing to work. The teenager has tan skin and hair bleached nearly blond by the sun; he's carrying yard tools.

"*¿Con qué te posito entro los Estados Unidos?*" Melissa asks.

"*Trabajo.*"

"*¿Qué clase trabajo?*"

"*En yardas,*" he answers. He was headed to Coronado as well.

An Economic Judgment

Melissa Lucio is not only a Border Patrol agent, but a mother and a taxpayer as well. She believes the influx of illegal immigrants could curtail her children's chances at prosperity. "When people talk about immigration issues as being racial," she says, "you have Hispanics as well as Anglos as well as other ethnic groups that will say the same thing: 'We need to be strong on immigration issues.' Why should my tax dollars and my anything be funding someone else?"

Melissa's family immigrated from Mexico a couple of generations ago. "My grandma jokes that I'm going to send her back over the border," Melissa says. She had what she describes as a typical, happy coming of age in El Paso. She met her first love, Rick, who's also Mexican American, in high school, and married him right after she graduated. Like several members of both of their families, Rick went into law enforcement, joining the Border Patrol. Melissa dreamed about the same thing for ten years before she decided to take the plunge. "I had thought about going to college and to the FBI behavioral science department, to pursue some forensics. But the more and more children I started having, I just started to see that dream being pushed further and further away," she says.

Melissa found out the Border Patrol was hiring when Rick told her about a career day he was coordinating—but he tried to discourage her from trying out. It was an arduous process. First she had to take a written test to get admitted to the academy. Then she had to get in shape. After seven years of bearing and raising five sons (Daniel, David, Derek, Dario, and Andrew—"we ran out of Ds," she says), she was two hundred and twenty pounds. She quit her job and lost forty before going into the academy, and another ten once she was there. When it came time for the induction ceremony, she received her badge from an officer who'd specially requested the honor—her husband "As he's pinning me he whispers in my ear, 'Oh Melissa, I never thought you would make it. You've never made me so proud.'" She beams. "It was absolutely great. It was amazing."

Now Melissa works just past the El Paso line in the Christo Rey area of New Mexico. Standing atop the hill that supports the huge statue of Christ, you can see Mexico, New Mexico, and Texas in panorama. You can also see the latest attempts to keep the border clamped down. Along the length of the border, construction crews are putting up an immense fence designed to eventually cover the entire U.S.-Mexico line. But Melissa for one is skeptical it will stop the crossings. "They'll just have to walk a little further," she says, to where mesas break the fence line.

Her division, which contains forty to sixty agents per day depending on scheduling, picks up about a hundred and fifty people per day, a thousand per week. It's labor-intensive work, particularly given the nature of the terrain. The El Paso Border Patrol region gained prominence in 1991 when Silvestre Reyes, the chief at the time, implemented a policy he called Operation Hold the Line. Instead of chasing border crossers after they walked over train tracks or through the Rio Grande (at the Juarez–El Paso border, the river is little more than a trickle in a concrete culvert), Reyes posted agents in vehicles along large stretches of the border. Their presence dropped the number of crossers at that juncture from eight thousand a day to virtually zero. But that meant more Mexicans who wanted to come to Texas chose to go through the New Mexico mountains. "You can't do that here. You'd have to have a ton of agents to watch every side of every hill. We have to be mobile," Melissa says.

It seems like an awful lot of work for each agent on an eight-hour shift to pick up the equivalent of three border jumpers a day. But the political stakes are far higher than those numbers would suggest. Tensions about immigration characterize the turn of this century as deeply as they marked the turn of the last one. But instead of Italians, Irish, and Jews who received a lukewarm welcome disembarking at Ellis Island in the late 1800s and early 1900s, Mexican Americans crossing into the border for points as far flung as New York and the Midwest are the immigrants under scrutiny today. . . .

The pickups don't always go smoothly. Some of the border crossers have passed out and nearly died from heat stroke or dehydration as they're being taken in; other times agents just find the bodies. (One agent tells me a gruesome, perhaps apocryphal

tale of finding a body whose eyes had literally popped out of the scorched head.)
Sometimes people resist or carry weapons. The agents also have to watch out for
cholos—gang members who can come from either side of the border, and who often
prey on those crossing the border to work. In a Wild West twist, some of the *cholos*
rob trains passing through the region. "A bandit will board the trains out West and
pilfer through first, and say, 'The Nike tennis shoes are here.' Then they have their
buddies, twenty or thirty or forty guys, shunt the track so the little computer tells the
train to stop. As soon as it stops, these guys start throwing the stuff down. They don't
care if the nine hundred ninety-nine dollar television cracks open because the good
ones will land somewhere and they will grab it and sell it. Or on the other hand, in
the next two weeks you'll arrest a bunch of people that are all wearing brand new
Nike tennis shoes."

Sometimes they prey on the individuals working along the border fence line.
As our day together draws to a close, Melissa gets a radio call from one of the men
erecting the new fence. He's worried because four men are approaching and he's
alone. "Ten-four. Horse patrol and myself will thirteen over there and check it out,"
Melissa radios back. As we approach, two men on powerful horses gallop parallel,
about twenty yards away. "I'm on the list for horseback," Melissa says. "I think it's
so cool." She surveys the situation as we approach. "These guys are definitely up to
no good." I ask how she can tell. "They don't have any bags, which means they're
not crossing. They don't have any water and they're just hanging around with no
attempt to go north." They might have wanted to get their hands on some of the
construction supplies, she figures.

Every eight weeks Melissa and the other agents change shift—days, evenings,
overnights (which start at midnight). Now she's working days and her husband is
working evenings, making it easy for him to take the kids to and from school. They
try to avoid both doing the evening shift, "because we've noticed that our kids'
grades drop."

To help out, Rick and Melissa have hired a live-in housekeeper, which is a
drama in and of itself. "I advertised for a housekeeper two years ago, [and] the first
thing off the bat was, 'Are you a U.S. citizen or a legal resident? If not, I work for
immigration and I can't hire you: And half the people would hang up. A quarter of
the people would say, 'I'm a border crosser,' but they were not permitted to work.
The lady we hired, she's late forties, great with the kids, teaching the kids Spanish,
and she's a legal resident, so it worked out really, really, well."

"So what's funny, a neighbor came up and said, 'Do you realize your house is
under surveillance?' I was like 'Excuse me?'" One day, when both husband and wife
were gone, an agent came to the home and asked their housekeeper for documents.
Neighbors came out to watch, and she waved right back at them to say "I'm still
here because I'm legal," Melissa says. The couple learned why the Immigration and
Naturalization Service suspected them when they talked the matter over with their
chief. A neighbor had phoned in with an elaborate tale how the housekeeper, supposedly illegal, had begged up and down the street for work and found it with the
Lucios. "It's just someone being vindictive. I thought, that is really terrible," Melissa

says. "At the time we lived in the Coronado Country Club area. They were really unhappy about Hold the Line because their maids couldn't come in illegally." As we head back into the station, I think again about the economics of the illegal immigration debate. The reality is that for every undocumented immigrant who finds low-wage work in America, there is somebody willing to hire that person. And some of the same people benefiting from below-market labor loudly decry illegal immigration at the same time.

The Politics of the Border

America likes to think its immigration laws are tough. And while they're arguably harsh on people who cross the border, most penalties on the businesses that hire illegal immigrants are modest. And people like the border crossers Melissa Lucio picked up often don't work for "businesses" at all, but everyday U.S. citizens who usually suspect the person they've hired to cut their lawn or babysit their kids doesn't hold a green card. America decries the waves of illegal immigration. But some Americans on the border and throughout the United States profit from the cheap labor these immigrants provide.

The economics of the border are full of conflict and duplicity, people who profit, people who lose, and people who lie about which camp they're in. Most important, the economics are deeply intertwined. Downtown El Paso, an unremarkable collection of modest office buildings and low-priced shops, is tethered by a bridge to downtown Juarez, Mexico. The Mexicans who cross the bridge come to work, visit, and shop. The Anglos going the other way often buy cheap groceries and pharmaceuticals (you can purchase Valium and Prozac without a prescription there), and college students hit the bars, where the words "drinking age" are meaningless. What happens when the Border Patrol cracks down on illegal crossings? Many downtown El Paso businessmen say their shops suffer, deprived of the day workers that used to buy clothes and consumer goods.

Many Mexican residents of Juarez aren't happy about the increasingly fortified border, either. El Paso and Juarez are separated by an unimpressive trickle of water that, amazingly enough, is part of the mighty Rio Grande river. A cement aqueduct, fenced on both sides, contains the water and separates the people. Painted on the concrete are signs decrying the border fortifications:

One reads OJO MIGRA (eyes are painted into the o's) ¡¡YA BASTA!!

Another says: POR CADA ILEGAL QUE NOS MALTRATEN EN LOS ESTADOS UNIDOS DE N. A. VAMOS A MALTRATAR UN VISITANTE GAVACHO. BIENVENIDOS LOS PAISANOS.

Their translations: "Look, Immigration—enough already!" and "For every illegal they mistreat in the United States, we are going to mistreat a visiting gringo. Welcome, countrymen."

It sounds like a bit of useless bravado, the "welcome, countrymen" sign. But the history of the Southwest is the history of what Mexico founded and America fought to win—not particularly fairly, either. Writes biographer Hugh Pearson:

In 1845, hewing to the strictures of Manifest Destiny we annexed the Republic of Texas, which had been part of Mexico. Its American settlers decided to introduce slavery into the territory, which was illegal in Mexico. Then, as gratitude for the Mexican government's inviting them to settle the territory and because they wanted to keep their slaves, they fought for independence. As former President and Gen. Ulysses S. Grant wrote in his memoirs, "The occupation, separation and annexation were, from the inception of the movement to its final consummation, a conspiracy to acquire territory out of which slave states might be formed for the American union."

After accepting the Texas republic's petition to be annexed by the United States, a dispute between the United States and Mexico ensued, regarding where the exact boundary of Texas lay. Mexican and U.S. patrols clashed somewhere along the disputed territory and the Unified States declared war on Mexico. In the process of fighting the war, U.S. troops captured from Mexico what is now New Mexico and what the Mexicans called Upper California. As conditions for surrender, Mexico was forced to cede all of the captured territory north of the Rio Grande River, and an agreed upon jagged imaginary line that now separates California, Arizona and New Mexico from Mexico. So today, Mexicans crossing into U.S. California are treated as illegal aliens if they don't go through the proper channels for entering territory that was originally theirs.

I didn't learn any of this in high school, and I'd wager that many Americans don't know it today. What happened doesn't change the fact that America has the right to control its borders, but it does cast into sharper relief the interconnectedness of these two nations. Texas was birthed from Mexico. But—defying the stereotypes that pervade much of the news coverage about the border—many Mexican Americans are now the ones guarding the border.

Silvestre Reyes headed the Border Patrol for the entire El Paso region. . . . I meet the solid, handsome fifty-year-old in the offices where he's running his campaign [for U.S. Congress] with the help of his twenty-five-year-old daughter. Even in his civilian clothes, he's got the demeanor of a law enforcement officer. Reyes grew up in a small farming town where his high school graduating class was made up of just twenty-six students. When he was a child, he served as a lookout against *la migra*—the Border Patrol—in the fields where Mexicans worked. He served in Vietnam, then worked as a Border Patrol agent for over twenty-five years. He believes that people's opinions about the border don't have anything to do with ethnic loyalty, but quality of life. "Hispanics, like every ethnic group in the country, have an expectation to be safe and secure in their neighborhoods," he says. "A Hispanic no more than anybody else appreciates undocumented people flowing through their backyards, creating a chaotic situation."

Still, Reyes says he'd like to find a way to benefit both Mexicans and Americans at the same time. "Mexican citizens don't want to come up here," he says. "They would rather stay home. But they stay home, they starve. We've got forces down in Mexico that want jobs, and people up here that want them to come up here. But the whole problem is, let's find a system that does it legally."

Despite its adverse effect on the El Paso economy, Reyes supports NAFTA as a way of increasing employment opportunities in Mexico. If things don't get better there, he reasons, illegal immigration will never stop. "Mexico has a surplus of manpower. I think 60 percent of Mexican citizens are under the age of twenty, if I remember my statistics right," he says. . . .

One policy he doesn't support is California's Proposition 187, which voters passed in 1994 in an effort, among other things, to prevent illegal immigrants from receiving government medical care or public education. Reyes calls the measure "illegal and unconstitutional. . . . Should we amend the Constitution in order to deny children born in this country their citizenships? I think we're crazy," he says. "What's gonna keep someone from going back retroactively and saying, 'You know, your father was born to illegal parents back in 1924. Therefore he was illegal, therefore you're illegal.'" (Such logic recalls a joke by Mexican-American comedian Paul Rodriguez, who says he supports making deportations for illegal immigration retroactive and shipping the Anglos back home.) The idea of barring education to undocumented children is "insanity running amok. The way that people enslave whole segments of our society is by keeping them ignorant. . . . To me it doesn't matter whether it's black or Hispanics or Chinese or whites or who it is. I think it's just wrong for any country to guarantee a subculture of ignorance. And that's what you're doing when you don't educate the kids."

The wording of California's Proposition 187 was also openly militaristic, reading:

> WE CAN STOP ILLEGAL ALIENS. If the citizens and the taxpayers of our state wait for the politicians in Washington and Sacramento to stop the incredible flow of ILLEGAL ALIENS, California will be in economic and social bankruptcy. We have to act and ACT NOW! On our ballot, Proposition 187 will be the first giant stride in ultimately ending the ILLEGAL ALIEN invasion.

Some advocates say the border has already become militarized, infringing upon the rights of citizens and legal immigrants. El Paso's Border Rights Coalition says that . . . half of the individuals who complained to their group about mistreatment by the Border Patrol, Immigration and Naturalization Service, and U.S. Customs were U.S. citizens, not legal or illegal immigrants. The group helped students at El Paso's Bowie High School file a class action suit. They alleged that Border Patrol agents were routinely harassing individuals on and near campus—in one case, arresting a group of students, U.S. citizens, who were driving to school. Today, the Border Patrol is operating under a settlement that requires they meet higher standards before detaining individuals, and limits searches at schools and churches.

Of course, the ultimate military-style solution would be to create a physical wall between Mexico and the United States. Reyes strongly disagrees with such a plan. "That's impractical, you know. The Berlin wall didn't seal, and that was using mines and barbed wire and guards and concrete, and all of that, and still people got out of there," he says. Yet as Reyes and I talk, construction on just such a wall is happening along the border near El Paso. While I'm out with Melissa Lucio, she shows me the early stages of the construction site. It's impossible to cover the whole border, of course. But . . . several miles of what Reyes calls the "impractical" solution stand completed.

■ ■ ■ ▧ **THE BORDER CROSSERS**

A Family Full of Contradictions

Gilberto, an eighteen-year-old undocumented immigrant from Chihuahua, has few marketable skills but one strong advantage on his side. He has family legally in the United States who are willing to help him. Gilberto is the brother-in-law of a naturalized U.S. citizen who emigrated from Hong Kong. Chiu, who went to college in the United States, met his wife Lorena, in a Juarez nightclub. Now they have two children, baby Jenny Anna and Andy, who turned three the day after I spoke with them. Both attend the University of Texas at El Paso, and they earn a living by running a home care facility for the elderly.

Gilberto helps out with the home care, meaning he's guaranteed a job as well as a place to stay far from the eyes of the Border Patrol. Like virtually all illegal immigrants, he's an unskilled laborer. Like many Mexicans, he finished the "secondario" level of schooling at fifteen and then started working. His first job was in a junkyard—hot, heavy work for very little money. Still, like a teenager, he used the remaining money he had to party rather than save. Asked if he's worried *la migra* will find him—something they did once before, as he was out and about—he shakes his head confidently, "No."

Chiu and Lorena's generous brick house is nestled in a pristine, upper-middle-class enclave undergoing rapid development. Bold and self-assured, Chiu strongly opposes illegal immigration, a position it's hard not to think deeply about when you see Gilberto sitting sheepishly on the other side of the table. "My brother-in-law, he's an illegal alien. He come and go whenever he wants. When you're talking about Hold the Line, it's only to make the government look good," Chiu scolds. "Washington, D.C., will furnish a lot of money for this project because it's very successful—you catch ten billion illegal aliens. Oh great job!" he sneers. "Now they have this Hold the Line thing, OK, and then they say, 'Nobody coming across.' But in the reality it's not true. In Mexico, if the people over there are making three to five dollars a day and if they cannot support their kids, do you think they would just sit there and die?"

Gilberto isn't in the dire straits many border crossers are. In fact, he originally entered not to stay but to fulfill teenage longings. "All the boys, they have the same dream: you know, they wanted to come and get some money and buy a truck, a nice truck," his sister Lorena translates, "and then go back to Mexico and spend one or two months or whatever on the money they saved up. Then after that, they come back to the United States again and work and get some more money. That's the way they think." Now Gilberto's changed his mind. He wants to stay in the United

States and become a nurse. "It's very important to learn to speak English, otherwise there's no way to find a job—well, maybe in El Paso a very low job. But I want to go further," he says. He's enrolled in a local high school, where his legal status proved no problem. "As a matter of fact, they are not allowed to ask you whether you have papers or not or whether you have a Social Security number or not, because if they do that they have violated federal law," Chiu says. "So they have to let him register although he's an illegal alien." In a clear example of how self-interest overrides politics, Chiu says that he's happy his brother-in-law can be enrolled, but that he is opposed to educating undocumented children. "When they do that they are inviting illegal immigrants to come to school here, you see. I would say no illegal immigrants to go to school in this country for free."

Neither Mexican nor American

A pensive seventeen-year-old named Diana finds herself in the opposite situation from Gilberto: with her near-perfect English and years of schooling in the United States, she seems culturally American, but this undocumented immigrant has no one to advocate for her or protect her. She's been caught between two worlds most of her life. Four years ago, Diana crossed into the United States at the Juarez–El Paso bridge that symbolizes the border so well. Now she's a senior at Fremont High School in Oakland, California. . . . Before crossing the Rio Grande, she spent her junior high school years near Durango, Mexico. And before that, from the ages of two until nine, she lived in the United States—attending American schools, playing with American toys, speaking both English and Spanish. Without a green card or citizenship, but with a keen understanding of American culture and her precarious position in it, she is neither fully American nor fully Mexican.

Diana remembers the day her family crossed over from Juarez to El Paso. "We used a raft to get across. It was really sunny that day. People were on the bridge watching us. They were like 'Oh look!'" she says. "I remember I saw this man with a little boy in his arms pointing at us." Once they got to El Paso, her family tried to blend in with the rest of the crowds in the downtown shopping area. "We crossed the street right in front of a Border Patrol car," Diana remembers. "The car stopped so we could cross the street! My Mom was praying and I was like, 'Mom, they're not going to do anything to us now.' They didn't."

While her experience in crossing the Rio Grande was a common one until recently, Diana's reasons for going back and forth between the United States and Mexico are personal and complex. Like most families who cross over from Mexico, Diana's came to work and make a better life for their children. Her father has a green card, so he was able to live and work legally; but he brought Diana, her mother, and Diana's older brother into the country without papers. Diana's father began drinking too much, and after living in the United States for several years, he decided to move the family back to Mexico and pull himself together. But there's little work near Durango, so he ended up going back to the United States to earn a living (taking Diana's teenage brother along with him) and sending money to the family back home. It was only once her father had stopped drinking that he decided to reunite the family, arranging for a "coyote"—or someone who smuggles people across the border—to bring Diana and the rest of the family north through Mexico, on a raft over the Rio Grande, and by truck out of Texas.

Diana was too young to remember the first time she crossed the border. She was only two years old, and friends of the family who had papers for their own toddler smuggled her in as their child. "People told me I kept saying, 'I want my mother.' They needed me to be quiet," she says. From two on, Diana lived in Chico, California, as a normal Mexican-American kid—almost. When I ask her if she knew she was an "illegal immigrant," she says, "That question really bothered me and came into my head in, I think, the second grade. Most of my friends would go to Mexico on their summer vacations to see their grandparents, and I would ask, 'Why aren't we going to Mexico?' My mother would say, 'We can't.' Then," she continues, "one time in school I said, 'Um, I'm illegal.' And my teacher said, 'Honey, don't say that out loud. You could get your parents in a lot of trouble.' That's when I started feeling a little inferior to other kids."

Sometimes she still does. "Not because of who I am but because of what I can't do," she says, quietly breaking into tears. One thing she can't do is apply to college, even though she's a solid student. Without legal residence papers, she has little hope of attending school or getting anything but the most menial of jobs. Her older brother tried enrolling in college, but after they repeatedly asked him for a Social Security number, he simply left. Now he plays in a band. "I want to get a green card so I can work, so I can go to school, so I don't need to worry about getting deported and everything. But we have to pay a lawyer seven hundred dollars for each person applying for the green card," money her struggling family doesn't have. After she gets a green card, she wants to become a citizen "because I would like to be heard in this country. I would like to vote and be part of the process."

The most wrenching part of her experience is that Diana knows she could have been a legal resident by now. In 1987, she says, "we could have gotten our papers through the National Amnesty Program," a one-shot chance for illegal immigrants to declare themselves to officials in exchange for a green card. "My mother applied for us, but my Dad [who was drinking] felt that if we went back to Mexico, everything would be for the best." She remembers the day they left the United States. "I had to leave all my friends and the things I had. We left everything: the furniture, my toys, my Barbies. I had to practically leave my life there."

Yet Diana credits the time she spent in Mexico with helping her reconnect with her heritage. She became close with her grandmother, was in the Mexican equivalent of junior ROTC, and won dramatic speaking contests, reciting poetry. "In Mexico, I always wanted to be the one with the best grades—always wanted to be the center of attention," she says. "Maybe because I believed in myself and what I did," she says. That sense of confidence is lacking in Diana today. But if she had stayed in Mexico, it would have been difficult for her to continue her education considering how little money her family had. Most of the girls Diana knew stopped going to school at fourteen or fifteen, got married to a farmer or laborer, and started a family.

So, in one sense, Diana feels she was lucky to return to the United States. But when she first arrived, she had a difficult time readjusting. She returned in time for ninth grade, which in Oakland at the time was still a part of junior high school. Teachers put her in an English as a second language program, probably because her shyness inhibited her from talking much. "It wasn't very helpful," she says. Luckily, as soon as one of her teachers found out how good Diana's English really was, Diana was moved into the regular track.

But Diana was dealing not only with educational displacement but ethnic culture shock. "In the ninth grade, there was only my Mexican friends . . . and we felt a little inferior to the rest." In her opinion, the Mexican kids broke down into two cliques: the "Mexican Mexicans," or hard-working immigrants, and the "little gangsters," or tough, Americanized teens. She hung out with the former—until tenth grade, when she went to Fremont and joined the Media Academy. There she made friends of several races. "When I got to Fremont there was African Americans, Asians, and Mexicans and everybody hangs out together and it was cool," she says.

What is heartbreaking to Diana today is that, though she loves school, she has little hope of continuing her education. She remembers a time that her teacher was leading them through an exercise in filling out college applications. "Everybody was like: 'Oh, I want to go to this place and I wanna go such and such and oh, my grades are good and everything.' My teacher was like, 'Aren't you going to fill out your applications?' And I was like, 'What for?'" Another girl in the class asked the question Diana was desperate to, but just couldn't. "What if you're not a legal resident?" Her teacher said to leave the Social Security number slot blank, but Diana says, dejected, "I didn't want to continue it.". . .

Still, "Regardless of all the barriers that are put between you and other people, America *is* the Land of Opportunity," says Diana. "No matter where you go, you will never find another place where even when you're not legal you can still get a job that pays you. There's no other place like it. In Mexico you can't even get a job. You depend on the crops on your land and live on what grows. There's nowhere for you to go, no McDonald's for you to hang out at. To me, it's better in America."

■ ■ ■ MEXICANIZING AMERICA?

The unspoken fear that underlies much of our policy about the border is that an influx of immigrants will "Mexicanize" America. But my journey through El Paso illustrates the complex culture of Mexican Americans, and just how unfounded the fears about "Mexicanization" are. Those living on the U.S.-Mexican border face some difficult political and economic questions: whether Americans can compete with the low-wage workers in Mexico; whether Washington lawmakers can truly understand the issues facing Americans on the border; and, for Mexican Americans in particular, whether they should feel some connection to the problems facing

Mexicans, or simply focus on their own issues. The influence of Mexican culture on America's should be seen as part of a continuum. Just as every immigration wave has shaped this country, so will the rise of the Latino population. In a best-case scenario, border towns like El Paso would help foster a rich appreciation for Mexican culture as *part* of American-style diversity.

The Animal Rights Crusade

James M. Jasper and Dorothy Nelkin

introduction ■ ■ ■ ■ ■

People tend to assume that their own values are good, right, and even moral. The more we are committed to a value, the more its arbitrariness recedes from sight and the more we assume its "rightness." An example is attitudes toward animals. In tribal and agricultural societies, people view animals instrumentally; that is, they think of animals as instruments to be used. A cow is to give milk, plow fields, and be eaten. A deer is to be hunted. A horse is for riding or to pull a plow or wagon. A dog is to pull a sleigh, to retrieve game, or to protect the home. The assumption—considered good, right, and moral—is that animals should be put into the service of humans.

These earlier societies—and their ideas—are remote from our own way of life. Because we face different circumstances, we have developed different attitudes about animals. Our attitudes are so different that we tend to see previous generations as misguided, even cruel and evil. For us, animals are to be loved and cuddled and cared for. They are to be taken to vets for their health care. They are to be fed nourishing and balanced food. They are to be bathed and groomed—even their teeth should be brushed and their nails clipped. Animals are sensitive and need to be protected. To treat their emotional problems, we even train animal psychologists.

Just as earlier generations assumed that their ideas about animals matched some universal morality, so do we. And we are convinced that our loftier perch gives us a superior view of life. Yet with attitudes toward animals still changing, coming generations may also shake their heads at our ideas. In the forefront of today's changing attitudes is the animal rights movement, the topic of this selection by Jasper and Nelkin.

Thinking Critically

As you read this selection, ask yourself:

1. How have ideas about animals changed over time? How are these changes related to urbanization?

2. Do you think that the treatment we give to an ant or cockroach should be less than that we give to a dog, cat, or horse? Why? What is the social origin of your attitudes?

3. In what sense is the animal rights movement similar to a religion?

Changes in beliefs about animals extend back to the growth of towns and mercantile values in the midst of the aristocratic, agrarian societies of sixteenth- and seventeenth-century Europe. A new urban middle class appeared, and by the nineteenth century it had changed daily life in Western Europe. The "civilizing process" that discouraged the new bourgeoisie from spitting on the floor, wiping their noses on their sleeves, and eating with their hands, represented an increased concern for the feelings and sensibilities of others. . . .

As urbanization removed many people from their direct dependence on animals as a resource, except as a means of transportation, close experience with animals other than pets declined. The bourgeois wife in town had fewer chickens to feed or cows to milk, so that her appreciation of animals came from her pet dogs. By 1700, people were naming their pets, often with human names (especially in England); pets appeared regularly in paintings; and some even received legacies when their owners died. When pets died, they (unlike farm animals) were never eaten; often they were buried in style, with epitaphs written by their owners. As the family home and its members became privatized and idealized, so did the family pet.

This new attitude toward animals had a distinct basis in social class, as Robert Darnton's description in *The Great Cat Massacre* dramatically suggests. The massacre occurred in the 1730s at a Paris printing shop where the wife of the master printer was "impassioned" of several pet cats. They were fed at the table with the family, while the printer's apprentices ate table scraps—the cat food of the time—in the kitchen. In symbolic rebellion, the apprentices and workers captured sacksful of pet and stray cats, held a mock trial, and hanged them all. Torturing cats was an old European tradition: a favorite pastime at many holidays was to set cats on fire, largely to hear their terrible "caterwauling." The apprentices' action dramatized the conflict between the traditional view of animals and the emerging sensibility of the wealthy classes. The new moral sensitivity began in the rising middle classes, but quickly conquered much of the aristocracy, and eventually—although not widely until the twentieth century—the laboring classes. In each case, its apostles were mainly women, priests, and the occasional philosopher who articulated the changing beliefs.

Before the nineteenth century, only a few individuals had expressed a heightened moral sensitivity toward animals. Margaret Cavendish, Duchess of Newcastle, wrote extensively in the 1650s and 1660s about the human tendency to tyrannize other species. Considered highly eccentric by her peers, she criticized the hunting of song birds and claimed that "the groans of a dying beast strike my soul." In the eighteenth century, pastors and poets such as Alexander Pope, John Gay, and William Blake attacked cruelty to animals, reinterpreting the biblical acknowledgment of man's dominion over nature to mean thoughtful stewardship rather than ruthless exploitation. As the age of democratic revolutions ushered in new standards of respect

Reprinted and edited with the permission of The Free Press, a division of Simon and Schuster, Inc., from *The Animal Rights Crusade: The Growth of a Moral Protest* by James M. Jasper and Dorothy Nelkin. Copyright © 1992 by James M. Jasper and Dorothy Nelkin. All rights reserved.

and dignity for the rights of individuals, new attention was paid to the treatment of animals. In the often-quoted words of Jeremy Bentham in 1789, the question to ask about animals ". . . is not Can they *reason*? nor Can they *talk*? but, Can they *suffer*?" Here was a new criterion, one that placed humans and animals in the same circle rather than drawing a boundary between them. . . .

The nineteenth-century expansion of industry and cities in Britain and America accelerated the speed of bourgeois moral sensibilities, including sympathy for animals, across all social classes. The realities of nature had little bearing on the lives of those in cities, who were free to project onto nature a pleasant, pastoral image that overlooked its cruelties and dangers. They could forget the violent, precarious lives of animals in the wild and exaggerate their innocence and goodness. The romanticization of nature was largely a reaction to industrial society and the passing of rural life. . . .

Animal rights activists act as moral entrepreneurs, igniting and then building on moral outrage. They appeal to widespread beliefs about the similarities between humans and animals, the love of pets as part of the family, and anxieties about encroaching instrumentalism. And they use shocking images of common practices that violate deeply held sentiments about decency and justice to convert people to the cause.

Shocking visual images are perhaps their most powerful tool. Monkeys in restraining devices, furry raccoons in steel traps, kittens with their eyes sewn shut, and other images of constrained mammals appeal to anthropomorphic sympathies. People's worst fears of a science and a technology out of control seem justified by photographs of animals probed with scientific devices—rats with syringes down their throats, cats with electrodes planted on their heads. A bright patch of red blood on a black-and-white poster catches the eye. . . .

Most moral shocks inform the viewer about what others—scientific researchers, circus trainers, cosmetics companies—do to animals. Some, like New Age consumer efforts, try to shock viewers into thinking about their own actions—their own contribution to animal cruelty. Where did the hamburger in the neat Styrofoam container come from? What was the original animal like? How did it live and how did it die? "Meat's no treat for those you eat!" What animal died to make your fur? "Are you wearing my mother on your back?" We are forced to think of animals, not as commodities, but as living beings with a point of view that we are invited to share.

Moral shocks are recruiting tools for protest movements, but the power of a shocking image is not by itself sufficient to build a movement. Membership generally requires time for activities, discretionary income to contribute, and a conviction that participants can make a difference. But shocks can be so persuasive that even people with no prior political experience become "converts." Moral crusades are often filled with recruits who have not been in other movements; the anti-abortion movement is one example. . . .

Moral truth requires missionary zeal. Those who believe they know the truth are often loud and shrill in their attacks. Fundamentalists hurl venomous labels at those who abuse animals. Scientists are "sadists," meat-eaters are "cannibals," factory farmers are "fascists," and furriers are "criminals." But even those who simply disagree with the fundamentalists become targets. At a public forum, Michael W. Fox of the Humane Society of the United States was asked whether there were any circumstances in which he would accept animal experimentation. He replied, "Just to ask that question indicates you are a speciesist and probably a sexist and a racist." Such labeling inevitably precludes further dialogue. . . .

The smug zeal of moral crusades is familiar. Seeing the moral world in black and white, many activists, especially those drawn into activism for the first time, are politically naïve and dismissive of majority sensibilities. In addition to saying that "A rat is a pig is a dog is a boy," PETA's [People for the Ethical Treatment of Animals] Ingrid Newkirk declared in a controversial statement, "Six million people died in concentration camps, but six billion broiler chickens will die this year in slaughterhouses." Others compare the plight of today's animals with that of African-American slaves before the Civil War. Those willing to grant moral rights to chickens easily make comparisons that offend mainstream tastes.

In the Gulf of St. Lawrence, the ice was said to have a red tinge after the seal hunt every March, when 100,000 seals were killed for their pelts. Most prized of all were the babies, which, for the first three weeks of life, have furry white coats. With their large eyes, they could bring out sentimental anthropomorphism in almost anyone. A Canadian film crew—expecting only to film seals in their natural habitat—caught part of the 1964 hunt, and the sight of baby seals being clubbed and spiked in the head caused outrage throughout the industrialized world and generated a major controversy, attracting the attention of both environmentalists and animal welfarists.

Brian Davies, then executive-secretary of the New Brunswick SPCA, merged his welfare perspective with the political arguments of environmentalists: "I discovered that an over-capitalized sealing industry was intent on killing the last seal pup in order to get a return on its equipment, and that those who profited from the seals gave not one thought to their suffering." Davis buttressed this critique of instrumentalism with an explicit anthropomorphic description: "Their hind flippers were like two hands crossed in prayer, and again, the five fingernails. I can well imagine why many biologists consider sea mammals the most advanced form of nonhuman life." Whether for anthropomorphic or other reasons, whales, dolphins, seals, and other sea mammals have aroused tremendous sympathies.

Davies later described the first baby seal he saw killed. "He was a little ball of white fur with big dark eyes and a plaintive cry . . . *he was only ten days old.* He went to meet, in a curious, friendly, and playful way, the first human he had ever seen and was . . . by the same human . . . clubbed on the head and butchered on the spot. He was skinned alive. I saw the heart in a body without a skin pumping frantically. From that very moment . . . ending the commercial whitecoat hunt was a cause that consumed me." As in a religious conversion, he knew his life would henceforth be devoted to what he called a "crusade against cruelty."

Those who believe that animals have absolute rights demand the elimination of all animal research. Condemning the instrumental rationality of science, they find it morally unacceptable to reduce animals to the status of raw materials, in pursuit of human benefit: "We don't consider animals to be a tool, the test tube with legs." Improving conditions is not enough, for as one poster puts it, "Lab animals never have a nice day."

Anti-vivisectionists insist that immoral methods can never be used to support even the most worthy goals. They support their impassioned argument by comparing laboratories to Nazi death camps: "For animal researchers, the ends justify the means. This argument has a familiar ring: Hitler used it when he allowed experiments to be done on Jews."

Farms have changed in recent decades. In 1964, British writer Ruth Harrison coined the term "Factory Farming" in her book *Animal Machines*. Describing the highly regimented conditions of slaughterhouses and the transport of animals by meat packing companies, she questioned the right of humans to place economic criteria over ethical considerations in the use of animals for food. Efficiency rules today's large farms. Chickens, which Americans consume at the rate of several billion a year, spend their lives in windowless buildings. They are subjected to intense light when they are young, because that stimulates rapid growth. They are kept in increasing darkness later in their seven-week lives, because this reduces their fighting with each other. Their beaks are cut off soon after they are born, so that they will do less damage to each other as they grow and fight. Each broiler chicken has about one half a square foot of space. Laying hens have the same space, but live longer, up to eighteen months, at which time they are sent to be slaughtered. Not just chickens, but pigs, veal calves, turkeys, and most other food animals are confined in small areas, often in darkness. Beef cattle spend their first six months in pastures, but then are shipped to cramped feedlots. These techniques have made American agriculture extremely efficient. . . .

Those who believe in the rights of animals as sentient beings support modest reforms, but only as a temporary measure, for their ultimate goal is to abolish altogether the production and consumption of meat. These groups have organized demonstrations and boycotts, picketed restaurants on Mother's Day, attacked turkey farms on Thanksgiving, and liberated restaurant lobsters. The ALF [Animal Liberation Front, a radical organization] has gone further, leaving butchers and slaughterhouses with broken windows and graffiti. Even remote ranches have had water systems broken, fences cut, and equipment damaged.

Both abolitionist and reformist organizations document the immorality of factory farming in brochures and magazines filled with gruesome photographs and ghoulish descriptions of cruelty in slaughterhouses and farms. These documents show contorted hens living their entire lives confined in wire cages so cramped that their toes grow around the wire. They describe the stressful conditions that cause pecking and cannibalism. Bulls are branded and castrated. Rabbits are "living machines" forced to produce eight to ten litters each year. Animals are crammed into trucks and shipped long distances to packing plants.

To highlight the immorality of industrial practices, the animal rights literature describes animals about to be killed for food or fun in human terms. Easily personified, veal calves are a favorite target of activists. Babies with large eyes, they are separated from their mothers ("yanked from their mothers' sides"), confined in stalls ("crated and tortured"), and kept anemic to produce lighter meat. Even lobsters are anthropomorphized: "They have a long childhood and an awkward adolescence. . . . They flirt. Their pregnancies last nine months and they can live to be over one hundred years old." They also have feelings and scramble frantically to escape the pot, "much the way I suppose I would sound were I popped into a pot and boiled alive.". . .

Animal activists direct their moral outrage primarily against large corporations. Their rhetoric is couched in terms of *we* and *they,* two sides separated by a vast moral chasm. Fur and meat producers are depicted as villains, profiteering without regard to pain, and willing to place economic over moral value. Agribusiness thrives "on the backs of the least empowered groups in our social structure: farm workers, future generations, and, of course, farm animals." Animal activists exploit a long tradition of rhetoric against capitalism and the factory system to link animal rights with other social and political issues like exploitation and deprivation for profit.

A Trans-Species brochure describes "New MacDonald's Farm" as a full-scale factory in which animals are enslaved, becoming machines to produce meat. John Robbins—author of *Diet for a New America,* heir to the Baskin Robbins Ice Cream Company, and the president of Earthsave—eulogizes pigs in "The Joy and Tragedy of Pigs," noting their high IQs, superior problem-solving abilities, and "sophisticated and subtle relationships with their human companions." Having described the human qualities of pigs, Robbins naturally criticizes "pork production engineers," who treat pigs like "machines." He quotes a trade journal, *Hog Farm Management:* "Forget the pig is an animal. Treat him just like a machine in a factory. Schedule treatment like you would lubrication. Breeding season like the first step in an assembly line. And marketing like the delivery of finished goods." The critique of factory farms, in which machines dominate the production process with no regard for animals, follows Karl Marx's nineteenth-century attack on the treatment of human labor in factories. Factory life turns living beings—humans or animals—into cogs in a relentless machine.

The campaign against furs has had far greater impact—especially on the attitudes of consumers. A New York City lawyer tells a reporter that she feels "very conflicted" about owning a fur, as her own son tells her she is doing something immoral. A fashion agent has no desire to wear her mink coat, for "it's asking for trouble." A travel consultant says she is "a little nervous about walking down a street and being pelted with eggs or paint." A business executive says that when she bought her mink coat it did not occur to her to think about how animals are bred or killed. "Now I am aware of the brutality of trapping an animal, and I would not wear a trapped fur."

Environmentalists and animal protectionists had once attacked the fur industry primarily because of the cruelty involved in trapping wild animals. This view still dominated their discourse in 1979, when the Animal Welfare institute published and widely distributed an exposé, *Facts on Furs,* that focused on leg-hold traps. But animal rightists equally condemn the ranching of fur animals, which now accounts for roughly 80 percent of furs sold. Although most ranched animals die from gas or lethal injection, critics claim that many foxes are still electrocuted by means of a clip on their lip and a probe in their anus. Such practices are seen as brutal and unwarranted, a blight on civilized society. . . .

Perhaps because protestors have had little success with ranchers, current anti-fur campaigns are aimed at those who wear furs more than at trappers, making department stores and fur salons the sites of protest. In 1987, Bob Barker, a popular television game show host, publicly refused to participate in a Miss U.S.A. pageant in which the women were to parade out in furs and remove them to reveal swim suits. One prize was to be a fur coat. The following year Barker attracted further media attention as the head of the Fur-Free Friday march in New York; he seemed to encourage demonstrators to spit on passersby wearing furs by saying that this tactic had been effective in changing public attitudes toward fur in Europe.

Demonstrators have picketed, spray-painted, and smashed the windows of fur stores, distributed the names and home addresses of furriers, harassed women by shouting or spitting on them, placed advertisements on subways and city buses, and sponsored fashion shows with the message "Real People Wear Fake Furs" and "Fake People Wear Real Furs." They have organized rock concerts, liberated beavers from fur farms, and held public memorial services for animals killed for furs. Graphic slogans provide effective moral shocks: "Somewhere There Are Animals Missing Their Paws," and "Wear the Bloody Side Out!" Like the anti-meat crusade, anti-fur films and photos dwell on the cruelty and pain inflicted on vulnerable and sensitive beings. A photograph of a rack of pelts is captioned: "A few moments ago, these were live, vulnerable beings capable of fear, happiness, hope, and pain." A sign on a New York City bus encourages empathy by portraying a trapped animal: "Get a Feel for Fur. Slam your hand in a car door." Some activists even oppose the wearing of wool, combining arguments based on pain (sheep may be nicked during shearing or may be cold once shorn) with rights talk (sheep should not be used for human ends).

Furriers launched a multimillion-dollar campaign against the animal protection movement. The movement has had even greater influence in European countries, where fur sales have drastically declined (fur sales have dropped 90 percent in the Netherlands, 75 percent in Britain and Switzerland since the early eighties), and Harrods, once boasting it sold every existing product, has abandoned its sale of fur coats. The industry defends itself as catering to consumer choice and protecting fundamental freedoms. A radio commercial by the fur industry asks the listener to imagine enjoying a steak dinner in a nice restaurant: "Suddenly there's a commotion. People are around your table jostling you. Shouting. Pointing at your steak and screaming that you are a killer." Ads in major newspapers proclaim, "Today fur. Tomorrow leather. Then wool. Then meat. . . ." The American Fur Industry/Fur Information Council of America ends with an appeal to American individualism: "The decision to wear fur is a personal one. We support the freedom of individuals to buy and wear fur. This freedom is not just a fur industry issue—it's everybody's issue." This defense of consumer choice as a fundamental freedom is as close to the high moral ground as the fur industry can come.

Furriers routinely label all animal activists as terrorists. Even the audience [members] at a "Rock Against Fur" concert were "supporting terrorism." When Beauty Without Cruelty published ads with a list of celebrities under the caption "Say NO to furs—They did," the Fur Retailers Council wrote to each person listed. It implied they were being used by terrorist groups, and warned them to "review the enclosed material recently sent to police chiefs and sheriffs throughout the U.S. calling attention to violence and revenue-producing campaigns that often have very little relationship to animal care." The materials included lists of break-ins and animal thefts. Labeling the movement the "Animal Rights Protection Industry," the Council also provided information on the net worth of various organizations such as Greenpeace and the ASPCA (American Society for the Prevention of Cruelty to Animals). Both animal rightists and their opponents denounce each other as large, powerful, and ruthless.

Amidst the moral confusions of contemporary culture, animal rightists offer a clear position based on a set of compelling principles. They offer moral engagement and commitment in a secular society with few opportunities to sort out one's values, appealing especially to those who reject organized religion as a source of moral tenets. Animals are a perfect outlet for moral impulses, for—unlike people—they seem incapable of duplicity, infidelity, or betrayal. Like children, they are innocent victims unable to fight for their own interests. Thus, protecting animals sometimes inspires the shrill tone, the sense of urgency, and the single-minded obsession of a fundamentalist crusade. Its members become missionaries, defining the world in terms of the treatment of animals. They see the world as good or evil, and the villain—the person who exploits animals—becomes a model of malice. . . . Convinced of the truth of their moral mission, many animal rights activists feel justified in using radical tactics as well as revolutionary rhetoric to serve their cause of abolishing all animal exploitation. . . .

Animal rights is but one of many controversies that have grown out of a clash of basic moral values, of competing world views. Unlike conflicts based on interests, such controversies cannot be fully resolved. Yet, raising basic questions that reflect widespread social and political concerns, moral crusades can never be dismissed. To stubbornly defend current practices is to encourage further polarization. To denounce the movement as irrational, kooky, or terrorist is to miss the popular appeal of its moral intuitions and political beliefs. If a solution is possible in such rancorous conflict, it will require good faith from both sides to ensure the dialogue and compromise basic to a democratic conversation.

Caught between Two Ages

William Van Dusen Wishard

introduction

As you read in the ninth selection, one of the world's most significant changes is the *globalization of capitalism*. Capitalism won the Cold War, and except for a couple of hold-outs (Cuba and North Korea), socialism has been vanquished. Victorious with its heady success, bringing even Russia and China into its fold, capitalism is expanding rapidly into every nook and cranny of the planet. The Least Industrialized Nations have become part of this process. Eyeing the material wealth of the industrialized West and Japan, they, like separated lovers, long to embrace capitalism. The Most Industrialized Nations, too, feel deep stirrings as they eye these nations' cheap labor and vast sources of natural resources. Amidst such intense desire, the affair has become so torrid that it is difficult to tell who is the seduced and who the seducer.

But not all Least Industrialized Nations—or at least not all the groups within them—feel this compelling attraction. Along with capitalism comes Western culture, which tears at identities and relationships that have been nourished for centuries. Some groups only mildly resist this threat to their traditional way of life, pushing back slightly to protect specific elements of what they have cherished. Others reject the affair entirely. Visualizing their entire way of life crumbling, and, fearful of a terrifying future they see arriving at such a dizzying pace, they act to preserve their traditional culture. Some, like the groups that support Al-Qaeda, strike back, hoping that by violence they can hold back the over-powering forces that, unleashed against them, are battering their cultures. As Wishard points out in this selection, living in these times of vast change is certainly easier for us whose cultures are dominant than it is for those whose cultures have been invaded.

Thinking Critically

As you read this selection, ask yourself:

1. Of the three trends that the author says are shaping our future, which do you think is the most powerful? The one most disruptive of traditional cultures? Why?

2. The author says that he views globalization positively. How can he come to such a conclusion in light of the many negative features he mentions?

3. What does the globalization of capitalism have to do with the possible extinction of the human species?

Nothing so dramatizes living between two ages as does the image of the fireball engulfing the World Trade Center, an image burned into the world's psyche September 11th. I'm not going to dwell on that event, except to say this. The image of the imploding World Trade Center must be seen as part of a panorama of images for its full significance to best be understood. The image, for instance, of death camps and crematoriums in Central Europe. The image of a mushroom cloud rising over the Pacific. Of Neil Armstrong stepping onto the Moon. Of Louise Brown, the first human to be conceived outside of the human body. Of a man standing near the summit of Mt. Everest talking on his cell phone to his wife in Australia. Of the first human embryo to be cloned. Of a computer performing billions of calculations in a second, calculations that could not have been performed by all the mathematicians who ever lived, even in their combined lifetimes. These are some of the images, representing both human greatness and depravity, that mark the end of one age and the approach of a new time in human experience.

It was in 1957 that Peter Drucker, who, more than any other person, defined management as a discipline, wrote: "No one born after the turn of the 20th century has ever known anything but a world uprooting its foundations, overturning its values and toppling its idols." So today I'm going to pursue Drucker's thought and suggest why I believe we're living at probably the most critical turning point of human history.

Between two ages. How are we to visualize the difference between those two ages? I offer some contrasts. From the dominance of print communication, to the emergence of electronic communication. From American immigration coming primarily from Europe, to immigration coming mainly from Asia and Latin America. From a time of relatively slow change, to change at an exponential rate. From economic development as a national endeavor, to economic development as part of a global system. From ultimate destructive power being confined to the state, to such power available to the individual. We could continue, but I think you see what I mean. We're in what the ancient Greeks called Kairos—the "right moment" for a fundamental change in principles and symbols.

Exactly what kind of era is opening up is far from clear. The only obvious fact is that it's going to be global, whatever else it is.

In the next few minutes I want to comment on three trends that are part of this shift between two ages. Let me start by stating my bias: I am bullish on the future. We've got unprecedented challenges ahead, clearly the most difficult humanity has ever faced. But I believe in the capacity of the human spirit to surmount any challenge if given the vision, the will and the leadership.

With this in mind, let's look at some trends, that are moving us from one age to the next.

First trend: For the first time in human history, the world is forging an awareness of our existence as a single entity. Nations are incorporating the planetary dimensions of life into the fabric of our economics, politics, culture and international relations. The shorthand for this is "globalization."

From "Caught Between Two Ages," *Vital Speeches of the Day*, January 15, 2002, pp. 203–211. Copyright © 2002 by William Van Dusen Wishard. Reprinted by permission of the author.

We all have some idea of what globalization means. In my view, globalization represents the world's best chance to enrich the lives of the greatest number of people. The specter of terrorism, however, raises the question as to globalization's future. Will the 1990's "go-go" version be one of the casualties of terrorism? Yes and no. The economic pace of globalization may slow down, and certainly reaction to America's "soft power"—what other nations see as the "Americanization" of world culture—will continue to grow. But other aspects may actually accelerate. For example, we're already seeing the increased globalization of intelligence, security and humanitarian concerns.

Aside from that, globalization is far more than just economics and politics: more than non-western nations adopting free markets and democratic political systems. At its core, globalization means that western ideas are gradually seeping into the social and political fabric of the world. And even deeper, globalization is about culture, tradition and historic relationships; it's about existing institutions and why and how they evolved. In short, globalization goes to the very psychological foundations of a people.

Look at what's happening. Nations are adopting such ideas as the sanctity of the individual, due process of law, universal education, the equality of women, human rights, private property, legal safeguards governing business and finance, science as the engine of social growth, concepts of civil society, and perhaps most importantly, the ability of people to take charge of their destiny and not simply accept the hand dealt them in life. For millions of people these concepts are new modes of thought, which open undreamt of possibilities.

Is this good? From our perspective it is. But what do other nations feel as America's idea of creative destruction and entrepreneurship press deeper into the social fabric of countries such as China and India; as American cultural products uproot historic traditions?

In the Middle East, American culture as exemplified by a TV program such as Baywatch generates a unique resentment. Such a program presents Islamic civilization with a different nuance of feminine beauty and the dignity of women. Baywatch, and American culture in general, lure Muslims into an awkward position. On the one hand, their basic human appetites respond at a primal level. So it becomes part of them. Yet on another level, they fear the invasion of this new culture is undermining something sacred and irreplaceable in their very social fabric. Yes, it's their own fault; they don't have to import such entertainment. Yet it all seems to be part of so-called "modernization."

All of which illustrates how hard it is for us Americans to appreciate the underlying differences between western ideas and the foundations of other nations. Take some of the basic contrasts between Asia and the west. The west prizes individuality, while the east emphasizes relationships and community. The west sees humans dominating nature, while the east sees humans as part of nature. In the west there is a division between mind and heart, while in the east mind and heart are unified.

I mention this to illustrate the deep psychological trauma nations are experiencing as they confront the effects of Globalization. We Americans, raised on the instinct of change, say, "Great. Let tradition go. Embrace the new." But much of the world says, "Wait a minute. Traditions are our connection to the past; they're part of our psychic roots. If we jettison them, we'll endanger our social coherence and stability."

Remember, it took centuries for our political, social and economic concepts to evolve in the West. They are the product of a unique western psychology and experience. Thus we cannot expect non-western nations to graft alien social attitudes onto an indigenous societal structure overnight.

Part of the upheaval created by globalization is the largest migration the world has ever seen, which is now under way. In China alone, 100 million people are on the move from the countryside to the city. In Europe, the OECD tells us that no country is reproducing its population; that the EU will need 180 million immigrants in the next three decades simply to keep its population at 1995 levels, as well as to keep the current ratio of retirees to workers.

As European population growth declines, and as immigration increases, the historic legends that are the basis of national identities tend to wane. As one British historian put it, "A white majority that invented the national mythologies underpinning modern European culture lives in an almost perpetual state of fear that it and its way of life are about to disappear." You realize what he means when you hear that the Church of England expects England to have more practicing Muslims than practicing Anglicans by next year. In Italy, the Archbishop of Bologna recently warned Italy is in danger of "losing its identity" due to the immigration from North Africa and Central Europe. This fear is the subtext for everything else we see happening in Europe today.

The question of identity is at the core of the world problem as globalization accelerates. It came sharply into focus in the 1960s when, for the first time in human history, we saw Earth from space, from the moon. An idea that had only existed in the minds of poets and philosophers suddenly became geopolitical reality—the human family is a single entity. We began to see national, cultural and ethnic distinctions for what they are—projections in our minds. We lost the clarity of identity—Herder's "collective soul"—that had given birth and meaning to nations and civilizations for centuries.

In my view, it's this continuing loss of identity—or the threat of it—that helps fuel terrorism. Granted, there's an individual psychotic aspect to any terrorist. But the context in which they live is a loss of a personal sense of identity, as well as a subsequent psychological identification with the God-image.

One aspect of globalization we sometimes find irritating is America's global role and the resulting world perception of America. This perception is shaped by many factors, some of which we control, many of which we don't. For example, nations have historically felt a natural antipathy toward the world's strongest empire, whoever it happened to be at the time. And make no mistake, we are perceived, at a minimum, as an empire of influence. That said, in my view no great nation has used its power as generously and with as little intention of territorial gain as has America. Nonetheless, if we don't understand what other nations feel about America, globalization will not succeed, and neither will the war on terrorism.

Consider a comment by the Norwegian newspaper, Aftenposten: "in Norway, Nepal, and New Zealand, all of us live in a world that is increasingly shaped by the United States." Now let's play with that thought for a moment and consider a hypothetical situation.

Imagine how we would feel if the world were increasingly shaped by, say, China. Suppose China had produced the information technology that is the engine of globalization, technology that we had to buy and incorporate into our social structure. Picture Chinese currency as the medium of world trade. Further envision Chinese as the international language of commerce. What if Chinese films and TV programs were flooding global entertainment markets, undermining bedrock American beliefs and values. Suppose China were the dominant military and economic world power. Imagine the Chinese having troops stationed for security and peacekeeping in over thirty countries around the world. What if the IMF and World Bank were primarily influenced by Chinese power and pressure. Suppose China had developed the economic and management theories that we had to adopt in order to compete in the global marketplace.

If this were the case, how would Americans feel? I'm not suggesting there's anything inherently wrong with U.S. world influence, I'm trying to illustrate the all pervasiveness of America's reach in the world in order to suggest why even our allies manifest uneasy concerns about America. Understanding this, and adjusting where warranted, is essential to the success of globalization, to say nothing of the future of America.

Consider another example. Think what it looks like to the rest of the world when we judge other nations on the basis of human rights and democracy, while at the same time systematically feeding our children a cultural diet considered by all religions and civilizations throughout history to be destructive of personal character and social cohesion. Two of America's foremost diplomats have commented on this anomaly. Zbigniew Brzezinski, former National Security Advisor to the president, writes, "I don't think Western secularism in its present shape is the best standard for human rights." He mentions consumption, self-gratification and hedonism as three characteristics of America's definition of the "good life," and then says, "The defense of the political individual doesn't mean a whole lot in such a spiritual and moral vacuum."

George F. Kennan, one of the giant U.S. diplomatic figures of the past half century, says simply, "This whole tendency to see ourselves as the center of political enlightenment and as teachers to a great part of the rest of the world strikes me as unthought-through, vainglorious and undesirable." I might add these comments were made before September 11th.

Such comments perhaps seem almost unpatriotic. But America's ability to provide world leadership may depend on whether we have the capacity to consider such reactions, and see what truth there may be in them. It's what the Scottish poet Robert Burns wrote: "Oh would some power the gift to give us, to see ourselves as others see us!"

I emphasize these points because if we're going to build a global age, it's got to be built on more than free markets and the Internet. Even more, it's got to be built on some view of life far broader than "my nation," "my race" or "my religion" is the greatest. Such views gave dynamism and meaning to the empires of the past. But the task now is to bring into being a global consciousness. It must have as its foundation some shared psychological and, ultimately, spiritual experience and expression. At the end of the day, globalization must have a legitimacy that validates itself in terms of a true democratic and moral order.

The second trend moving us between two ages is a new stage of technology development. This new phase is without precedent in the history of science and technology.

At least since Francis Bacon in the 1600's we have viewed the purpose of science and technology as being to improve the human condition. As Bacon put it, the "true and lawful end of the sciences is that human life be enriched by new discoveries and powers."

And indeed it has. Take America. During the last century, the real GDP, in constant dollars, increased by $48 trillion, much of this wealth built on the marvels of technology.

But along with technological wonders, uncertainties arise. Let me interject here that in 1997 I had a quadruple heart bypass operation using the most sophisticated medical technology in the world. So I'm a believer. Nonetheless, the question today is whether we're creating certain technologies not to improve the human condition, but for purposes that seem to be to replace human meaning and significance altogether.

The experts tell us is that by the year 2035, artificial robotic intelligence will surpass human intelligence. (Let's leave aside for a moment the question of what constitutes "intelligence.") And a decade after that, we shall have a robot with all the emotional and spiritual sensitivities of a human being.

Not long after that, computers—will go at such a speed that the totality of human existence will change so dramatically that it's beyond our capability to envision what life will be like. But never fear, we're told. The eventual marriage of human and machine will mean that humans will continue as a species, albeit not in a form we would recognize today.

Thus arrives what some would-be scientific intellectuals call the "Post-human Age." I emphasize, this is not science fiction. It is the projection of some of our foremost scientists.

Let's move from the general to the specific. Consider a remark by the co-founder of MIT's artificial intelligence lab and one of the world's leading authorities on artificial intelligence: "Suppose that the robot had all of the virtues of people and was smarter and understood things better. Then why would we want to prefer those grubby, old people? I don't see anything wrong with human life being devalued if we have something better." Now just absorb that thought for a moment. One of the world's leading scientists ready to "devalue human life" if we can create something he thinks is better. Setting aside the question of who decides what "better" is, to me, devaluing human life is a form of self-destruction.

The editor of *Wired* magazine says we're in the process of the "wiring of human and artificial minds into one planetary soul." Thus, he believes, we'll be the first species "to create our own successors." He sees artificial intelligence "creating its own civilization."

These are not "mad scientists." They're America's best and brightest, and they believe they're ushering in the next stage of evolution.

In sum, we're creating technology that forces us to ask what are humans for once we've created super intelligent robots that can do anything humans can do, only do it a thousand times faster? Why do we need robots with emotional and spiritual capability, and what does that have to do with the seventy percent of humanity that simply seeks the basic necessities of life? What will it mean to be able to change the genetic structure not just of an individual child, but also of all future generations? Do we really want to be able to make genetic changes so subtle that it may be generations before we know what we've done to ourselves?

What we're talking about is a potential alteration of the human being at the level of the soul. This is a work proceeding absent any political debate, certainly without the assent of elected leaders. Yet it will change the definition of what it means to be a human being. It's the silent loss of freedom masquerading as technological progress.

Many other questions come to mind, but two in particular. Will it happen, and what is driving this self-destructive technological imperative?

On the first question—will it happen—my guess is probably not. In my judgment, there is a major issue the technological visionaries disregard. That is the question of how much manipulation and accelerated change the human being can take before he/she disintegrates psychologically and physiologically.

What we're experiencing is not simply the acceleration of the pace of change, but the acceleration of acceleration itself. In other words, change growing at an exponential rate. The experts tell us that the rate of change doubles every decade; that at today's rate of change, we'll experience 100 calendar years of change in the next twenty-five years; and that due to the nature of exponential growth, the 21st century as a whole will experience almost one thousand times greater technological change than did the 20th century.

I hasten to add that these are not my projections. They are the views of some of America's most accomplished and respected experts in computer science and artificial intelligence.

Onrushing change is already producing mounting dysfunction. The suicide rate among women has increased 200% in the past two decades. Thirty years ago, major corporations didn't have to think much about mental health programs for employees. Now, mental health is the fastest growing component of corporate health insurance programs. Think of the corporations that now provide special rooms for relaxation, naps, music or prayer and meditation. The issue now for corporations is not so much how to deal with stress; it's how to maintain the psychological integrity of the individual employee. . . . Books are now written for eight and nine year old children advising them how to recognize the symptoms of stress, and to deal with it in their own lives. . . .

Now, project forward the predicted increased speed of computers and the resulting ratcheting up of the pace of life over the next decades, and you end up asking, "How much more of this can the human metabolism take?" It's not the case that sooner or later something will give way. The multiplying social pathologies indicate that individual and collective psychological integrity is already giving way.

The second question is, what's driving this self-destructive activity? Certainly we as consumers are a major part of it. We're addicted to the latest electronic gizmo; whether it's the ubiquitous cell phone to keep as in touch with everyone everywhere, or one of those Sharper Image CD players you hang on the shower head so you can listen to Beethoven while taking a shower.

But let me offer three views that suggest a deeper story. Consider the comment of a former Carnegie-Mellon University computer scientist hired by Microsoft as a researcher. In an interview with the *Washington Post,* the good professor said, "This corporation is my power tool. It is the tool I wield to allow my ideas to shape the world."

My power tool. What clearer expression of ego-inflation could there be?

A second comment comes from the editor of *Wired* magazine, who famously wrote, "We are as gods, and we might as well be good at it." The Greeks had a word for identifying ourselves with the gods—hubris, pride reaching beyond proper human limits.

Perspective on all this comes from within the scientific community itself.

Freeman Dyson is one of the world's preeminent theoretical physicists. He talks about the "technical arrogance" that overcomes people "when they see what they can do with their minds."

My power tool; we are as gods; technical arrogance. The Greeks had another word that was even stronger than hubris. Pleonexia. An overweening resolve to reach beyond the limits, an insatiable greed for the unattainable. It is what one writer terms the "Masculine Sublime," which he describes as the "gendered characteristics out of which the myths of science are molded—myths of masculine power, control, rationality, objectivity."

From the earliest times, everything in human myth and religion warns us about overreaching. From the myths of Prometheus in ancient Greece, to the Hebrew story of Adam and Eve; from the Faust legend to Milton's *Paradise Lost;* from Mary Shelley's *Frankenstein* to Stevenson's *Dr. Jekyll and Mr. Hyde;* from Emily Dickinson to Robert Oppenheimer's lament that "in some sort of crude sense, the physicists have known sin"; through all these stories and experiences that come from the deepest level of the human soul, there has been a warning that limits exist on both human knowledge and endeavor; that to go beyond those limits is self-destructive.

No one knows exactly where such limits might be. But if they don't include the effort to create some technical/human life form supposedly superior to human beings, if they don't include the capacity to genetically reconfigure human nature, if they don't include the attempt to introduce a "post-human" civilization, then it's hard to imagine where such limits would be drawn.

Keep in mind that myths are more than fanciful stories left over from the childhood of man. They emanate from the unconscious level of the psyche; that level which connects us to whatever transpersonal wisdom may exist. It's a level at which, as quantum physics suggests, there may exist some relationship between the human psyche and external matter. There may be some fundamental pattern of life common to both that is operating outside the understanding of contemporary science. In other words, we may be fooling around with phenomena that are, in fact, beyond human awareness; possibly even beyond the ability of humans to grasp. For at the heart of life is a great mystery which does not yield to rational interpretation. This eternal mystery induces a sense of wonder out of which all that humanity has of religion, art and science is born. The mystery is the giver of these gifts, and we only lose the gifts when we grasp at the mystery itself. In my view, Nature will not permit arrogant man to defy that mystery, that transcendent wisdom. In the end, Nature's going to win out.

Some people are already searching for the wisest way to approach such potential challenges as the new technologies present. Bill Joy, co-founder and former chief scientist of Sun Microsystems, suggests we've reached the point where we must "limit development of technologies that are too dangerous, by limiting our pursuit of certain kinds of knowledge." His concerns are based on the unknown potential of genetics, nanotechnology and robotics, driven by computers capable of infinite speeds, and the possible uncontrollable self-replication of these technologies this might pose. Joy acknowledges the pursuit of knowledge as one of the primary human goals since earliest times. But, he says, "If open access to, and unlimited development of, knowledge henceforth puts us all in clear danger of extinction, then common sense demands that we re-examine even these basic, long-held beliefs."

The third trend moving us between two ages is a long-term spiritual and psychological reorientation that's increasingly generating uncertainty and instability. This affects all of us, for we're all part of America's collective psychology, whether we realize it or not.

The best measure of America's psychological and spiritual life is not public opinion polls telling us what percentage of the population believes in God. Rather, it's the content and quality of our culture. For culture is to a nation what dreams are to an individual—an indication of what's going on in the inner life.

In my judgment, what's really going on is that the world is experiencing a long-term spiritual and psychological reorientation similar to what happened when the Greco-Roman era gave way to the start of the Feudal Age. That was a time of great disorientation and searching. The cry "Great Pan is dead," was heard throughout the ancient world as the traditional gods lost their hold on the collective psyche. The Greco-Roman world became awash in countless new religions and sects vying for supremacy.

Not too different from our times, beginning with Nietzsche's cry, "God is dead." When we look at what's happening today we see 1500 religions in America, including such anomalies as "Catholic-Buddhists." Beyond that, we see a smorgasbord of spiritual/psychological fare as seen in the popularity of books such as *The Celestine Prophecy* or the *Chicken Soup* series, in the rise of worldwide fundamentalism, in numerous cults such as "Heaven's Gate," in the New Age phenomenon, in interest in Nostradamus, in crop circles, in the supposed "Bible Code," in conspiracy theories, in fascination with the "other" as seen in movies such as "Planet of the Apes" or "Tomb Raiders," in the search for some extraterrestrial intelligence to save us from ourselves, and last but certainly not least, in terrorism, which, at its core, is a demonic hatred expressed in spiritual terms.

What happened in the Rome–early Feudal Age shift was played out over centuries. What's happening today has, yes, been evolving over the past few centuries. We see it first manifested in the emergence of the Faust legend; then in the Enlightenment's enthronement of the Goddess of Reason in Notre Dame and the ensuing acceptance of rationalism as life's highest authority; and in our own time in the ethos of "meaninglessness" that has virtually defined 20th century Western culture. But what's happening today—due to the 20th century electronic information technologies—is probably unfolding at a more rapid pace than the shift in the fourth-fifth-sixth centuries. For information technologies transmit not only information, but psychological dynamics as well.

While there are millions of devout Christians and Jews in America and Europe, the Judeo-Christian impulse is no longer the formative dynamic of Western culture, especially among the so-called "creative minority." Even so calm a journal as the *Economist* opines, "The West is secular." One need only look at the changing relationship between the roles of the priest and the psychologist to see what has been happening. Earlier in the 20th century, if someone had personal problems, he or she went to the priest for advice. Gradually that changed, and people started going to their psychologist. Recently, the leader of the Roman Catholic Church in England and Wales said that as a background for people's lives, Christianity "has almost been vanquished." His language mirrored a statement by the Archbishop of Canterbury who declared Britain to be a country where "tacit atheism prevails." *Newsweek* recently described Europe as a "post-Christian civilization." Throughout the continent, *Newsweek* reported, "churches stand empty."

Part of the psychological reorientation taking place is the breakup of our collective inner images of wholeness. For example, we used to talk about "heaven," which denoted the transcendent realm, eternity, the dwelling place of the gods. Now we just speak of "space," which has no spiritual connotation. We used to talk of "mother earth," which had a vital emotional association. From time immemorial, nature was filled with spirit. Now we just speak of "matter," a lifeless nature bereft of gods.

Thus transcendent meaning—which is the source of psychological wholeness is diminished. The function of symbolic language-words like "heaven" and "mother earth"—is to link our consciousness to the roots of our being, to link our consciousness to its base in the unconscious. When that link is devalued or discarded, there is little to sustain the inner life of the individual. So, few people are inwardly fed by any primal source of wholeness. In effect, our symbolic life and language have been displaced by a vocabulary of technology, a vocabulary that's increasinaly devoid of transcendent meaning. The effect is a weakening of the structures that organize and, regulate our life-religion, self-government, education, culture and the family.

As a result, the soul of America—indeed, of the world—is in a giant search for some deeper and greater expression of life. Despite the benefits of modernization, technological society offers no underlying meaning to life. Thus the search taking place is both healthy and normal—given the seminal shift to an entirely new epoch that is occurring as we speak.

What we're discussing is at the core of the crisis of meaning that afflicts not only America and Europe, but Asia as well. For example, the *Washington Post* reports from Beijing, "Across China people are struggling to redefine notions of success and failure, right and wrong. The quest for something to believe in is one of the unifying characteristics of China today." A report from the East/West Center in Hawaii notes the decline in family and authority in Asia, and concludes by saying, "Eastern religion no longer is the binding force in Asian society." So it's a global crisis of meaning we're talking about.

Let me briefly summarize what we've been discussing. (1) Globalization possibly the most ambitious collective human experiment in history; (2) a new stage of technology the objective of which is to supplant human meaning and significance; and (3) a long-term psychological and spiritual reorientation. These are only three of the basic changes determining the future. And it's because of the magnitude and significance of such trends that I suggest the next three decades may be the most decisive thirty-year period in human history. . . .

Name Index

Subject Index